THE REVENGERS' COMEDIES

Born in London in 1939, Alan Ayckbourn spent most of his childhood in Sussex and was educated at Haileybury. Leaving there one Friday at the age of seventeen, he went into the theatre the following Monday and has been working in it ever since as, variously, a stage manager, sound technician, lighting technician, scene painter, prop-maker, actor, writer and director. These talents developed thanks to his mentor, Stephen Joseph, whom he first met in 1958 upon joining the newly formed Library Theatre in Scarborough. He was a BBC Radio Drama Producer from 1965 to 1970, returning to Scarborough to take up the post of Artistic Director of the Theatre in the Round, left vacant after Stephen Joseph's death in 1967. Since that time, he has premièred over thirty of his plays, first at the Library Theatre and, from 1976 onwards, at the company's new converted base, the Stephen Joseph Theatre. Over twenty of his plays have subsequently been produced either in the West End or at the National Theatre. They have been translated into thirty-two languages and have been performed in virtually every continent of the globe, receiving many national and international awards in the process.

THE REVENGERS' COMEDIES
ALAN AYCKBOURN

faber and faber
LONDON · BOSTON

First published in 1991
by Faber and Faber Limited
3 Queen Square London WC1N 3AU

Photoset by Parker Typesetting Service, Leicester
Printed by Clays Ltd, St Ives plc

A CIP record for this book
is available from the British Library

ISBN 0-571-14358-X

2 4 6 8 10 9 7 5 3 1

The Revengers' Comedies was first performed in Scarborough at the Stephen Joseph Theatre in the Round on 13 June 1989. The cast was as follows:

HENRY BELL	Jon Strickland
KAREN KNIGHTLY	Christine Kavanagh
LORRY DRIVER	Jeff Shankley
WINNIE	Doreen Andrew
NORMA	Claire Skinner
OLIVER KNIGHTLY	Adam Godley
LADY GANTON	Ursula Jones
COLONEL MARCUS LIPSCOTT	Donald Douglas
PERCY CUTTING	Martin Sadler
COUNCILLOR DAPHNE TEALE	Alwyne Taylor
ANTHONY STAXTON-BILLING	Rupert Vansittart
IMOGEN STAXTON-BILLING	Elizabeth Bell
LYDIA LUCAS	Frances Jeater
TRACEY WILLINGFORTH	Claire Skinner
MRS BULLEY	Doreen Andrew
BRUCE TICK	Jeff Shankley
HILARY TICK	Alwyne Taylor
GRAHAM SEEDS	Frank Lazarus
VERONICA WEBB	Ursula Jones
JEREMY PRIDE	Frank Lazarus
FIREMAN	Jeff Shankley
EUGENE CHASE	Rupert Vansittart
MOTOR-CYCLIST	Jeff Shankley

Directed by	Alan Ayckbourn
Designed by	Roger Glossop
Lighting by	Mick Hughes

The Revengers' Comedies was subsequently performed at the
Strand Theatre, London, on 16 October 1991 (Part I) and
17 October 1991 (Part II). The cast was as follows:

HENRY BELL	Griff Rhys-Jones
KAREN KNIGHTLY	Lia Williams
LORRY DRIVER	Raymond Sawyer
WINNIE	Doreen Andrew
NORMA	Rose Keegan
OLIVER KNIGHTLY	Adam Godley
LADY GANTON	Lavinia Bertram
COLONEL MARCUS LIPSCOTT	Jeffrey Wickham
PERCY CUTTING	Raymond Sawyer
COUNCILLOR DAPHNE TEALE	Hazel Ellerby
ANTHONY STAXTON-BILLING	Rupert Vansittart
IMOGEN STAXTON-BILLING	Joanna Lumley
LYDIA LUCAS	Lavinia Bertram
TRACEY WILLINGFORTH	Nina Young
MRS BULLEY	Doreen Andrew
BRUCE TICK	Jeff Shankley
HILARY TICK	Hazel Ellerby
GRAHAM SEEDS	Geoffrey Whitehead
VERONICA WEBB	Jennifer Piercey
JEREMY PRIDE	Geoffrey Whitehead
FIREMAN	Christopher Birch
EUGENE CHASE	Nicholas Palliser
MOTOR-CYCLIST	Christopher Birch
Directed by	Alan Ayckbourn
Designed by	Roger Glossop
Lighting by	Mick Hughes

CHARACTERS

HENRY BELL (forty-two)
KAREN KNIGHTLY (twenty-five)
LORRY DRIVER (forties)
WINNIE, a servant (sixty)
NORMA, a servant (sixteen)
OLIVER KNIGHTLY, Karen's brother (twenty-one)
LADY GANTON (sixty)
COLONEL MARCUS LIPSCOTT (sixty)
PERCY CUTTING (forty-five)
COUNCILLOR DAPHNE TEALE (forty-four)
ANTHONY STAXTON-BILLING (thirty-eight)
IMOGEN STAXTON-BILLING (thirty-seven)
LYDIA LUCAS, her assistant (late thirties)
TRACEY WILLINGFORTH, a secretary (early twenties)
MRS BULLEY (fifties, voice only)
BRUCE TICK (thirty-five)
HILARY TICK, his wife (thirty-five)
GRAHAM SEEDS (fifty, voice only)
VERONICA WEBB (forty-eight)
JEREMY PRIDE (fifty-five)
FIREMAN
EUGENE CHASE, an executive (thirty-five)
MOTOR-CYCLIST

CONTENTS

PART ONE

ACT I

Prologue Midnight. Albert Bridge, sw3

ACT II

PART TWO

ACT III

ACT IV

PART ONE

ACT I

PROLOGUE
Midnight.

*Albert Bridge, SW3. Perhaps a little river mist. Distant traffic, a
ship's siren.* HENRY, *a man in his early forties, appears in a pool of
street light on the bridge. He is wrapped in an overcoat and scarf. He
is hunched and miserable. He stares over the edge, deciding whether to
jump. From his expression, it's evidently a long way down. He says a
little silent prayer, as though asking forgiveness, and makes to climb
over the railing. He is uncomfortably straddled across the railing and
in some discomfort when he hears a woman's voice from the darkness.*

KAREN: (*Calling*) Help . . . Help . . . Please help me . . .
    (HENRY *stops and listens, rather startled.*)
    Please help . . . somebody . . .
HENRY: (*Calling, tentatively*) Hallo?
KAREN: (*Calling back*) Hallo . . .
HENRY: (*Calling again*) Hallo?
KAREN: Would you stop saying hallo and come and help me,
    please? I've got myself caught up here . . .
HENRY: Oh, right. Hang on, there . . . Just hang on . . .
    (*He starts to clamber back on to the bridge.*)
KAREN: I don't have any option. I've been hanging here for
    hours.
HENRY: Just one very small second . . .
    (HENRY *moves to the source of her voice. As he does so, we make
    out* KAREN *for the first time. She is in her mid-twenties. She
    wears a woolly hat and a lightweight coat over an evening dress.
    She is hanging outside the bridge railing. All that seems to be
    keeping her from falling is the belt of her coat, which has become
    entangled with the ironwork.* HENRY *reaches her.*)
    Oh, Lord. How can I . . .?
KAREN: (*Trying to indicate*) Do you see? Something's caught – I
    think it's the belt of my coat . . .
HENRY: Oh, yes, yes. Look, I think I'd better . . . (*Flustered*)
    Look – er . . . Yes, yes. I think I'd better try and – er . . .

3

Would you mind if I – tried to lift you . . .?

KAREN: You can do what you like – just get me off this bloody
bridge . . .

HENRY: Yes, yes, right . . .

(*He studies the problem.*)

KAREN: Can you see? I think it's my belt . . .

HENRY: Yes, yes, so it is. I think I'd better get that free before
I . . .

(*He starts to untangle the belt.*)

KAREN: Careful . . .

HENRY: Yes. Only I don't want to tear your coat, you see. If I
tried to lift you over as you are, I might damage it . . . It's a
very nice coat . . .

KAREN: (*Sarcastically*) Well, that's very considerate of you . . .
Thank you.

HENRY: (*Finally freeing the belt*) Right. There you go, all free.

KAREN: Aaaarh!

(*The sudden release of the belt all but causes her to lose her
balance and topple over the edge. She grabs at the first available
handhold, which happens to be Henry's scarf.*)

HENRY: (*Choking*) Hurrgh!

KAREN: (*Screaming*) Hold on to me, for God's sake!

HENRY: (*With difficulty*) Hould hoo hossibly het ho hof hy harf?
Hi han't –

KAREN: Don't let go . . .

HENRY: Hi han't . . .

KAREN: What?

HENRY: Hi han't heathe . . .

KAREN: Well, give me something else to hold. (*Angrily*) Quickly,
you're so useless . . . You're so totally, totally useless . . .
What are you doing on this bridge, anyway?

(HENRY *manages to put his arms under hers and around her
middle.* KAREN *releases his scarf.*)

HENRY: (*Much relieved*) Ah! Thank you. OK, I'm going to try
and pull you over. Ready?

KAREN: Right.

HENRY: And – heave . . .

(HENRY *hauls at her.* KAREN *reacts.*)

4

KAREN: Aaargh! Careful!

HENRY: Sorry. It's a question of leverage . . .

KAREN: Well, could you use another bit of me to lever with?

HENRY: Yes, I'm sorry, I didn't mean to . . . (*He finds another grip.*) That better?

KAREN: Fractionally. Those are only my ribs.

HENRY: And two–six! Hup!
(*He starts to heave her over.*)

KAREN: (*Reacting*) Hah!

HENRY: (*Another heave*) Hip!

KAREN: Hoo!

HENRY: Sorry, is this hurting?

KAREN: No, it's quite nice, actually. Keep going.

HENRY: (*A final heave*) Hoy!

KAREN: Huf!
(*He finally half lifts, half drags her over the railing.* KAREN *finishes sitting on the bridge.* HENRY *regains his breath.*)
God! That was terrifying.

HENRY: Close thing.

KAREN: It certainly was. (*She shudders. She looks around her as if searching for someone.*)

HENRY: You all right?

KAREN: Thank you very much.

HENRY: Not at all.

KAREN: You saved my life.

HENRY: Well . . .

KAREN: I must owe you something . . .?

HENRY: No.

KAREN: Something. A drink, at least?

HENRY: (*Looking at his watch*) It's half past twelve.

KAREN: Half past twelve?

HENRY: Yes.

KAREN: (*Angrily*) My God! Half past *twelve*?

HENRY: Yes.

KAREN: I don't believe it.

HENRY: How long had you been there?

KAREN: Since twenty past eight.

HENRY: Lord.

5

KAREN: Half past twelve! It's unbelievable.
    (*Pause.*)
HENRY: Well . . .
KAREN: This is Chelsea Bridge, isn't it?
HENRY: No, this is Albert Bridge.
KAREN: Albert Bridge?
HENRY: Yes.
KAREN: You sure?
HENRY: Positive.
KAREN: Sod it!
HENRY: What?
KAREN: Nothing.
    (*Another pause.*)
HENRY: Er . . . How did you come to get there?
KAREN: Where?
HENRY: Where you were. Hanging like that? How did you get
    there? Do you mind my asking?
KAREN: Well, obviously, I was trying to throw myself off.
HENRY: *You* were?
KAREN: Only I managed to make a complete mess of that, too.
    Like everything else in my life . . . (*Suddenly despairing*) Oh,
    God . . .
    (*She hunches up, tearfully, a pathetic huddle on the pavement.*)
HENRY: (*Ineffectually*) Oh, come on, now . . .
KAREN: You can leave me, it's all right. Leave me here. I'm just
    so pathetic . . .
HENRY: Look, perhaps I could see you home . . .?
KAREN: Go away. Just leave me here . . .
HENRY: I can't do that.
KAREN: I'll be all right. I expect.
HENRY: I can't leave you here like this.
KAREN: (*A little cry of self-pity*) Oh . . .
HENRY: (*Soothingly*) Sssh!
KAREN: Oh!
HENRY: Please let me . . . at least get you on your feet. You'll
    catch your – you'll catch your cold sitting there.
    (KAREN *lets* HENRY *help her to her feet.*)
    There.

KAREN: (*Holding on to him*) Thank you. You're very kind.

HENRY: (*Slightly embarrassed*) No, not really. I just –

KAREN: I'm sorry I called you useless. I didn't mean that.

HENRY: No, as it happens you were right. I am a bit useless, really.

KAREN: Yes? Is that how you see yourself? Useless?

HENRY: Most of the time.

KAREN: Well. That makes two of us, then, doesn't it?
(*She smiles a little.*)

HENRY: (*Smiling too, despite himself*) I suppose it does.
(KAREN *evidently decides to pull herself together. She scrabbles in her mac pocket and eventually finds a tissue.*)

KAREN: Come on . . .

HENRY: (*Startled*) Where to?

KAREN: I'll take you somewhere for a drink. Come on.

HENRY: But nothing will be open.

KAREN: I know somewhere that's open. It's all right, it's not far . . .
Do you have your car with you?

HENRY: I don't have one.

KAREN: Mine's parked along there . . . Come on, we both need something. Unless you've other things you'd sooner be doing?

HENRY: (*Looking back at the river*) Er, no. No.

KAREN: Great. (*Turning and extending her hand*) By the way. Karen.
Karen Knightly.

HENRY: (*Shaking her hand in turn*) Henry. Henry Bell.

KAREN: Splendid. Then follow me, HenryBell.

HENRY: Where are we going?

KAREN: (*Disappearing into the darkness*) Just as far as the bypass, that's all . . .

HENRY: Ah. (*As he follows her off, puzzled*) What bypass?
(*The lights dim and almost immediately return to reveal –*)

SCENE I
2.30 a.m.

A table in the corner of a transport café. Faint jukebox music and the sound of an electronic game machine. Chatter from unseen lorry drivers.
HENRY *appears carrying two very large mugs of tea. He sets these on the*

table. He yawns, something he is wont to do throughout the scene. He removes his coat and scarf and, after a careful examination of two chairs, places the items on one and sits on the other. We see he is wearing a neat, conventional suit. He looks around him. He smiles at someone nervously and looks away self-consciously. He tries his tea and nearly scalds his mouth. The chatter in the room suddenly ceases. So does the game machine. Just the thud of the jukebox. The cause of this lull enters. KAREN *has evidently been freshening up. She has removed her hat and let her hair loose. She is now carrying her coat, revealing a chic, if somewhat incongruous, strapless evening dress. She seems quite unaware of the effect she has caused.* HENRY, *gaping, rises as she approaches. She really does look quite something.*

KAREN: (*Dropping into the chair opposite him*) Sorry I've been so long, HenryBell. Just taken a proper look at myself. I looked frightful. Is this tea? Terrific. Just what I needed.

HENRY: It's very, very hot. Be careful.

KAREN: Great. (*She takes a great gulp, apparently immune to heat.*) Mmm! They don't make tea like this anywhere else but here.

HENRY: Where exactly are we?

KAREN: About – twenty miles from Salisbury. Why?

HENRY: No. No reason. It just seems quite a way to come just for a cup of tea, that's all.

KAREN: (*Sipping her tea*) Worth it, though.

HENRY: Oh, yes. (*Slight pause.*) Glad we didn't decide to have alcohol. We'd probably have finished up at Land's End. (*He laughs a little at his joke.*)

KAREN: (*Seriously*) Why, is there a good pub there?

HENRY: I've no idea.

KAREN: I'm game to go if you are.

HENRY: No. No . . .
   (*He sips at his tea tentatively. A silence. The music plays for a second.* KAREN *listens.*)

KAREN: Oh, God, this is wonderful, this one. I love it. What is it? The Hollies?

HENRY: (*Blankly*) Pardon?

KAREN: Or is it Brian Thing and the Thingies?

HENRY: I don't know, I . . .

8

KAREN: (*Turning and yelling to someone*) Who's this, do you know? Is it the Hollies?

FIRST VOICE: (*Off*) What's that, darling?

KAREN: This music. Is it the Hollies?

SECOND VOICE: (*Off*) It's the Everlys, sweetheart.

KAREN: The Everly Brothers. Of course it is. Thank you.

SECOND VOICE: (*Off*) Any time, sweetheart, it's my pleasure.

FIRST VOICE: (*Off*) Make sure that's the only pleasure you give him and all, darling . . .

(*A lot of laughter.* KAREN *seems amused. She obviously enjoys such attention, unlike* HENRY, *who looks even more embarrassed. He looks at his watch.*)

KAREN: Have you got to be somewhere, HenryBell?

HENRY: What?

KAREN: You keep looking at your watch, I wondered if you had to be somewhere?

HENRY: No, I was – I was just wondering – how I was going to get back, that's all.

KAREN: What's the time?

HENRY: Half past two.

KAREN: It's OK. I'll take you back. Don't worry. Where are you? Chelsea?

HENRY: Er . . . more Fulham, really.

KAREN: Fulham. Fine. Easy.

HENRY: (*Yawning*) Is that convenient for you? Excuse me.

KAREN: Anywhere's fine for me.

HENRY: Where do you have to go?

KAREN: Me? (*Vaguely*) Oh, the other side of Dorchester.

HENRY: Dorchester? The one in Dorset?

KAREN: Have you been there?

HENRY: Do you mean – do you mean you'd drive me all the way back to London and then drive all the way to Dorset? Tonight? You'll kill yourself . . .

KAREN: Why not? What else was I going to be doing?

HENRY: Ah, yes. Point taken.

KAREN: (*Tearful*) God, I'm so unhappy, you know . . .

HENRY: Yes? (*Pause.*) Do you want to talk about it?

KAREN: (*Suddenly angry*) No!

9

(They sit in silence. HENRY *is becoming wary of her ever-changing moods.* KAREN *sings along with the music. Occasional, wordless, discordant notes with no attempt at the melody.)*

HENRY: I – I don't know if this would help at all but . . .

KAREN: Yes, I'm sure there is a God, vicar, thank you very much.

HENRY: No, I wasn't going to say that – what I was going to say is, Karen – you're not alone. That's all.

KAREN: I know I'm not alone. There's millions of the buggers everywhere. That's half the trouble.

HENRY: *(Patiently)* No, I meant – tonight. When you were trying to – end it all . . . You weren't the only one.
    (KAREN stares at him.)
    I was just about to do the same thing, you see. Jump off that bridge.

KAREN: *You* were?

HENRY: I don't know if that helps at all . . .

KAREN: I saved your life, then?

HENRY: I think you did.

KAREN: Well . . . *(She raises her mug.)*

HENRY: *(Joining in the toast)* Yes.

KAREN: Would you have really jumped, HenryBell? Really?

HENRY: *(Considering)* Yes. Then I would have done. At that moment, probably. Not now.

KAREN: The moment's passed?

HENRY: It has.

KAREN: Are you glad you didn't?

HENRY: *(Smiling at her)* Yes. Yes, I am.

KAREN: *(Smiling back at him)* So am I.

HENRY: You're glad you didn't jump?

KAREN: Oh, yes, that too. But I'm glad you didn't.

HENRY: Thank you. *(A pause.)* It's just everything suddenly conspires against you at once, doesn't it? It all becomes insoluble.

KAREN: Insuperable.

HENRY: Right. I don't know how you feel. Every now and then, I just get this overwhelming sense of the futility of it all. Of the sheer uselessness. Do you get that feeling?

KAREN: No.

HENRY: Ah.

KAREN: I don't think I'd kill myself simply because I couldn't think of a reason for living.

HENRY: You wouldn't?

KAREN: No. I can always find a good reason for living.

HENRY: In that case, why would you ever want to kill yourself?

KAREN: I'd kill myself when I had a very good reason for doing so. A stronger reason than the reason I had for living. There is a difference, I promise you there is.

HENRY: (*Uncertain*) Yes. Yes, I can see there probably is.

KAREN: Why did you? Want to do it?

HENRY: As I say. Things. I don't want to bore you with details. My wife – she'd recently left me and – I was just about getting over that . . .

KAREN: Did she go off with another man?

HENRY: No. She just went. She found it – me – too much. All of a sudden.

KAREN: Have you any children?

HENRY: Yes. One. Well, hardly a child. He's left home, now. Working in Holland.

KAREN: When did your wife leave?

HENRY: Oh, a year ago.

KAREN: You waited that long to jump off a bridge?

HENRY: No, as I was saying. I'd just about got over her going. I'd come to terms with that. I'd sold the house. Got a little flat. Mastered the microwave. I mean, Marianne and I – we were fond of each other, don't get me wrong – but it was familiar-fond rather than loving-fond – if you know what I mean. A bit routine. Appallingly routine, if you want the truth. We never rowed – we never disagreed – we never – did anything very much except – sit. I wasn't really surprised when she went. Not deep down. It was the . . . I don't know . . .

KAREN: Loneliness?

HENRY: Pointlessness. So I hurled myself into my work. I enjoyed my work. I was good at it.

KAREN: Was?

HENRY: That's it, you see. I've just been fired. Sorry. Made redundant. Sounds nicer. I cleared my desk this evening –

yesterday evening – I had a glass of sherry with the department. And I left quietly by the side door. After fourteen years, and without much home life to speak of, that really did leave a bit of a hole. I had suddenly moved on from a state in which things seemed faintly pointless, to one where I could no longer see any point to them at all.

KAREN: Where did you work?

HENRY: Lembridge Tennit. If that means anything.

KAREN: Can't say it does. What line are they in?

HENRY: Everything, really. From biscuits to bicycles. You'd know the brand names.

KAREN: Oh, I see. One of those. Multinationals.

HENRY: Multi. Multi. Multi.

KAREN: Polluting the rivers, poisoning the atmosphere and secretly funding right-wing revolutionaries.

HENRY: Those are the chaps.

KAREN: Why did they fire you?

HENRY: Oh. All the jargon. Redefining the job profile. Rationalizing the department. Restructuring the management team. Which essentially meant either get promoted or – get out. And, innocent that I was, so certain that I'd been doing a good job, I sat there fully expecting to be promoted.

KAREN: Being good is never enough in itself . . .

HENRY: How right you are. (*He pauses.*) How right. It's not just a matter of doing a good job. Or even doing the best you can. No. It's no good taking work home with you and sitting seven nights a week ruining your eyesight for no extra money. No point at all in covering for colleagues who aren't doing the job they're paid to do because they're taking three-hour lunchbreaks five days a week and rolling in absolutely legless after fifteen double scotches at four thirty in the afternoon. That's never enough. You've also got to be working the system. Chatting up the right people. Buying the drinks that matter. Arranging the cosy little dinner with the boss's P.A. Taking the right lift at the right moment with the right people. Going down – hallo, Mr Pride, sir – fancy bumping into you, remember me? Losing the right game of squash. Missing the right putt. Winning the right rubber. Licking the right shoes. Sending the right Christmas cards. Driving the right car. Choosing the right suit. Wearing the right bloody underwear. Screwing the right secretary . . . (*He stops.*) Sorry.

KAREN: (*Simply*) It's just a game, that's all.

HENRY: And you either play by the rules and win, like he did. Or you ignore them and lose, like me.

KAREN: He?

HENRY: What?

KAREN: You said he. Who's he?

HENRY: (*Through grated teeth*) Tick.

KAREN: Sorry?

HENRY: (*Barely able to say the name*) His name is Bruce Tick. I've never hated anyone in my life, you know. Well, not since I was a child – but then you hate people all the time at that age – but Bruce Tick I actually hate now. He smiled at me and stole my job. Even as he was smiling he was stealing my job. But do you know the worst thing of all? The worst thing was – *everybody knew he was doing it* – and no one – *no one* thought to . . . People I'd worked with for fourteen years. *Friends!*

KAREN: Yes.

HENRY: That's what hurt. That hurt more than anything. (*Calming down*) Yes, I came very near to murdering Mr Bruce Tick, I can tell you.

KAREN: (*Seriously*) You should have done. Why didn't you?

HENRY: (*Assuming she is joking*) What? And give him the satisfaction of sitting up there on his cloud afterwards, sipping Glen Whatsit, while I'm down here breaking rocks in a quarry? No, thanks.

KAREN: Good point.

HENRY: No, to hell with them all, I say. Except Elaine, of course. (*He yawns.*) Excuse me.

KAREN: Elaine?

HENRY: My secretary. That was. You know what she did? The minute she heard they were firing me, Elaine marched right in there and handed in her notice.

KAREN: Was she in love with you?

HENRY: Elaine? Good Lord, no. Respectable, happily married

13

lady. Six years to go till retirement. Everything to lose and she just didn't care. She marched in there and she told them.

KAREN: Good for her.

HENRY: She said to them: 'I can no longer continue to work for a firm who could reward fourteen years of unswerving loyalty with such contemptuous disdain.'

KAREN: She sounds quite a woman.

HENRY: She is. Well, at least she's been spared from working for Bruce Tick.

KAREN: I don't like the sound of him at all.

HENRY: He's – repellent.

(HENRY *simmers. A silence.*)

But then, I am slightly prejudiced.

KAREN: I knew someone like that once.

HENRY: Really? Bad luck.

KAREN: Yes.

(*Pause.*)

HENRY: Who was he?

KAREN: Her name was Imogen Staxton-Billing.

HENRY: She sounds absolutely appalling.

KAREN: She is. What sort of woman – what sort of wife – would be frigid and inept enough to drive her own husband out of his house into the arms of another woman – a woman who really did appreciate him and gave him love and warmth and comfort and sex – and then, at the very last minute, this wife refuses to let him go. Instead uses all her wiles and cunning and cheap little wifely blackmailings – flaunting their two grotesquely repulsive kids – in order to lure him back into her barren, lumpy iceberg of a bed. What sort of woman do you think would do that?

HENRY: Sounds like an Imogen Staxton-Billing sort of woman to me.

KAREN: Right.

(*A pause.*)

HENRY: You don't think that he might have . . . The husband might have . . . been a bit to blame, as well?

KAREN: Who?

HENRY: The husband?

14

KAREN: Anthony Staxton-Billing?

HENRY: Yes. You don't think he might have decided, after all, to give the marriage another go? Decided to go back to his wife? Is that a possibility? I mean, I was just hoping to perhaps help you to see her in a better light . . . (*He trails away.*)

KAREN: (*Dangerously*) If you don't mind my saying so, that is a very, very ignorant thing to say.

(*A pause.*)

Sorry, HenryBell.

HENRY: That's quite all right.

(*A silence – mainly because* HENRY *can't think of anything to say.*)

KAREN: No, you couldn't possibly say that if you'd met the ageing, comatose, bovine Imogen Staxton-Billing. Bouncing, bonny, horsey, dung-smelling niece of one Colonel Marcus Lipscott, DSO, VSOP and twiddly bits. She worked it. Somehow she worked it. She had little Tony running home to Mummy. She cheated.

(*She reflects.*)

(*Calmly*) I was standing at that station with three suitcases. For hours and hours and hours. And he never came. *Three* suitcases. Can you imagine that?

HENRY: (*Yawning, despite himself*) That's terrible. Excuse me.

KAREN: It was. It was terrible. Wait for me, darling. The trains were coming in. And then the trains were going out. And then they were coming in again. And I was just standing there. Like an old, unwanted – chocolate machine. With three suitcases. Can you imagine how I felt?

HENRY: Yes. How awful. (*A pause.*) Which station was this?

KAREN: (*Furiously*) I don't know which station. I can't remember which bloody station. How do you expect me to remember the station, for God's sake? (*Weeping openly now, as her voice gets increasingly loud*) How could he do that to me? How could he do that to *me*? I'll kill her!

(HENRY *looks around nervously. They are beginning to attract attention.*)

(*Screaming*) AAAAAAAAAAAAAAAAAAAAAAAAAAAHHHHHHHHH!

(*A large figure looms into view. It is a* LORRY DRIVER. *He stares at* HENRY *suspiciously.*)

LORRY DRIVER: Spot of bother is there, mate?

HENRY: No, no, no. We're fine. Don't worry.

LORRY DRIVER: (*To* KAREN) Is he giving you any trouble, love?

KAREN: No, it's all right.

LORRY DRIVER: Sure?

KAREN: Yes.

LORRY DRIVER: (*A bit disappointed*) All right. (*To* HENRY) Don't give her any trouble, mate, all right?

HENRY: I'm not going to.

LORRY DRIVER: If there's one thing I can't stand in this world it's a man maltreating a pretty young girl, all right?

HENRY: Absolutely. (*He yawns.*) Sorry.

LORRY DRIVER: (*Leaning close to* KAREN) All right then, love? You all right? You let me know if he causes you any more trouble, all right? I'll come and sort him out for you, all right? You just give me a shout. I'll be just over there if you need me, all right? All right, then?

KAREN: (*Irritated by all this*) Oh, just bugger off, will you? Go away!

LORRY DRIVER: (*Outraged*) Oy, oy, oy, oy, oy . . .

KAREN: Look, go away. We're having a private conversation, all right?

LORRY DRIVER: (*Departing truculently*) No need for that. No need for language like that. (*To* HENRY, *threateningly*) You'd better watch her language, mate. If you don't want to get sorted out. All right?

(*The* LORRY DRIVER *goes – a Knight of the Road rebuffed.*)

KAREN: I can't stand men like that. Right. (*Shouting in the direction of the* LORRY DRIVER) Who do they think they are, anyway? (*Pushing aside her mug*) I can't drink any more of this, it's foul. If I don't have a vodka soon, I'll die.

(*She rises and starts to put on her coat.* HENRY *rises, too, glancing at his watch.*)

HENRY: We still won't find anywhere open. It's only just after three a.m.

KAREN: It's all right, I know somewhere.

HENRY: Would I be right in thinking it's just the far side of Dorchester?

KAREN: You got it in one, kid.
  (*She goes out swiftly.* HENRY, *still struggling into his coat and yawning, follows her. He turns in the doorway and nods to the unseen drivers.*)
HENRY: Goodnight .
  (*A barrage of abuse and shouting. He exits hurriedly. With scarcely a break, the lights rapidly cross-fade to – *)

SCENE 2
5.00 a.m.

Furtherfield House. The hall. Seemingly this is a very large place indeed. The hall is the size of a football pitch. We see some area of it. A couple of chairs or a sofa, to give an idea of the scale. Somewhere, a huge front door is heard to slam. Immediately, KAREN *enters, pulling off her hat and coat as she does so.* HENRY *follows, totally awed by the unexpected.*

KAREN: (*Yelling*) Winnie! Winnie! (*To* HENRY) Sling your coat anywhere. I think we'd be better off here in the hall, it'll be freezing in the drawing rooms. (*Yelling again*) Winnie! Wakey, wakey!
HENRY: It's only five o'clock, maybe people aren't . . .
KAREN: Winnie!
  (WINNIE *appears in her dressing-gown. She is the old family retainer, gentle, uncomplaining, with a soft-spoken Dorset accent.*)
WINNIE: Just a minute, Miss Karen . . . Here I am.
  (*She gathers up their coats during the next.*)
KAREN: Winnie, dearest, could you find us a bottle of nice champagne?
WINNIE: Champagne. Right, Miss Karen.
KAREN: (*To* HENRY) Anything to eat?
HENRY: No, not at this time of the morning. (*Yawning*) Excuse me.
KAREN: No, I'm not hungry either. Just the champagne.
WINNIE: Right. Just the champagne. Morning, sir.

17

HENRY: Good morning. This is very kind of you.

KAREN: Winnie, this is Mr Henry Bell. Known as HenryBell.

HENRY: How do you do?

KAREN: We'll have two glasses, Winnie.

WINNIE: Right you are, Miss Karen.

(WINNIE *goes off*.)

HENRY: What an amazing house. Wonderful. It's yours?

KAREN: Well, my family's. Yes.

HENRY: Who lives here? Besides you?

KAREN: Well, mostly my brother. That's my brother Oliver – he's generally around somewhere – then other people trail in and out from time to time. And then there's people like Winnie and things.

HENRY: Do you have a lot of servants?

KAREN: (*Vaguely*) No . . . Well. A few. I don't have much to do with any of that side, really.

HENRY: Your parents don't live here, then?

KAREN: (*Casually*) No, they're both dead. There was an accident. And they died.

HENRY: Oh dear. What sort of accident?

KAREN: (*Slight pause*) I'm not allowed to talk about that.

HENRY: Ah.

(WINNIE *enters with a tray, two glasses and a bottle of Dom Perignon*.)

KAREN: This isn't an ancestral home or anything, if that's what you're thinking.

HENRY: Oh, I see. (*He yawns*.) Excuse me.

WINNIE: Want me to open it, Miss Karen?

KAREN: Well, we don't want to sit here staring at the bottle, do we, Winnie? (*To* HENRY) Some revolting old landowner built it in about 1850. My grandfather bought it in about 1910, spent a fortune doing it up and then promptly died and left it to my father.

HENRY: I couldn't see it all in the dark. How many rooms?

KAREN: No idea.

WINNIE: There's fifty-eight rooms, sir, including the servants' quarters and the old nurseries.

HENRY: Fifty-eight. Goodness.

WINNIE: There's twenty-five bedrooms, not counting the master bedroom. Twelve bathrooms. A billiard room, two drawing rooms, dining room, a west study, an east study . . .

KAREN: Yes, thank you, Winnie. (*To* HENRY) You get the idea, anyway.

WINNIE: (*Giving* KAREN *a glass*) Miss Karen.

KAREN: We don't use half the place. I mean, the billiard room is where Oliver keeps his motor bike.

WINNIE: He's got a whole race track now and all.

KAREN: Has he? Oh well, I can't keep up with him these days.

WINNIE: (*Giving* HENRY *a glass*) Sir.

HENRY: Thank you very much indeed. Delicious.

WINNIE: Anything else, miss?

KAREN: No, Winnie, you can go back to bed now. Thank you.

WINNIE: Nearly time to get up, I think. Sleep well then.

HENRY: Thank you.

(WINNIE *goes off again*.)

Good health.

KAREN: Good health, HenryBell.

HENRY: Mmm. Lovely.

(KAREN *studies him for a second*.)

KAREN: HenryBell . . . While we were in the car. I had rather an exciting idea.

HENRY: (*Yawning*) Sorry, did I doze off during the drive? I think I did.

KAREN: You did. You've had your night's sleep. So you can keep awake now.

HENRY: I'm afraid I'm going to have to go to bed, properly. Very soon. Somewhere or other.

KAREN: (*Ignoring him*) Answer me this –

HENRY: I presume one of your twenty-five bedrooms is free –

KAREN: If I hadn't met you – if you hadn't met me – where would you be?

HENRY: Home in bed, probably.

KAREN: (*Angrily*) Oh, do be serious.

HENRY: I'm sorry.

KAREN: I hate silly men. I can't stand them.

HENRY: What about silly women?

19

KAREN: (*Ignoring him*) Answer me. Where would you be? Where would we both be? I will tell you. Floating in the Thames. That's where we'd be. Only we're not. Thanks to you, I'm here. And thanks to me, you're here. True? Or false?

HENRY: Yes. I mean, true.

KAREN: We've both been given a reprieve. We're playing extra time. I don't know for how long – I may be run over tomorrow. You may drop dead tonight . . .

HENRY: I probably will, in a minute . . .

KAREN: But for now, we're here. Alive when we should be dead. And owing that life to each other. And do you know the most crucial thing of all that occurred to me? It must have been *meant*. Something, some force, some power was operating tonight. It saw what you and I were trying to do and it said, not yet, not yet. I need these people. These two people are still necessary. They are still an essential part of the world. They are still in play. They are still there on the board. But the question is, why? For what reason?

HENRY: (*Yawning*) I don't know, no idea.

KAREN: Think.

(*A pause.*)

Well?

HENRY: I haven't a clue.

KAREN: We both said it. Back there in that café. We sat there and we both experienced that same feeling.

HENRY: We did?

KAREN: Yes.

HENRY: What feeling?

KAREN: (*Drawing close to him, softly*) Revenge, HenryBell, revenge.

HENRY: Revenge?

KAREN: (*Excitedly*) That's why we're being kept alive, HenryBell, you and I. Why we weren't allowed to die. We're unquiet spirits, if you like, with unfinished business. The wrongs that have been done to us have got to be put right. We're never going to rest, either of us, until we've done that.

HENRY: (*Intrigued*) You actually believe that?

KAREN: My psychiatrist told me once that revenge was the most powerful driving force in the human psyche . . .

HENRY: You're seeing a psychiatrist?

KAREN: Oh, years ago.

HENRY: Ah.

KAREN: I was just a baby.

HENRY: A baby? You had feelings of revenge when you were a baby?

KAREN: Well, ten, twelve – I don't know. The point is – you and I – we still have purpose.

HENRY: Revenge?

KAREN: Yes. Can't you feel it in you? It's a terrific feeling, HenryBell, if you can harness it. Use it. Creatively.

HENRY: I don't see how one could possibly do that.

KAREN: Nor did I. Till just now in the car. Then I had this brilliant idea. Oh, it's so exciting . . . (*Taking up the bottle*) Have some more champagne . . .
(*She pours some into his glass, regardless.*)

HENRY: (*In vain*) Just a drop . . .

KAREN: What you were saying earlier gave me the idea. You said, if you did what you felt like doing and went into your office and murdered Mr – whateverhisnameis –

HENRY: Tick. Bruce Tick.

KAREN: Then your victory would be very short-lived indeed because you'd probably spend the rest of your life in gaol.

HENRY: Quite so.

KAREN: Similarly, were I to run down Imogen Staxton-Billing on the zebra crossing as she trundled her monstrous brood to school or to put strychnine into her feeding trough, then the finger of suspicion would very rapidly point at me. The same problem would apply.

HENRY: (*Yawning*) Yes.

KAREN: Keep awake, I'm nearly there. But what – here it is – what if we swapped?

HENRY: Swapped?

KAREN: I took on your revenge. You took on mine. I put pay to Mr Tick. You put pay to Mrs Staxton-Billing.

HENRY: That's ridiculous –

KAREN: It's brilliant. No motive. No trace. Cold, calculated revenge.

HENRY: You mean, kill them?

KAREN: No. Not necessarily. Just – teach them. Give them as good as they gave.

HENRY: How?

KAREN: That's half the fun of it. We'd both have to work it out for ourselves. Find a way. Size up our prey and seek out their weaknesses. Choose our method. And – thwunk!
(*She brings her fingers together like a gin trap.*)

HENRY: What's – thwunk?

KAREN: That's the trap closing on them, HenryBell. Isn't it a brilliant idea?

HENRY: It's – absurd. I mean how could I – I couldn't – No. Could you . . . ? Honestly?

KAREN: I could.

HENRY: You really could?

KAREN: All I'd need is a way in. Just an intro.

HENRY: There you are, then. That's impossible to start with. I couldn't introduce you to Bruce Tick . . . Hallo, Bruce, I'd like you to meet the instrument of my revenge . . .

KAREN: No, of course you couldn't, that would ruin the whole thing.

HENRY: I don't even know where he lives. It's somewhere miles out.

KAREN: You know where he works, though.

HENRY: So?

KAREN: I'll get myself a job with the firm.

HENRY: A job? What sort of a job?

KAREN: I don't know. A secretary or something.

HENRY: Have you ever been a secretary?

KAREN: No.

HENRY: Well, you can't just walk in and be a secretary, you know. You need shorthand and typing and degrees in word-processing. All sorts of things these days.

KAREN: Oh, I could bluff all that.

HENRY: Don't be ridiculous. (*Half to himself*) Mind you, a lot of them seem to.

KAREN: You don't like the idea, then.

HENRY: No, I don't.

(*A silence.* KAREN *sulks.*)

Look, Karen. It wouldn't work. (*Pause.*) It really wouldn't.

KAREN: You're a wimp.

HENRY: Probably.

KAREN: What have you got to lose? Nothing. What's the worst
that could happen? Imogen Staxton-Billing might slap your
face. Better than being fished out of the Thames by the river
police any day. But you'd prefer to go on being trodden on
by the Mr Ticks of this world, would you? Fine. They'll be
happy. They don't expect you to fight back, so they'll hardly
be surprised when you don't, will they? (*Pause.*) Wimp.

HENRY: (*Tired and angry*) Look, it just wouldn't work.

KAREN: Wet.

HENRY: Complete dreamland.

KAREN: Weed.

HENRY: Childish.

KAREN: Wally.

HENRY: (*Shouting*) Look, will you stop that! I'm sorry. I've had
enough. I'm sorry. I'm very tired and I want to go to bed.
I'm sorry.

(*A pause. He controls himself.*)

(*Quietly*) I'm sorry.

KAREN: Are you frightened because you think you couldn't do it,
or because you think I couldn't do it?

HENRY: I think it's out of the question for both of us even to try.

KAREN: (*Wheedling*) But supposing – supposing – I tried,
HenryBell . . . I mean, it needn't involve you at all – no one
need trace me to you – Look, say I managed to get in there –
into your firm somehow and – say that somehow I got close
to Mr Tick – Then would you be prepared to give it a try
from your side?

HENRY: (*A slight pause*) Why? Why do you want to do this?

KAREN: The greatest feeling in the world, HenryBell. Revenge.
Pure, unadulterated revenge. Not weedy little jealousy. Not
some piddling little envy. But good, old-fashioned,
bloodcurdling revenge. Just picture it, HenryBell. What I
could do to him, once I got close to your Mr Tick . . . Can't
you see it?

23

HENRY: My God, I think I can, almost . . .

KAREN: It'll be him standing on that bridge instead of you . . .
And there won't be someone like me there to rescue him,
either. I'll just drive past on the other side of the road. And
as I go by, I'll lean out and say – by the way, Mr Tick,
HenryBell sends you his regards. Isn't that a beautiful
thought?

HENRY: (*Softly*) Fairly attractive, I must say.

KAREN: Think about that.

HENRY: I will.

(*He yawns. She refills his glass.* HENRY *is still abstracted.*)

KAREN: Did you say your secretary had resigned?

HENRY: Elaine? Yes.

KAREN: Presumably they'll have to replace her, won't they?

HENRY: I suppose so. They'll probably advertise the post, in due
course.

KAREN: When will they get someone?

HENRY: Oh, weeks. Knowing the pace that place moves.

KAREN: Big, is it?

HENRY: Lembridge Tennit? Huge. They've got thirty-two floors
in that building alone.

KAREN: What will they do till they get someone permanent?

HENRY: I don't know. Probably get a temp.

KAREN: A temp?

HENRY: Temporary secretary. From an agency. Just to fill in.

KAREN: I could do that.

HENRY: (*Yawning*) You couldn't. Believe me. You really
couldn't.

KAREN: Maybe I could talk to your Elaine . . .

HENRY: What for?

KAREN: Do you have her address?

HENRY: Yes, I do actually. Why?

KAREN: Is she on the phone?

HENRY: (*Yawning again*) Yes, yes . . . I'm sure she is.

KAREN: Ring her.

HENRY: Now?

KAREN: Now.

HENRY: I'm not ringing anyone now. It's five thirty in the

24

morning, for God's sake . . .

KAREN: Then later on. Tell her I want to see her. Tell her I need to talk to her . . .

HENRY: Oh, heavens . . .

KAREN: Will you do that?

HENRY: (*Yawning*) I'm so tired, you've no idea . . .

KAREN: Will you do that?

HENRY: Karen, please let me go to bed . . .

KAREN: (*Slapping him awake*) HenryBell, listen to me . . .

HENRY: I agree. Yes, I agree to everything.

KAREN: Will you give me her number?

HENRY: (*Yawning uncontrollably*) Yes, yes, anything. I'll give you anything you want – just let me go to bed . . .

KAREN: Give it to me . . .

HENRY: (*Producing his wallet*) Here.

KAREN: Is the number in here?

HENRY: (*His eyes half closed*) Yes, in the address book . . .

KAREN: This is a wallet.

HENRY: (*Yawning*) Oh . . . ooo . . . ot . . . air . . . (*He takes back the wallet and puts it away.*) . . . it . . . ear . . . (*He produces an address book from his other inside pocket.*) . . . air . . . is . . .

KAREN: (*Examining the book*) What's Elaine's surname?

HENRY: Oh God, I've told you everything I know . . . let me sleep . . .

KAREN: HenryBell, what's her surname?

HENRY: . . . ith . . .

KAREN: Ith? What I–T–H?

HENRY: No . . . Smith . . .

KAREN: Smith . . . (*Finding it*) E. Smith.

HENRY: (*Snuggling up on the sofa*) Mmm . . .

KAREN: (*Keeping the book*) Good. Good. Good boy . . .

HENRY: (*Sleepily*) Good boy . . .

KAREN: (*Helping him up*) Come on, HenryBell. Bedtime now. Don't go to sleep yet. Up you come. Come on. I'll take you up to bed.

(KAREN *starts to lead him off.* HENRY *is reeling with tiredness.*)

HENRY: Bedtime . . .

KAREN: That's it. Upstairs now . . .

HENRY: Upstairs now . . .

KAREN: Come on. You can come and sleep in my bed. You can come and sleep with me . . .

HENRY: Oh, no. Please no. I just need to sleep . . .

KAREN: Come on. We'll have a nice time now, shall we?

HENRY: Oh, please no. Not that. Please . . .

KAREN: Come on, HenryBell, that's it. You mustn't go to sleep yet, we've got to celebrate . . .

HENRY: (*Despairingly, as he is led away*) Oh God, please. Anything but that . . .

(*They go off. Once again the lights cross-fade swiftly and we move to –*)

SCENE 3
3.00 p.m.

The dining room at Furtherfield House. Afternoon sun is streaming in through large windows. Faint birdsong from outside. Distant sounds of mowing. A clock ticks somewhere. The room is dominated by a (predictably) large table. It is laid for one. NORMA, *a young parlourmaid, probably no more than sixteen, enters. She is evidently waiting to serve breakfast. She straightens the cutlery a fraction, tweaks the table arrangement of flowers and walks to the window and watches whoever it is who is mowing.* WINNIE *enters and looks at* NORMA. NORMA *catches her eye and hurries out.* WINNIE *moves to the table and restraightens the cutlery and the flowers. She also has a look out of the window. In a moment,* HENRY *enters. He has on a large dressing-gown and larger slippers. He looks rather lost.*

HENRY: (*Seeing* WINNIE) Ah.

WINNIE: Afternoon, sir.

HENRY: Ah. Is it?

WINNIE: Lovely day again.

HENRY: Yes. You haven't by any chance seen my clothes?

WINNIE: Clothes?

HENRY: Yes.

WINNIE: No, I'm afraid not, sir.

26

HENRY: Only they were taken off me – I took them off me – myself last night and they're nowhere in sight this morning. It's very odd.

WINNIE: Very odd, sir.

HENRY: Yes. Well.

WINNIE: It might be that Miss Karen took them, sir.

HENRY: Really?

WINNIE: It might be. She did have a bag when she went.

HENRY: Went?

WINNIE: Out, sir.

HENRY: Where?

WINNIE: I wouldn't know at all, sir.

HENRY: Oh.

WINNIE: She did take her car, that I do know.

HENRY: Ah, then she could have gone anywhere, couldn't she? At the rate she drives she's probably in Cornwall.

WINNIE: A law unto herself, sir, Miss Karen.

HENRY: Yes. Still, until she gets back with my suit, I'm afraid I have to wear this. I hope nobody minds.

WINNIE: That's the late master's gown, sir. I'm sure you'll be very welcome to it. Now, would you care for some breakfast, sir?

HENRY: Well, yes, I think I would. Thank you.

(WINNIE *holds out the chair while he sits at the table. As he goes to sit, a fluttering sound above their heads.* HENRY *instinctively ducks.*)

WINNIE: Oh, those birds. They fly in here through the windows and then they haven't the sense to fly out again. Shoo! Shoo! There, now.

HENRY: (*Sitting*) Thank you. I'm afraid I'm terribly late down. My watch has stopped. I've no idea of the time.

WINNIE: It's just gone three ten, sir.

HENRY: Three ten? Good Lord.

WINNIE: So long as you slept well, sir.

HENRY: Yes, I did, I did. Eventually I did, anyway.

WINNIE: What would you care for, sir? I'm afraid we didn't lay out the sideboard with there just being the one of you here, sir. When we have a house full we have it all laid out there, you see. It's a lovely sight.

HENRY: It must be, yes.

(*The bird swoops again.* HENRY *evades it.*)

WINNIE: How about eggs and bacon, sir? That suit you?

HENRY: Oh, well now, that sounds rather . . .

WINNIE: Or scrambled eggs? Poached eggs? Boiled eggs? Omelette? Kidneys? Kedgeree? Ham? Kippers? A little bit of smoked haddock?

HENRY: No, no. Eggs and bacon sound just the thing.

WINNIE: Cornflakes?

HENRY: Perfect.

WINNIE: Or Weetabix? Crispies? Puffed Wheat? Shredded Wheat? Sugar Puffs? Rice Crispies? Muesli?

HENRY: No, no. Cornflakes.

WINNIE: Tea or coffee?

HENRY: Tea. (*Quickly*) Indian. Just as it comes. With milk. White toast. Marmalade. Thank you.

WINNIE: Butter?

HENRY: Yes, please. Unsalted.

WINNIE: Or margarine?

HENRY: Butter.

WINNIE: Thank you, sir. Won't be a moment. Newspaper is there, sir.

HENRY: Thank you.

(WINNIE *goes out.* HENRY *takes a deep breath. All in all, he's feeling rather cheerful. The bird divebombs him again. He flaps it away with his napkin. He rises and retreats to the window, ducking and weaving. The bird gives up and apparently perches somewhere high in one corner of the room.* HENRY *relaxes. He, too, watches the mowing. He takes deep breaths. He hears the sound of approaching crockery. He hastily resits.* NORMA *enters with a tray with milk, sugar, a silver bowl full of cornflakes and a separate bowl for* HENRY *to eat them out of.* NORMA *is evidently still learning her job. She frowns throughout in concentration, breathing heavily as she goes about her tasks. Her tongue tends to stick out when she attempts anything especially difficult.* WINNIE *shadows* NORMA *throughout, talking her through every action in a low, barely audible voice.*)

WINNIE: (*Quietly*) Put it down just there.

28

(NORMA *puts the tray down.*)

That's it. Now give the gentleman the bowl.

(NORMA *goes to give* HENRY *the large bowl.*)

No, not that bowl. The other bowl. Give the gentleman the other bowl.

(NORMA *goes to give* HENRY *the smaller bowl.*)

HENRY: (*Anticipating this, in an encouragingly helpful tone*) Thank you.

WINNIE: No, no, no. Not from that side. You don't serve from that side, ever, now do you?

(NORMA *takes the bowl back and moves round to* HENRY's *other side.*)

That's it. That's better.

(HENRY *gets the bowl again.*)

HENRY: Thank you again.

WINNIE: Now serve the cornflakes. Serve the gentleman with the cornflakes.

(NORMA *takes up the silver bowl and moves around to* HENRY's *other side.*)

That's it. Good girl. Good girl. Don't get nervous, he won't bite you.

NORMA: Cornflakes, sir?

HENRY: Yes, thank you very much.

(NORMA *now attempts silver service on the cornflakes. It is nail-biting stuff. Each serving gives him about eight cornflakes at a time. She is very nervous.* HENRY *watches her, scarcely daring to breathe. The bird divebombs them a couple of times.* WINNIE *continues her back-seat advice in a low monotone.*)

WINNIE: That's it, carefully, carefully, carefully. Never mind about the bird.

(NORMA *shoots cornflakes over the table. She attempts to rescue them. So does* HENRY.)

(*Sharply*) No, don't try to pick them up. Leave them there.

(HENRY *and* NORMA *both stop at once.*)

No point in picking them up now, is there? Keep going.

(HENRY *gets another eight cornflakes.*)

NORMA: Is that sufficient, sir?

HENRY: (*Relieved*) Yes, yes. That's perfect.

(*He stares at his nearly empty bowl.*)

WINNIE: Milk and sugar now. Milk and sugar.

HENRY: Oh, now look, I can easily do that myself. Please.

(*But* NORMA *is on a pre-programmed course. She carries the tray round to* HENRY.)

NORMA: (*Holding firmly on to the jug*) Milk, sir?

HENRY: Thank you.

NORMA: Say when, sir.

(NORMA *attempts another difficult feat, holding the tray in one hand and the milk jug in the other. The milk dribbles out in a thin trickle.*)

HENRY: (*Waiting till he has enough milk*) Er . . . er . . .

NORMA: That sufficient, sir?

HENRY: (*Doubtfully*) Yes, yes. Thank you.

(*The cornflakes are barely damp.*)

WINNIE: Now the sugar. Serve the sugar.

(NORMA, *like a high-wire artiste, manages to get the milk jug back on the tray and pick up the sugar.*)

NORMA: Sugar, sir?

HENRY: Thank you.

NORMA: Say when, sir.

(*She scatters an enormous amount of sugar over Henry's flakes.*)

HENRY: (*As she does this*) Yes – right, wo! wo! Thank you.

NORMA: That sufficient, sir?

HENRY: Perfect.

NORMA: Thank you, sir.

WINNIE: That's it, now take the rest of that out with you. Off you go.

NORMA: I'll serve you your bacon and eggs in a moment, sir.

HENRY: Er look, I think, actually, I've changed my mind. I don't think I want bacon and eggs, after all.

NORMA: Right, sir.

HENRY: Just the tea and toast.

NORMA: Right, sir.

WINNIE: (*In her usual undertone*) You better tell cook he doesn't want it. Tell her the gentleman's changed his mind.

NORMA: Right.

(NORMA *goes out carefully, as before.*)

30

WINNIE: (*Confidentially*) You'll have to bear with Norma, sir. She's just learning.

HENRY: Ah. I see you've had a fire out there.

WINNIE: Beg your pardon, sir.

HENRY: The building or whatever it was out there. I see you've had a fire.

WINNIE: Oh yes, sir. That'll be the old summer-house.

HENRY: Oh yes. What happened? How did it get burnt down?

WINNIE: (*Darkly*) There was a fire, sir. Just a fire.

(*Somewhere along the hall, the sound of* NORMA *dropping the tray and contents on the parquet floor.*)

Excuse me, sir. Newspaper's just there, sir.

(WINNIE *goes out.* HENRY *tries to scrape a little of the sugar off his cornflakes. He nibbles at a few but they aren't very appetizing. The sound of a sports car outside the window. A scrunch of tyres as it comes to a squealing halt on the gravel drive.* HENRY *looks towards the window, startled. The front door slams, off.*)

OLIVER: (*Yelling, off*) Winnie!

(WINNIE *immediately hurries through.*)

WINNIE: (*As she passes, to* HENRY) Excuse me, sir. That'll be Master Oliver.

HENRY: (*Uncomprehending*) Ah.

(NORMA *hurries through after* WINNIE.)

NORMA: (*As she passes through, to* HENRY) Master Oliver.

(*Voices from the hall. After a second,* OLIVER *strolls in. A tall young man in his early twenties. He is wearing evening dress with a white jacket. He throws himself into the chair at the other end of the table.*)

OLIVER: Hi!

HENRY: (*Rising*) Good afternoon.

OLIVER: Good God! Is it really?

(WINNIE *and* NORMA *re-enter. They are carrying, separately, two halves of a Victorian jardinière.* WINNIE *carries the top while* NORMA *struggles behind her with the base.*)

NORMA: (*As she passes, to* HENRY) Tea's just coming, sir.

HENRY: (*Alarmed by her exertions*) Thank you. Can you manage – ?

OLIVER: Winnie, run us a bath, will you, there's a sweet.

31

WINNIE: (*As she goes*) Yes, Master Oliver.

OLIVER: Careful with that. I'll have to take it back. When I find out where it came from.

(WINNIE *and* NORMA *go out. Pause.*)

Found the thing on my back seat. I've been chatting away quite merrily to it all the way home under the impression it was a passenger. Come down with Karen, did you?

HENRY: Yes. Last night. Early this morning. I'm Henry Bell.

OLIVER: Oliver Knightly. I'm her bro.

HENRY: Yes. Hallo.

OLIVER: Hi. I've just been to this party.

HENRY: Oh yes.

OLIVER: Just now. Dragged on and on. Very dull.

HENRY: Oh dear.

OLIVER: Still going, I think. They held it in an aquarium.

HENRY: Really. How unusual.

OLIVER: I'll tell you one thing. The fish were having a far better time than we were, I can promise you that.

(NORMA *enters with another tray. This time it contains a silver teapot, milk, sugar and teacup, etc.*)

I mean, I don't know your views on Dolphin Shows but I've just about had them up to here . . .

HENRY: Well . . .

NORMA: Tea, sir?

HENRY: (*Vainly*) It's all right, I can –

(NORMA *grasps firmly hold of the teapot.*)

OLIVER: I mean, you've seen one. Know what I mean?

HENRY: I suppose so.

OLIVER: I mean, nice enough creatures they may be but with a very limited repertoire. I don't care how many nude girls they tow round on rubber rings.

NORMA: Milk, sir?

HENRY: Just a little, please.

(*The bird flutters above their heads.* HENRY *ducks again.*)

OLIVER: (*Squinting upwards*) Oh, that's a wren. Do you see? Lovely birds.

NORMA: Sugar, sir?

HENRY: No. Thank you.

NORMA: Thank you, sir. Toast is just coming, sir.

HENRY: Thank you.

(NORMA *goes out, leaving the tray.* HENRY *takes advantage of her absence to adjust the colour of his tea during the next.*)

OLIVER: I must have a bath in a minute. I tend to think we have some people coming round.

HENRY: Oh, really?

OLIVER: I seem to remember we have. Today's Saturday, isn't it?

HENRY: (*Ducking as the bird apparently divebombs him*) Yes.

OLIVER: Then we definitely have.

HENRY: Ah. I wonder if you perhaps know where Karen has gone to?

OLIVER: Haven't the foggiest, sorry. I mean, she disappears for months on end sometimes.

HENRY: Oh. Does she?

OLIVER: Looking for her, are you?

HENRY: It's just that she has my clothes, you see.

OLIVER: Your clothes?

HENRY: My suit. And my shoes. And my shirt. So I've nothing to put on. Nothing at all.

OLIVER: Well, you're welcome to anything of mine. Just help yourself.

HENRY: That's very kind of you but I'd rather like to get my own clothes back, really.

OLIVER: (*Sleepily*) How come she's waltzed off with your suit? Was she wearing it?

HENRY: No. I don't think so, anyway. It's a very complicated story . . .

OLIVER: (*Settling back in his chair*) Uh-huh?

HENRY: We met on this bridge last night, you see. Albert Bridge actually. And . . . well . . .

OLIVER: Mwuhuhuh . . .

(OLIVER *has fallen asleep. He snores very gently.*)

HENRY: Ah.

(HENRY *drinks his tea while* OLIVER *slumbers on.* NORMA *comes on with her tray, this time containing toast, butter, marmalade, etc. She sees* OLIVER *and tiptoes the rest of the way.*)

33

NORMA: (*Whispering*) Toast, sir?

HENRY: (*Whispering back*) Thank you. Now, I know with this I really can help myself, you see, so don't –
(*Another sports car draws up outside at speed. Another squeal of brakes.* NORMA *freezes.* WINNIE *hurries through to the hall.*)

WINNIE: (*As she passes through*) That'll be Miss Karen.

NORMA: Miss Karen.
(*She hurries out after* WINNIE. HENRY *quickly helps himself to toast. Voices from the hall. In a moment,* KAREN *enters. She is now in rather stylish day clothes. She appears amazingly fresh for someone who can't have slept at all.*)

KAREN: Hallo!

HENRY: (*Rising*) Ah, Karen, thank heavens . . .

KAREN: HenryBell. (*She kisses him.*) You look lovely. That suits you. Are they all looking after you?

HENRY: Yes. Karen, where are my clothes? I can't find my clothes.

KAREN: Wait, wait, wait. Just wait and see what I've bought.
(WINNIE *and* NORMA *enter with innumerable carrier bags and parcels.*)
(*Indicating her purchases*) Behold! I have not been idle.

HENRY: Good grief.

KAREN: (*To* WINNIE *and* NORMA) Dump them down, just dump them down. (*Seeing* OLIVER) Oh, just look at that. Isn't that sweet? Has he been there long?

HENRY: Just a moment or two.

KAREN: He's like a dormouse. He sleeps anywhere. (*Shouting into his face*) OLIVER!
(OLIVER *stirs in his sleep but fails to wake.*)
Hopeless. I'm parched. Winnie, do we have some white wine open?

WINNIE: I can open one, miss.

KAREN: Bring us a couple of glasses, there's a dear.

WINNIE: Yes, miss.
(HENRY *makes a feeble protest.* WINNIE *goes out, followed by* NORMA.)

KAREN: (*Sotto*) That was a beautiful night last night. You were fantastic.

34

HENRY: Was I?

KAREN: (*Kissing him rather offhandedly*) We must do it again some time. Now, to prove I had not forgotten you . . . (*She rummages among the bags.*) Now which one was it? Oh yes. *Voilà!*
(*From one of her bags, she produces a man's suit, new and on a hanger. It is modern and positive in design and colour. Certainly something that* HENRY *would never dream of wearing. She holds it up for him to look at.*)
What do you think?

HENRY: (*Incredulous*) You're going to wear that to the office?

KAREN: Of course not. It's for you.

HENRY: Me?

KAREN: Do you like it?

HENRY: I'm not wearing that.

KAREN: It's gorgeous. I picked it specially. They took it out of the window for me.

HENRY: I wouldn't be seen dead in that.

KAREN: (*Throwing the suit down, sulkily*) Oh well, walk around naked then, see if I care.

HENRY: Where's my suit?

KAREN: I went to a lot of trouble for that.

HENRY: Karen, where is my suit?

KAREN: I don't know. In a rubbish bin somewhere. I don't know.
(NORMA *comes on with a tray with a bottle of white wine and glasses.* WINNIE *follows her.*)

WINNIE: (*Sotto, to* NORMA) That's it, just put it down there.

HENRY: A rubbish bin?

NORMA: Wine, miss?

KAREN: Thank you.

HENRY: What rubbish bin? Where?

KAREN: I don't know. Somewhere in Oxford Street. I wasn't lugging that hideous suit all the way back with me.

NORMA: (*Hovering at Henry's elbow*) Wine, sir?

HENRY: (*Ignoring* NORMA) Oxford Street? Why did you take it to Oxford Street?

KAREN: How else was I to know your size? (*Tearfully*) I got you a shirt and everything to match.

35

NORMA: (*Patiently*) Wine, sir?

HENRY: I was perfectly happy with the suit I had.

WINNIE: (*Sotto to* NORMA) Other side, girl. You're serving him from the wrong side again.

HENRY: I was very fond of that suit. I'd had it for years.

KAREN: Obviously.

NORMA: (*Appearing at* HENRY's *other elbow*) Wine, sir?

HENRY: No, I don't want any wine. Go away. I just want my suit.

KAREN: Then you'll have to go to Oxford Street and get it, won't you? I'm not doing any more for you, that's it.
(*She sits and glares into the middle distance.* HENRY *can't cope with that at all.* OLIVER *snores.*)

WINNIE: (*Sotto, to* NORMA) Ask the gentleman if he's had sufficient, then.

NORMA: Have you had sufficient, sir?

HENRY: (*Testily*) Yes, yes, yes.

NORMA: Thank you, sir.

WINNIE: (*Sotto, to* NORMA) Clear away, then. Start clearing away.
(NORMA *starts to clear away Henry's breakfast.* OLIVER *snores.* KAREN *sulks.*)

HENRY: (*Softly, to* KAREN) I'm sorry. Look, I'm sorry. I don't want to seem ungrateful. It's just I was – (*Aware of the others*) I was rather fond of that suit. It had seen me through some good times. And yes, it has to be said, some pretty rotten ones as well.
(KAREN *sulks on.* HENRY *perseveres.*)
You see, I don't think that particular sort of suit would suit me at all. You see?

KAREN: You haven't even tried it on.

HENRY: No, but I can pretty well tell just from looking at it, you see. If I was in a shop, shopping, I'd catch sight of it and I'd say straight away, look, that really isn't my sort of suit.

KAREN: You might at least try it on. I bought it specially.

HENRY: Yes, OK, OK. I'll certainly go and try it on if you like . . .

KAREN: You will?

HENRY: But I'm afraid you're in for a bit of a laugh if I do. It's going to make me look pretty silly.

36

KAREN: (*Brightening, getting up*) How do you know till you've tried? Come on, try it.

HENRY: All right, yes. Right . . .
(HENRY *picks up the suit rather gingerly and makes as if to leave the room. During the next,* WINNIE *and* NORMA *go out with the tray.*)

KAREN: Wait, wait. We need all the bits. Just a second. (*She rummages in the bags again.*) Shirt!
(*She produces a very jolly shirt.*)

HENRY: (*Eyeing it*) Ah.

KAREN: Tie!
(*She produces a tie in similar vein.*)

HENRY: Oh, my God . . .

KAREN: Not your sort of tie, either?

HENRY: I didn't say that.

KAREN: Shoes!
(*Some very un-Henryish (slip-on) shoes.*)

HENRY: Oh-ho! Yes. Those are interesting, aren't they? I'll go upstairs . . .

KAREN: Here's all right. Why not here?

HENRY: Here? But –
(*He indicates* WINNIE *and* NORMA.)

KAREN: It's all right, there's nobody here. Oliver's sound asleep. I won't look . . .

HENRY: (*Reluctantly*) All right.
(*He starts to get dressed, rather like a bather on a crowded beach.* KAREN *talks to him as he does this.* HENRY *starts by putting on the trousers under his dressing-gown. Only then does he remove this and put on the shirt.*)

KAREN: Now, let me tell you what I've been up to. First, I've been to see your Elaine Smith.

HENRY: (*Struggling into the trousers*) You have?

KAREN: It's all right, I rang her first. She was a little bit suspicious to start with but once she heard the whole story – how you'd nearly jumped off that bridge and how I stopped you in the nick of time –

HENRY: You told her all that?

KAREN: Of course. She was horrified. (*Admiring the trousers*) God,

37

those are going to look terrific on you. Elaine said anything I could do to get back at Bruce Tick – and anyone else in that firm come to that – and give him one from her, too. She's ace. No wonder you liked her. Absolutely invaluable. She told me masses about the ins and outs of the firm. Who's having who, who's got their knife into who. My God, the place is an absolute rats' nest. Elaine said it was amazing you survived as long as you did.

HENRY: Really? (*He is doing up the shirt now.*)

KAREN: (*As he does this*) Oh, that's gorgeous. You're going to look an absolute knockout.

HENRY: (*Sceptically*) Oh, yes?

KAREN: Anyway, she gave me absolutely priceless information. And most important of all, the inside secrets of how to cope with the dreaded Mrs Bulley.

HENRY: Who on earth's Mrs Bulley? Oh, her . . .
(*He starts to tie his tie.*)

KAREN: Mrs Bulley is the key to the whole secretariat. She alone can hire and she alone can fire. If I can win her heart, I can work for anyone in the building. She is the dragon that guards the gates.

HENRY: Yes, that pretty well describes her.

KAREN: Her name strikes shivers through the typing pool. But I think I've got the measure of her penchant. Nice, plain sensible girls with very little make-up in drab wool suits cut just below the knee, plain stockings and flattish shoes. That's her type. Mrs Bulley does not care for the flash.
(HENRY *now has on the trousers, shirt and tie.*)
(*Applauding*) Oh, yes, yes, yes!

HENRY: (*Coolly*) Socks. Any chance of some socks? Or have you bought me some tartan tights . . . ?

KAREN: Socks! Damn! I knew there was something. (*Yelling*) Winnie! (*To* HENRY) Hang on. The point is Elaine Smith, apparently, was Mrs Bulley's blue-eyed girl. She's going to phone her first thing Monday morning and recommend me.

HENRY: This is madness . . .

KAREN: HenryBell . . . Remember our agreement.

HENRY: What agreement?

KAREN: The agreement we consummated last night . . .
HENRY: Oh, that agreement.
KAREN: Yes. That agreement.
> (WINNIE *and* NORMA *enter.*)
> Winnie, can you run upstairs and get me some socks from
> Master Oliver's room.
WINNIE: Yes, miss. (*To* NORMA) Run upstairs and get some
> socks from Master Oliver's room . . .
NORMA: (*Going off*) Right.
KAREN: Better bring a selection.
WINNIE: Bring a selection.
NORMA: Yes, miss. I'll bring a selection.
> (NORMA *goes off.*)
KAREN: (*Resuming*) So, anyway, after that I had this shopping
> trip – you wait till you see *my* suit, it's fabulous – after that, I
> even had time to call on a couple of friends who've very
> kindly agreed to give me a reference. And here I am. Not a
> bad day's work, eh?
HENRY: How on earth did you find people to give you a
> reference?
KAREN: (*Smiling evasively*) Oh, they owed me a favour.
> (HENRY *finally tries the jacket on. He has everything now except
> shoes and socks.*)
> Let's have a look at you, Henry Bell.
> (HENRY *stands self-consciously.*)
> Oh, yes. *Yes!*
> (NORMA *returns with two or three pairs of brightly coloured
> socks.*)
> Ah, good. Thank you. Now then . . .
> (KAREN *holds up a couple of pairs and rejects them.*)
> No . . . no . . . (*Finding some that are reasonably appropriate*)
> They'll do for now.
HENRY: (*Taking the socks*) Thank you. Yes, these should set the
> whole thing off nicely. All I need now is the crazy car and the
> bucket of whitewash.
> (HENRY *sits and pulls on the socks.* KAREN *sets aside the rejects.*)
> (*Struggling with the socks*) I'm sure this is going to look
> extraordinary.

39

KAREN: Nonsense.

(HENRY *slips on the shoes and rises. The women admire him.*)
Wonderful.

HENRY: What?

KAREN: Turn round.

(HENRY *does so.*)
Terrific.

HENRY: Really?

KAREN: Really.

HENRY: Really?

KAREN: Yes.

WINNIE: Oh yes.

NORMA: Yes.

(HENRY *still has his doubts but is rather flattered by their attention. It's doubtful whether so many women have ever given him this much attention at one time before.*)

HENRY: Well, I . . . It's certainly not something I would have . . . Still I suppose . . . (*Smiling at them*) Well.

KAREN: (*Smiling back*) It's the start of a new life, HenryBell. A new life. A new you.

HENRY: (*Preening himself ever so slightly*) Yes, you're absolutely right. What the hell. Ha!

(*At this point,* OLIVER *snorts and wakes up. The first thing he sees is the new improved* HENRY.)

OLIVER: Wah! God! Who on earth are you?

HENRY: Hallo, again.

OLIVER: Have we met?

HENRY: Yes. Henry Bell. I was having breakfast when you dozed off.

OLIVER: Oh, yes. What have you done to yourself? You seem to have had a new paint job.

KAREN: Hiya, Oll . . .

OLIVER: (*Seeing her for the first time*) Oh hi, Ka. How're things?

KAREN: Terrif.

OLIVER: Good-o. Going to have a bath. Did you run that bath, Winnie?

WINNIE: Yes, Master Oliver. Be a bit cold now, I dare say.

OLIVER: Oh, dear. Run another one somewhere else, will you? Use a different tank.

40

WINNIE: Yes, Master Oliver. (*Sotto, to* NORMA) Come and help run the bath, now.

(WINNIE *and* NORMA *go out, taking the rejected socks. They leave the wine tray, which* OLIVER *now spots.*)

OLIVER: Oh great, wine. (*Holding up* HENRY's *unused glass*) This anyone's?

HENRY: No.

OLIVER: I'd better get changed. Those people are coming.

KAREN: What people?

OLIVER: Oh, you know. All those people. Cheers.

KAREN: What people? I'm busy.

OLIVER: The charity fête festival freedom thing committee. You know. The ones who meet here all the time. The one I'm on. They want to use the meadow.

KAREN: Oh. That committee. Yes.

OLIVER: They've always got something on. I said we'd lend them the meadow, again.

KAREN: Isn't Imogen Staxton-Billing on that committee?

OLIVER: Probably. I think they both are, aren't they?

KAREN: Anthony as well?

OLIVER: Think so.

KAREN: (*To* HENRY) Your chance.

HENRY: What?

KAREN: To meet them.

HENRY: You mean they're both coming here? To this house? Him and his wife? With you here? Won't that be – ?

KAREN: Presumably they thought I'd be away . . .

OLIVER: Yah. I'm sure they did.

HENRY: All the same . . .

KAREN: This is the country, HenryBell. You can't stop seeing people just because you've slept with one of them. You'd end up a hermit. It's a wonderful chance for you to have a look at her. See what you make of her.

HENRY: Yes.

KAREN: Your first sight of the enemy.

HENRY: Now, wait a minute. I haven't yet declared war . . .

KAREN: Just a look. No harm in looking, is there?

HENRY: No.

OLIVER: What's all this?

KAREN: Go and have your bath.

OLIVER: Right-o. Will you organize some cake or something for them? They usually expect a bun or two.

KAREN: Oliver.

OLIVER: Yah?

KAREN: Listen, when they come, would you mind if we introduced HenryBell as your friend rather than mine?

OLIVER: HenryBell? Who's HenryBell?

HENRY: Me. Henry. Bell.

OLIVER: Oh, yes. Why's that?

KAREN: I'd just rather they thought he was your friend. And not my friend.

OLIVER: (*Doubtfully*) Well, I don't know. What sort of friend?

KAREN: I don't know. Any sort of friend . . .

OLIVER: He doesn't look much like any friend of mine. Not wearing a suit like that. No offence, sorry . . .

HENRY: That's quite all right. I don't think any friend of mine would wear a suit like this, either.

KAREN: (*Beadily*) Well, I know plenty of mine who would.

OLIVER: Then he'd better be a friend of yours, then.

KAREN: (*Shouting*) I don't want him to be a friend of mine, I want him to be a friend of yours.

OLIVER: (*Shouting back*) Well, he bloody well can't be a friend of mine. I'm damned if I want a friend wearing a suit like that.

HENRY: (*Shouting with them*) Listen, if it helps I'll take the thing off –

KAREN: (*Fiercely*) DON'T YOU DARE TAKE IT OFF.
(*A pause.*)

OLIVER: (*Calmer*) Tell you what. He could be something else altogether.

KAREN: (*Testily*) What?

OLIVER: I don't know. He could be from – from our accountants.

HENRY: In a suit like this?

OLIVER: Oh, yes . . . Most of them wear suits like that.

KAREN: That's brilliant. You can be from . . . What are their names?

OLIVER: Haven't the faintest idea. One of them's called Dennis, I think.

KAREN: No, the name of the firm.

OLIVER: Dennis and Co. I don't know. Dennis, Dennis and Dennis.

(*He laughs.*)

KAREN: Don't be stupid. I hate men when they're stupid.

(NORMA *has entered with* WINNIE *just behind her.*)

NORMA: Your other bath's run, Master Oliver.

OLIVER: Oh, yah. Good-o.

KAREN: I'll tell you who would know what they were called. John would know.

OLIVER: John?

KAREN: John Brackett.

OLIVER: Oh yes. He'd know. He knows everything.

KAREN: Phone him. Find out what they're called.

OLIVER: I'm going to have a bath. You phone him.

KAREN: (*Angrily*) Oliver!

OLIVER: (*As he goes*) They'll all be here in a minute.

(OLIVER *goes out.*)

KAREN: Winnie. I want you to phone Mr Brackett, our solicitor. All right?

WINNIE: Yes, miss.

KAREN: Ask him could he tell you the name of our accountants. All right? Have you got that?

WINNIE: Accountants. Right, miss.

(*She goes.*)

KAREN: (*After her*) Oh, and get their address as well.

(*To* HENRY) You ought to know where you work. In case anyone asks you.

HENRY: I can't tell lies like that.

KAREN: All right. I'll tell them you're a failed suicide that I dragged off a bridge to spend the night with me. How about that?

HENRY: (*Weakly*) Oh, God. All right.

(*A doorbell rings.*)

KAREN: They're here. Come on.

HENRY: Where?

KAREN: Just say hallo to them.

HENRY: Now?

KAREN: Just quickly, come on. It won't take a second. They're having a committee meeting, you won't have to be with them for long.

HENRY: What do I say?

KAREN: Say hallo, that's all . . .

(*Before they can leave the room,* NORMA *has ushered in two of the guests. First,* LADY GANTON, *a woman in her sixties. Then* COLONEL MARCUS LIPSCOTT *of similar age.*)

NORMA: Lady Ganton and Colonel Lipscott, miss.

KAREN: Hallo, Ursula. How lovely to see you.

LADY GANTON: Karen, dear. What a wonderful surprise. We didn't expect you.

(*They kiss.*)

You're looking wonderful.

KAREN: Thank you.

LADY GANTON: Wonderful.

KAREN: Marcus.

MARCUS: (*Slightly less warmly*) Hallo, Karen. (*Kissing her*) Good to see you. Understood you were in London.

KAREN: No, we – came back . . . last night, suddenly. May I introduce Henry Bell?

LADY GANTON: Hallo.

HENRY: (*Shaking hands*) How do you do?

KAREN: This is Lady Ganton. Ursula Ganton. And this is Colonel Marcus Lipscott. Henry Bell.

MARCUS: How do you do?

KAREN: (*Pointedly*) Marcus is Imogen's uncle. I may have mentioned her to you, HenryBell. Imogen Staxton-Billing's uncle.

HENRY: Oh yes, right. That Imogen Staxton-Billing.

MARCUS: Oh, you know Imogen, do you?

HENRY: No, I'm afraid not.

LADY GANTON: You'll see her in a minute, I expect. She'll be at the meeting. (*To* HENRY) Are you coming to the meeting?

KAREN: No, Henry's from our accountants. He's just here looking at our books.

LADY GANTON: Oh, I thought you might have been a sponsor.

From the brewery. You look as if you're from the brewery.

HENRY: No, I'm afraid I'm not from the brewery.

LADY GANTON: Pity.

(*The doorbell rings.*)

KAREN: Will you excuse me?

HENRY: (*Panicking at being abandoned*) Er . . .

KAREN: Won't be a minute . . .

(KAREN *goes out. In a moment, voices are heard outside.*)

MARCUS: Did you say you were a turf accountant?

HENRY: No, no. Just an accountant. I'm looking at the books.

MARCUS: Really? You look more like a bookie. What sort of firm is it?

HENRY: Oh, it's a very – trendy sort of place.

LADY GANTON: Jolly good. I don't think we can ever have enough of that, do you?

MARCUS: Enough of what?

LADY GANTON: Trendiness. God bless the young people. They brighten up this world, that's what I say. In my day, we all looked dreadfully dull and dressed exactly like our mothers.

MARCUS: I didn't dress like my mother.

LADY GANTON: And then rows and rows of identical men. All in shiny dark blue suits. I mean, whoever decreed that accountants should all wear shiny dark blue suits?

HENRY: Exactly. That's precisely our policy . . .

(*The doorbell rings again. In a moment, fresh voices are heard.*)

MARCUS: (*Suspiciously*) Where is this place you work for?

HENRY: Oh . . .

(*He points vaguely at the ceiling.*)

MARCUS: What's the name of it?

HENRY: That's a wren, surely. Up there. Look.

LADY GANTON: Oh yes . . . Do you feed them?

HENRY: Oh yes, rather.

LADY GANTON: Well, don't. You'll never get rid of them. They'll be nesting up there next.

(PERCY CUTTING *enters – a small unassuming man in his forties in a shiny dark blue suit.*)

MARCUS: Ah, Percy. Come over here. Meet Mr Bell. Now that's the sort of suit I expect an accountant of mine to wear. Like the one Percy's wearing. Percy, this is Mr Bell. Mr Bell, this is Percy Cutting.

PERCY: Hallo.

HENRY: How do you do?

MARCUS: Now, Percy, would you believe, this chap's an accountant?

PERCY: No. I don't think I would necessarily. Not at a glance, certainly.

HENRY: No, well . . .

(*He laughs.*)

PERCY: Where do you work then? Carnaby Street?

(*He laughs.*)

HENRY: (*Sharing the joke*) No, no.

MARCUS: I've just been trying to find that out.

LADY GANTON: He's being rather secretive about it.

HENRY: No, no. There's no secret. No secret at all.

LADY GANTON: Who do you work for, then?

HENRY: Er . . . It's on the tip of my tongue . . .

LADY GANTON: I don't think he knows.

(*At this moment,* WINNIE *arrives at his elbow with a piece of paper on a tray.* MARCUS *and* LADY GANTON *move away under the next and start talking together.*)

WINNIE: (*To* HENRY) Excuse me, sir . . .

HENRY: Excuse me.

WINNIE: The – information you asked for, sir.

HENRY: The – oh yes, thank you. (*He reads it swiftly.*) Thank you.

(WINNIE *goes out again.*)

PERCY: Not bad news, I hope?

HENRY: No, no. Where were we? Oh, yes. Where I work. I work with – Ullworth, Gladys and Thrace.

PERCY: Don't you mean Ullworth, Gledhouse and Thrace?

HENRY: Gledhouse. Sorry, did I say Gladys? Gledhouse.

PERCY: I know them well. We used to have dealings with them at one time. You still in the same place then, are you?

HENRY: Oh yes, you bet. We're still in – in – (*he peaks at the paper but can't read the writing*) – still in good old – Strewth Street.

PERCY: Really? You used to be in Straight Street in my day.

HENRY: Oh yes, we are. Don't get me wrong. The main bunch of us are still in good old Straight Street. But a few of us have moved into our new annexe just round the corner in Strewth Street.

PERCY: Ah well, after my time that must have been. I don't know Strewth Street at all.

HENRY: No, it's very, very narrow.

PERCY: Old man Stackwood still soldiering on, is he?

HENRY: (*Affectionately*) Oh yes, yes. Bless his old heart.

PERCY: Miserable old sod, isn't he?

HENRY: Oh, yes. And we're mighty glad to be working round the corner in Strewth Street, I don't mind telling you.

PERCY: I bet. I bet. I can see you've worked with old Stackwood.

HENRY: You can say that again.

PERCY: Amazed he'd let you come to work in a suit like that, though.

HENRY: Well, all sort of things go on in Strewth Street that he doesn't know about, I can tell you.

PERCY: Tell me now, I've always wanted to know . . .

(HENRY *is rescued from the remorseless* PERCY *by the entrance of more guests.* KAREN *comes in with* DAPHNE TEALE, *a buxom woman in her mid-forties with bright red hair. Following them,* ANTHONY *and* IMOGEN STAXTON-BILLING. ANTHONY, *in his late thirties, has relied for a fraction too long on his youthful good looks to give him the reputation as the local ladies' man. His wife,* IMOGEN (*despite Karen's slanderous description of her*) *is, at thirty-seven, attractive too – though the trials and tensions of the past few years have left their mark on her. One might describe her as a desperately neglected English rose. She is certainly not at her best this afternoon. She has, after all, just been confronted unexpectedly with* KAREN.)

KAREN: (*Calling to the beleaguered* HENRY) Henry?

HENRY: (*Gratefully*) Yes?

KAREN: Come and meet some more people.

HENRY: (*Hurrying over*) Yes, of course.

KAREN: Henry. This is Councillor Mrs Teale.

DAPHNE: (*A blunt plain local speech*) Daphne Teale, how do you do?

HENRY: Hallo, Henry Bell.

KAREN: Henry's from our accountants. And this is Anthony and Imogen Staxton-Billing.

(*She immediately moves away to the other group.*)

HENRY: Ah, hallo.

ANTHONY: (*Cursorily*) 'Llo.

(*They shake hands.*)

HENRY: (*Turning to* IMOGEN) Hallo, Henry Bell.

(IMOGEN *scarcely looks at him but gives him the most peremptory of greetings and handshakes.*)

IMOGEN: (*Glacially*) Hallo.

DAPHNE: Did she say you were an accountant?

HENRY: (*Defensively*) Yes.

DAPHNE: Oh. (*She looks him up and down.*) Not local, are you?

HENRY: No. London.

DAPHNE: Yes, I thought as much. Excuse me, I just want a word with . . .

(*She drifts away to the other group.*)

HENRY: (*Charmingly*) Of course. (*Turning to the* STAXTON-BILLINGS) Well. A lot of people to meet all of a sudden.

IMOGEN: (*Ignoring him, to her husband*) Did you know she was going to be here?

ANTHONY: Who?

IMOGEN: You know who I'm talking about?

ANTHONY: No idea at all.

IMOGEN: I'm talking about that little toad, Karen Knightly. Who do you think I'm talking about?

ANTHONY: Oh, Karen. That's who you're talking about.

(*Slight pause.*)

HENRY: Did you have far to come?

IMOGEN: (*Ignoring him still*) God, you bastard. You let me come to this house and walk straight in to her. And you never even warned me she'd be here.

ANTHONY: Oh, do put a cork in it . . .

IMOGEN: I mean it's so cruel, Anthony. Don't you realize how cruel it is? Don't you honestly realize?

ANTHONY: Oh, God. It's one of those afternoons, is it?

(*He starts to move away.*)

IMOGEN: Anthony . . .

ANTHONY: Goodbye.

(*He goes to talk to* DAPHNE *who has joined up with* PERCY. *Pause.*)

HENRY: (*Trying again*) What's this committee in aid of then? Is it for some charity?

IMOGEN: What? Are you talking to me?

HENRY: Er . . . yes. I was . . . I was just . . .

IMOGEN: Listen, I don't think we have a thing in common, do we? I'm sure you have nothing to say that would be of the slightest interest to me. And there's nothing whatever that I want to talk to you about. So why don't you just run away and practise your small talk with somebody else?

(HENRY *is totally staggered by her rudeness. Before he can even begin to think of a retort,* IMOGEN *moves away from him. At the same time,* MARCUS *calls everyone to order.*)

MARCUS: Ladies and gentlemen, I think we're all here – are we all here?

PERCY: Yes, I think so.

MARCUS: Right. Shall we move through to the library and get under way, then? I understand Oliver's on his way down. If you'd all like to follow on. Tea and biscuits are promised, I am assured, imminently.

LADY GANTON: Hooray!

(*General chatter as the assembly starts to move off.* HENRY *moves away but keeps his angry gaze on* IMOGEN. KAREN, *having seen everyone out ahead of her, turns back in the doorway to* HENRY.)

KAREN: (*Softly*) Well, what did you make of her? Mrs Staxton-Billing?

HENRY: (*Through gritted teeth*) Mrs Staxton-Billing? Well . . .

KAREN: So is it on? Our agreement?

HENRY: (*Still smarting*) Oh yes. Most definitely it's on.

KAREN: (*In a gleeful whisper*) Revenge?

(*She extends her hand to him.*)

HENRY: (*Taking her hand, grimly*) Revenge.

(*Blackout.*)

ACT II

SCENE I
9.30 a.m.

*The following Monday morning. The skyscraper offices of Lembridge
Tennit. The outer area of the offices of Mrs Bulley (Head of Personnel
– Brackets Secretarial). The distant buzz of office activity – fax
machines, telex, duplicators, printers, phones, etc. Seated at the
secretary's desk is* LYDIA, *Mrs Bulley's secretary. Probably in her
mid- to late thirties she is, in keeping with her boss's preference, very
demure and proper. There are a couple of other reception-type seats.
On one of these sits* TRACEY, *a very attractive young woman in her
early twenties. She is gazing rather nervously at one of the magazines
provided. She is here for an interview. Lydia's phone rings.*

LYDIA: (*Answering the phone*) Good morning, Mrs Bulley's
    secretary . . . Oh, hallo, Mr Southland . . . She's just on the
    other line at present, Mr Southland . . . Would you like to
    hold or shall she call you back? . . . Right you are, thank you,
    Mr Southland, she shouldn't be long . . .
    (*She hangs up. She flashes a smile at* TRACEY.) She won't keep
    you waiting a moment.
TRACEY: 'K you.
    (LYDIA *busies herself at her desk. In a moment,* KAREN *enters.
    She, too, is dressed for the interview but to do so she has
    somewhat altered her image. She is wearing an unflattering suit,
    minimal make-up, her hair scraped back and flat shoes. She
    carries a hefty handbag. The overall impression is that she has
    tried to make herself as plain as possible. Yet, as with all
    Karen's varying personas, the impression is of someone ringing
    the changes within their own multiple personality, rather than
    inventing a totally new character.* KAREN *approaches the desk.
    *TRACEY *stares at her faintly incredulously.*)
KAREN: (*In very dainty tones*) Good morning.
LYDIA: Good morning. Can I help you?
KAREN: Yes, I hope you can. I have an appointment to see Mrs
    Bulley at nine forty-five.

LYDIA: (*Reaching for the list*) Oh yes. Your name is – ?

KAREN: Knightly. Miss Knightly.

LYDIA: Initial?

KAREN: K. Just plain K. I believe Miss Smith telephoned about me earlier?

LYDIA: Oh yes, of course. Would you like to take a seat over there?

KAREN: Yes, I would. I've been here for ages hunting high and low for this office.

LYDIA: Oh dear, yes, it is a big building.

KAREN: It certainly is. I've been going up and down in that lift like a yo-yo. (*To* TRACEY) Good morning.

TRACEY: (*Uncommunicatively*) 'Llo.

KAREN: You waiting, too?

TRACEY: Yeah.

LYDIA: Mrs Bulley won't keep you a moment . . .

KAREN: Thank you . . .

LYDIA: (*Glancing at her phone*) Yes, she's off the line now.
(*A voice comes from the intercom on her desk.*)

MRS BULLEY: (*Fiercely*) Lydia . . . Lydia, come in here a minute.

LYDIA: (*Pressing down a key and replying*) Coming, Mrs Bulley.
(*To the others*) Just one moment . . .
(LYDIA *gathers up her notebook and goes into the inner office. We hear the start of the conversation before the door closes behind her.*)

MRS BULLEY: (*Angrily, off*) Lydia, will you please tell me what on earth is going on?

LYDIA: I'm not quite sure what you mean, Mrs Bulley . . .
(*The conversation is cut off. Slight pause.* TRACEY *continues to study her magazine.*)

KAREN: I don't know why I'm applying for this job. I really don't. I'm the last person who'll get it, I know I am. (*Pause.*) I mean, I'm not even remotely what they're looking for. (*Pause.*) I know I'm not. (*Pause.*) A girl I met in the lift, she described to me exactly what they were looking for and it certainly wasn't my type, I can tell you that. (*Pause.*) I'm not remotely what they're looking for at all.
(*A pause.* TRACEY *refuses to be drawn.*)

51

I mean, if you don't mind my saying so, I think you stand a far better chance than I do. (*Pause.*) I'm sure you're far more approaching very nearly the type they're approximately looking for.

(*A pause.*)

TRACEY: (*Drawn at last*) What type are they looking for?

KAREN: Oh. You know. Out front.

TRACEY: Out front?

KAREN: Apparently this job has a very high public profile.

TRACEY: Does it?

KAREN: Apparently. It surprised me, but there you are.

TRACEY: It's just secretarial, isn't it?

KAREN: Oh yes. But it's market analysis, you see. Which involves a great deal of entertaining of clients and socializing and so on.

TRACEY: (*Surprised*) Really?

KAREN: Oh yes. Which of course means they want someone with personality and glamour and buckets of sex appeal. All the sort of things that don't naturally come up my particular alley, I'm afraid.

TRACEY: Nobody told me that.

KAREN: (*Confidentially*) Well, the point is I don't think we're supposed to know.

TRACEY: Why not?

KAREN: They want to see us in our natural state. They don't want us putting on airs. It has to be innate, you see, innate. So this girl was telling me in the lift.

TRACEY: Well . . .

KAREN: I'm afraid I'm innately rather quiet . . . Pity. I'd have liked all that overseas travel . . .

TRACEY: Overseas travel?

KAREN: Still. (*She sits unhappily.*) C'est la vie, n'est-ce-pas?

TRACEY: Pardon?

(*After a moment,* TRACEY *goes for her bag. She looks to see if* KAREN *is watching her but apparently she isn't.* TRACEY *checks her appearance in her mirror. She starts to go over her make-up. More lips, more eyes, more blusher. She fluffs her hair. She goes mad with the scent. She hitches her skirt up another inch or so.*

She practises the odd moue. LYDIA *comes out of Mrs Bulley's office looking rather flushed.*)

MRS BULLEY: (*Off*) . . . well then, find out who did, Lydia.

LYDIA: Yes, Mrs Bulley. (*Composing herself*) Miss Willingforth?

TRACEY: Yes?

LYDIA: Would you go in now, please.

(TRACEY *shimmies to the door.* LYDIA *frowns at her disapprovingly.* TRACEY *winks at* KAREN, *who gives her the thumbs up.* TRACEY *goes into the inner office.*)

MRS BULLEY: Ah, Miss Willingforth? Close the door, will you?

LYDIA: (*Half to herself*) Well, I don't know how I'm supposed to know, I'm sure . . .

KAREN: I beg your pardon?

LYDIA: Why half these wretched girls haven't turned up for their interviews.

KAREN: Really?

LYDIA: I mean, they've all been going back to their agencies and saying that someone here's been telling them at the front desk that they need to speak fluent Russian. I mean, who on earth would tell them that? Ridiculous. (*Sniffing*) I don't think that one's going to last long. If there's one thing Mrs Bulley can't stand it's perfume. She even objects to my talc.

KAREN: Well, I only hope the aroma of my coal-tar soap's worn off, then. I'm afraid I'm rather addicted to it.

(*They laugh. The office door opens and* TRACEY *comes out looking rather upset.*)

MRS BULLEY: (*Off*) . . . thank you. I should try the club just round the corner, dear. They're always on the lookout for new hostesses. Next.

TRACEY: (*Muttering*) Old bitch . . .

(*She glares at* KAREN, *who only smiles at her demurely.*)

(*In a low tone*) I'll get you for that . . .

KAREN: (*Quietly and sweetly*) Oh, yes? I'd like to see you try, you brainless litle bimbo.

(*Something in* KAREN'S *expression makes* TRACEY *hurry out rapidly.*)

MRS BULLEY: (*Off*) Next. Come along. Come along.

LYDIA: Miss Knightly . . .?

KAREN: Thank you, you've been so helpful.

(KAREN *crosses to the office door, smiles at* LYDIA *and goes inside.*)

MRS BULLEY: (*Off*) Miss Knightly?

KAREN: Mrs Bulley? How do you do? So nice to meet you. I'll close the door, shall I?

(*The door closes. The voices cut off.*)

LYDIA: (*Smiling to herself*) What a nice woman . . .

(*The lights fade and the office scene changes quite rapidly to bring us to –*)

SCENE 2
10.00 a.m.

The grounds around Furtherfield House. A wooded part. Dappled sunlight. Birds sing. HENRY *appears. He is out for a mid-morning walk. He has on another, less extreme, country outfit. One he's presumably found about the house. He has a home-made stick and has been stepping out. He stops now, rather breathless. He sits on a convenient log and looks up at the trees with pleasure and listens to the birds. The life of a country squire is one he's never experienced before. He's enjoying it. His peace is disturbed by the sound of a light motor-bike engine, revving and spluttering as it approaches.*

OLIVER: (*Off*) Go on, go on, keep going, keep going, you stupid creature . . .

(*The engine finally stalls. Silence.*)

(*Off*) Oh, knickers.

(OLIVER *enters pushing the bike. Both he and it are very muddy.*)

(*Unsurprised, as ever, at seeing* HENRY) Oh, hi!

HENRY: Hallo.

OLIVER: (*Stopping*) Stupid machine keeps stalling. I think there may be something in the fuel. A bit of grit, possibly.

HENRY: Or a ploughed field.

OLIVER: Yes. Scrambling. It's great fun.

HENRY: Looks it.

OLIVER: When the weather's filthy, then I prefer to race around the house. But today, it's just too good to be cooped up indoors, don't you agree?

HENRY: Absolutely.

OLIVER: Care for a go?

HENRY: No, thanks.

OLIVER: Also a great way to hunt rabbits.

HENRY: Don't they tend to hear you coming?

OLIVER: Yah, they tend to. But you can always get the deaf ones. (*He laughs.*) Right. See you later.

HENRY: See you later.

OLIVER: (*Shaping to give his machine a running start*) Come on, you stupid creature . . . Hup!
(*He trots off and, fairly soon after he is out of sight, the engine bursts into life.*)
(*Off, triumphantly*) Yee – haw!
(*The engine revs, recedes a little, then splutters and stops again.*)
(*Distant*) Oh, knickers.
(HENRY *smiles. The birds resume singing. He stands and is about to resume his walk. He takes a couple of paces and then –*)

IMOGEN: (*Off, urgently*) Whoa . . . ! Whoa . . . ! Whoa, boy! Easy, Silas . . . Easy! Silas, don't be so bloody pig-headed! Whoa, Silas . . . Whoa! Whoa, Silas . . . ! (*A cry.*) Sil-a-a-a-a-a-as . . . !
(*The sound of a body crashing into the bracken. The triumphant whinny of a horse. Silence.* HENRY *stands riveted.* IMOGEN *groans in pain.*)
(*Faintly, in pain*) Oh, shit. Oh, bollocks. You are a bastard, Silas. How could you do this to me? Again? Oh . . . oh . . . Everything's broken . . . Oh!

HENRY: (*Peering into the undergrowth*) Hallo.

IMOGEN: Oh!

HENRY: Hallo . . . you all right?

IMOGEN: No. Who's that?

HENRY: (*Moving towards the sound of her*) Me. Hallo.
(IMOGEN *crawls into the clearing on all fours. She is almost as muddy as* OLIVER *was. She has obviously landed full length on her side. She has mud all down one side from face to toe. She is, of course, in full riding kit.*)

55

IMOGEN: (*As she crawls*) Ooo! Eee! Ooo! Aaaa!

HENRY: (*Seeing her*) Oh my word, let me . . .

(*He takes her arm and tries to help her to her feet.*)

IMOGEN: Who's that, is that . . . ? (*Seeing who it is*) Oh, it's you.

HENRY: Come and sit over here and get your –

IMOGEN: (*A great cry of pain as she tries to stand on her ankle*) Yarr!
Ooh! No. Not on that one. Let me sit down.

HENRY: Here.

(*He guides her down. She sits on the log.*)

IMOGEN: Thanks.

HENRY: Is your – horse all right? I presume that was a horse you
were riding?

IMOGEN: He's been called other things. No, my horse has never
been better, thank you. Laughing his head off all the way
home.

HENRY: Oh.

IMOGEN: Take a tip. Never own a horse with a sense of humour.
Hallo, you're –

HENRY: Henry Bell.

IMOGEN: Yes. Imogen Staxton-Billing. We met at the weekend,
didn't we?

HENRY: Yes.

IMOGEN: I – seem to recall being rather rude to you. I'm sorry.

HENRY: Oh, no.

IMOGEN: It wasn't the best of days. That's my only excuse.
(*Slight pause.*) It's no excuse at all really, but that's the only
one I can offer you.

HENRY: Please, forget all about it.

IMOGEN: Someone said you were Karen Knightly's accountant.
Is that right?

HENRY: Yes.

IMOGEN: Yes. Well, you see I rather jumped to the conclusion
that you and she were together – if you know what I mean.

HENRY: Oh no.

IMOGEN: You're not?

HENRY: Not really.

IMOGEN: Not really? What's not really?

HENRY: Not at all.

IMOGEN: Glad to hear it.
> (HENRY *stares at her*. IMOGEN *stares back at him for a moment*.)
>
> (*Suddenly*) Do you think you could possibly help me?

HENRY: How do you mean?

IMOGEN: Up.

HENRY: Up. Yes, of course. I'll help you to the house.
> (*He helps her to her feet*.)

IMOGEN: No, it's quite all right. I'll totter home. It's not far. Ah!
> (*She winces as she tries to put weight on her ankle*.)

HENRY: You couldn't possibly totter anywhere. Here. (*He lends her his shoulder*.) Come on. Up to the house.

IMOGEN: Is Karen there today, by any chance?

HENRY: (*Rather guiltily*) No – she's – in London. I think.

IMOGEN: Ah. OK.
> (*She allows* HENRY *to lend her support*.)

HENRY: That's it. That's it. When we get back we can phone a doctor.

IMOGEN: No, it's all right. If I bathe it, it'll be fine. It's only a sprain . . .

HENRY: (*As they go*) Now we don't know that necessarily . . .

IMOGEN: Yes, honestly, I'm sure it is. I've got absolutely pathetic ankles. I'm constantly doing this sort of thing. You always feel such a fool, too . . .
> (*As they go, the lights cross-fade again and we return once more to –*)

SCENE 3
10.30 a.m.

The Lembridge Tennit building. This time, the outer area of Bruce Tick's office. In many ways similar to the other office we have seen. The phone on the desk is ringing.
> LYDIA *and* KAREN *enter. They stand in the doorway.*

LYDIA: (*Evidently concluding a brief tour*) . . . and, finally, this is Mr Tick's office. This is where you'll be working.

KAREN: Oh, how lovely and light.

LYDIA: That'll be your desk . . .

KAREN: It's all so beautifully decorated, isn't it?

LYDIA: (*Rather doubtfully*) Yes . . .

(BRUCE TICK, *an overweight, mid-thirties dynamic executive, comes whirling in from his inner sanctum.*)

BRUCE: (*Yelling to no one in particular*) . . . three billion profit at the last quarter you'd think we could afford someone to answer the bloody phones . . . (*Answers phone.*) Hallo . . . Bruce Tick speaking . . . Tell me all . . . Hallo, sweetie . . . Good morning to you . . . (*Listens.*) . . . Uh-huh . . . uh-huh . . .

(*As he speaks, he gives* KAREN *and* LYDIA *the briefest of glances, failing to note who they are at all.*)

(*To them*) Sorry, beautifuls, won't keep you a moment. (*Into phone*) Yes, my sweet. Yes . . . yes . . . Well, rest assured it will be with you tomorrow morning. At the latest. This is my first day, I have barely unpacked the briefcase and the place is like early-closing day on the *Marie Celeste* . . . Yes, yes, right. Will do, sweetie. Will do. Love to Helga . . . Hilda, rather . . . Yes, will do. Bye.

(*He slams his hand down on the phone and immediately punches up an internal number.*)

LYDIA: Mr Tick . . .?

BRUCE: (*To the phone*) I don't believe this . . . (*As he punches another number, to* LYDIA) Just one moment, I'll be right with you, my sweet . . . (*Into phone*) Rachel, I have been trying since nine, I cannot get a reply from Mrs Bulley's office. I think she has finally taken an overdose of formaldehyde and pickled herself. Would you be a sweetie and stick your head out of your office and tell that twelve-ply plank of an assistant of hers that I want a secretary *now*, not tomorrow. I don't care if its stocking seams are crooked and it looks like the rear end of a turnip, I need someone now. OK? Thank you so much, my sweet. Nothing personal. My love to Derek when you see him . . . Dennis, rather . . . Will do.

(*He puts down the phone.*)

LYDIA: Mr Tick . . .?

BRUCE: My sweetie. I am so sorry. Now, what can I do for you . . .?

LYDIA: Mr Tick, this is Miss Knightly. She'll be helping you out until we've advertised for a permanent appointment.

BRUCE: Miss Knightly, you come like the relief of . . . (*He looks at her for the first time*) . . . relief of . . . (*His voice trails away.*)

KAREN: How do you do, Mr Tick.

BRUCE: Yes. Welcome. Sit down. Please. Help yourself to a desk.

LYDIA: Well, I'll leave you then. Anything you want, Karen, just phone me on 961, all right?

KAREN: Thank you, Lydia, I will.

LYDIA: Bye.

KAREN: Bye.

BRUCE: (*Who has been staring at KAREN in disbelief*) Er . . . Linda . . .

LYDIA: Lydia.

BRUCE: Lydia. Er . . . (*To KAREN*) Excuse me. (*To LYDIA, confidentially*) This is just temporary, I take it?

LYDIA: Yes, as I say, just until . . .

BRUCE: Only I don't think I can work with that for long.

LYDIA: Well, we did the best we could, Mr Tick. Mrs Smith left very suddenly, as you know . . .

BRUCE: (*Indicating KAREN*) I mean, really. Couldn't you find anything better than that . . .

LYDIA: (*In a fierce undertone*) There was very, very little choice, Mr Tick. We're very lucky to get her.

BRUCE: Who's very lucky?

LYDIA: She's very highly qualified, she has excellent references and if you lose her we cannot guarantee you a replacement until Wednesday at the earliest. So please try and work with her.

BRUCE: All right. All right.

LYDIA: (*To KAREN*) Bye.

KAREN: *A bientôt.*

(LYDIA *goes out.* BRUCE *turns to cope with* KAREN, *who sits demurely at her new desk.*)

BRUCE: Well now, Miss . . . I suppose we'd better start by getting each other's names. I'm Bruce Tick. Call me Bruce. And you're —

KAREN: Karen Knightly. Call me Karen . . .

BRUCE: (*A little confused by her pronunciation*) Kieron?

KAREN: No, Karen.

BRUCE: Oh, *Karen*.

KAREN: (*Giggling*) Kieron's a boy's name.

BRUCE: (*Laughing*) Yes, of course it is . . . (*Under his breath*) Jesus. (*Briskly*) Right. Now, Karen. I don't know you. You don't yet know me. We're both new here. This is my first day. This is yours. We're going to have to do a certain amount of learning as we go, all right? Thinking on our tootsies, OK?

KAREN: Yes, Bruce.

BRUCE: Now, there's a few things you ought to know about me straight away. I work hard and I play hard. All right?

KAREN: Yes, Bruce.

BRUCE: I don't like half-measures, pissing about or pussyfooting around, all right?

KAREN: You believe in calling a spade a spade, Bruce?

BRUCE: A what?

KAREN: A spade.

BRUCE: Oh, a spade, yes. I'm hard but I'm fair. All right? You support me, Kieron, you give me that hundred and five per cent I'm asking for and I promise you, you will have a ball, baby. But you let me down, Kieron and . . . (*He brings his hand down on her desk*) . . . OK. You know what I mean? (*He repeats the gesture.*)

KAREN: Oh yes, I do, Bruce.
(*She repeats his gesture.*)

BRUCE: (*Faintly suspicious*) Right. Now this will be our typical day. I shall be here. Day in day out, rain or shine, five days a week at a whisker before nine a.m. You will do the same. I don't want excuses that the tube's broken down or the buses are on strike. Remember, I'll have slogged in from Sunningdale, so that won't wash with me.

KAREN: No, Bruce.

BRUCE: At nine sharp we cope with correspondence. Is your shorthand good?

KAREN: Lightning, Bruce.

BRUCE: It'll need to be. We'll work a hard, hard morning together until half past twelve. At which point, the demands of this job are such that I need to be out of this office, wheeling and dealing elsewhere. So from then on, back here at homebase, it'll all be down to you, Katherine. All right?

KAREN: Absolutely, Bruce.

BRUCE: The next time you see me then will be at half past four to cope with messages, when I'll expect my letters typed and ready for signature. As for going-home time – well, let me say this – (*Significantly*) don't ever expect to go home until the day is finished, all right? The boyfriend can wait, the hairdo can wait. Business first. Yes?

KAREN: Yes, Bruce.

BRUCE: If you don't like the sound of that, you'd better walk out through that door now.

KAREN: Oh, no.

BRUCE: Sure?

KAREN: No. I think I'll find working with you a tremendous challenge.

BRUCE: I hope you do. I hope you do, Kerry. All right, shall we get under way? I've a pile of letters on my desk, shall we start with those?

KAREN: Yes, of course.

BRUCE: Good girl. I want to make one call, then I'll buzz you, all right?

KAREN: Yes, Bruce.

BRUCE: Five minutes. Get yourself a pencil, go to the loo and prepare yourself for a long, hard slog.

(BRUCE *goes into his office. When he is gone,* KAREN *gives a slightly over-the-top shudder of disgust.*)

KAREN: Yeerrk!

(*She then springs into action. Opens her bag and produces a personal cassette player/recorder. Also her address book and a small portable radio phone. She finds a number and keys it in.*)

Hallo . . . Elaine . . . It's Karen Knightly . . . Yes . . . I got it . . . Absolute doddle . . . Isn't she . . . yes . . . but Elaine, he's *revolting* . . . yeerrrrk . . . yes . . . Listen . . . I can't talk long . . . About the letters . . . if I bike the tape over to you

61

by about one o'clock can you have them typed and back to me by four fifteen? . . . Yes . . . Sure. (*Opening her desk drawer*) Yes, there's some here . . . fifty sheets of headed paper . . . both sizes. Yeah . . . Please *yes*, the envelopes as well . . . I couldn't possibly cope with those . . . right. (*She opens another drawer.*) Yes . . . per letter, yes . . . do you want it in advance? . . . yes, sure, either way suits me . . . yes . . . bye.

(KAREN *disconnects. On the spur of the moment, she decides to make another call. She punches another number (two keys only) and waits.*)

Winnie? It's Miss Karen . . . Is Mr Bell there? . . . Is he? *Is* he? Wonderful. Listen, Winnie, don't disturb him then . . . Just give him a message from me, all right? . . . Are you ready . . . Karen is condition red . . . red, all right? R–E–D. Yes.

(*The intercom on her desk buzzes.*)

OK. Must go, Winnie. Bye.

(*She puts away the phone in her bag and grabs up a pencil and rummages in the drawer for a notebook.*)

BRUCE: (*From his office*) Katie! Come on, come on!

KAREN: Coming, Bruce . . .

(*She switches on her recorder, sets it to record, puts it back in her bag and takes that, together with her notebook and pencil, into* BRUCE's *office. As she does this* –)

BRUCE: (*Yelling once more*) Katie! Shift your bum, girl.

KAREN: Yes, I'm coming, Bruce. (*To herself as she hurries out*) Yeeeerrrk!

(*The lights cross-fade to reveal* –)

SCENE 4
11.30 a.m.

A drawing room at Furtherfield House. IMOGEN *is seated. She has removed one riding boot and sock and is resting her injured foot on a stool. Her face is still muddy.* NORMA *is kneeling, dabbing at Imogen's foot with a bag of ice.* HENRY *stands watching anxiously.*

HENRY: Is that any better at all?

IMOGEN: Well, it doesn't hurt as much.

HENRY: Good, good.

IMOGEN: But then I have lost all sensation in my entire leg.

HENRY: I think the ice is good for it, though.

IMOGEN: Well, I'll take your word for it. I feel like a deep-frozen chicken.

HENRY: (*Gallantly*) You don't look like a deep-frozen chicken.

IMOGEN: God knows what I look like . . . (*To* NORMA) Thank you. Honestly, that's just terrific.

NORMA: That sufficient, madam?

IMOGEN: Thank you. Ample.

(NORMA *rises and stands a little apart from them, holding the ice bag, uncertain what to do next.*)

HENRY: You're sure you won't see a doctor?

IMOGEN: Not unless it gets worse. I may have to ask you for a lift home, though.

HENRY: Ah.

IMOGEN: That a problem?

HENRY: I don't drive, I'm afraid.

IMOGEN: Ah. That is a slight snag. Oh listen, if you get someone to phone our place, Anthony should be back for his lunch round about now. He could pick me up.

(WINNIE *enters carrying a tray with a piece of paper on it.*)

HENRY: Yes, I'm sorry I couldn't be . . . Ah, Winnie, would you phone Mrs Staxton-Billing's husband and ask him if he'd be so kind as to come and run her home.

WINNIE: Yes, sir, I will, sir. There's a telephone message here, sir. (*With a look at* IMOGEN) From Miss . . .

HENRY: Oh, yes. Thank you.

(HENRY *takes the piece of paper and glances at it briefly.*)

(*Pretending to make sense of it*) Uh-huh. Uh-huh. Thank you, Winnie.

(NORMA *is starting to shiver badly.*)

IMOGEN: (*Noticing this*) I say. Is this girl here all right?

HENRY: Norma? Are you all right, Norma?

NORMA: (*Teeth chattering*) Yes, sir.

WINNIE: It'll be with holding the ice, sir.

63

HENRY: Good Lord. For heaven's sake, put it down, girl.

WINNIE: It's all right, sir. I'll deal with that. (*Sotto, to* NORMA)
Come on then. In the kitchen. Throw the ice away in the
sink and save the bag. Off you go. That's it.
(NORMA *goes out, still shivering.*)
She's very young, you see, madam. She's still only learning.

IMOGEN: Yes.

WINNIE: She'll be better when she's older.

IMOGEN: Yes. I hope she makes it.

WINNIE: I'll telephone straight away, sir.
(WINNIE *goes out.*)

IMOGEN: (*Casually*) Are you staying down for a bit?

HENRY: (*Guardedly*) Yes.

IMOGEN: Good. Well, I must – we must – repay your hospitality.
For being so gallant.

HENRY: (*Laughing*) Ha. Well.

IMOGEN: Perhaps you'll come round and have a drink with us.

HENRY: Thank you. That would be lovely.

IMOGEN: We live just down the hill there. We have the farm.

HENRY: Ah. Your husband's a farmer?

IMOGEN: Yes. (*Pause.*) Amongst other things.

HENRY: Ah-ha. (*Pause.*) I don't know anything about farming.

IMOGEN: No, well. Nor do I really. My family were in textiles.

HENRY: Oh, were they? Wool?

IMOGEN: I beg your pardon?

HENRY: Were they in wool?

IMOGEN: (*Puzzled*) No, I don't think so.

HENRY: Cotton?

IMOGEN: No. I think it was mostly sort of nylon, really.

HENRY: Ah.

IMOGEN: Daddy made an awful lot of money out of it, whatever it
was. I'm afraid I never took much interest. He sold the
business, anyway, while I was still fairly young. Then he
retired.

HENRY: (*Interested*) Uh-huh.

IMOGEN: Then he died.

HENRY: (*Sympathetically*) Ah.

IMOGEN: And left it all to me.

HENRY: (*Brightening*) Oh, well.
  (*Pause.*)
IMOGEN: And I seem to have given most of it to Anthony. Who's
  busy spending it as fast as he can.
HENRY: On the farm?
IMOGEN: (*Laughing sarcastically*) Not likely. The whole place is
  falling down. No, please. Don't get the wrong impression –
  he hasn't frittered it all away or anything like that. Well, not
  much of it. No, he's put a lot of it into my uncle's firm.
  That's my Uncle Marcus. Who was there the other day as
  well. Did you meet him?
HENRY: Colonel Lipscott?
IMOGEN: That's him. Anyway, Anthony's a director with his
  firm. A business which seems to eat money non-stop. God
  knows how much longer they'll stay afloat.
HENRY: What do they do?
IMOGEN: They make pipes.
HENRY: What, briar pipes, you mean? That sort?
IMOGEN: No, concrete pipes. Huge things. Round, you know.
HENRY: Oh yes.
IMOGEN: Sewage and so on.
HENRY: I see. Literally throwing your money down the drain,
  then?
  (*He laughs.*)
IMOGEN: (*Unsmiling*) Yes, I suppose that could be quite funny.
  In other circumstances I'd probably find it a hoot myself.
HENRY: Sorry.
  (IMOGEN *suddenly gives a sob. It is quite unexpected and startles*
  HENRY.)
  Er . . . Anything the – ?
IMOGEN: No. No. No.
  (WINNIE *looks in.*)
WINNIE: Mr Staxton-Billing is on his way, madam.
IMOGEN: Thank you.
  (WINNIE *goes.*)
HENRY: You all right?
IMOGEN: Yes. I think it's this house. I shouldn't have come here.
  Whenever I come here it does things to me. It's knowing that

65

... You probably know – if you don't then someone's bound to tell you sooner or later – that Karen Knightly is my husband's mistress. Had you heard that? Of course you had. Karen must have told you. She doesn't care, she tells everybody.

HENRY: (*Cautiously*) I heard that she was.

IMOGEN: Was?

HENRY: But not any longer.

IMOGEN: Who told you that?

HENRY: That's what I heard.

IMOGEN: They still are.

HENRY: Are you sure?

IMOGEN: (*Snapping*) Of course I'm sure. I'm not a fool.

HENRY: No.

IMOGEN: I may fall off horses and let other women screw my husband but I'm not a complete fool, you know.
(*She starts to cry in earnest now.*)

HENRY: Oh now, come on . . .

IMOGEN: (*Sobbing*) Oh God, my foot hurts – it hurts so much . . .

HENRY: Your foot?

IMOGEN: (*Rocking to and fro*) It's so painful, you've no idea.

HENRY: Shall I rub it?

IMOGEN: What?

HENRY: Shall I rub it? Would you like me to rub it?

IMOGEN: I don't care . . . I don't care any more . . .

HENRY: (*Taking her foot*) Here. (*He rubs away at her ankle.*) That better? That doing the trick?
(IMOGEN *suddenly leans forward, seizes him and pulls him to her, hugging him fiercely.*)

IMOGEN: Oh, hold me. Just hold me, please.

HENRY: Yes, right, right.

IMOGEN: Please hold me.

HENRY: Yes, yes, I've got you . . .

IMOGEN: (*A great pent-up cry of grief*) Aaah!
(*She rocks to and fro in his arms.* HENRY *clings on to her. He has very little option. Slowly the crying subsides. She stops her rocking and releases him.* HENRY *also lets go.*)
(*Much calmer*) Thank you. Thank you very much. You're a very understanding man.

66

HENRY: (*Modestly*) No, it's just . . .

IMOGEN: You don't know how much I needed that cry. It's silly. I hadn't had one for ages. Well, on my own when I'm feeding the pigs or something but that's not the same thing at all, is it? You really do need someone else, you see. A lot of women I know have girl friends. I'm sure that's one of the reasons they have them. Someone to cry with. I don't have any for some reason. Anthony saw them all off. He either made passes at them or shouted at them. He didn't like me having them, anyway. Now all I can do is sit on my own with the kids while he's off boozing with all his hearty men friends. When he's not here, servicing Miss . . .

HENRY: (*Gently*) I don't think you'll find he's with Karen, any more.

IMOGEN: (*Growing angry again*) Well, he's certainly doing it with someone and it bloody well isn't with me, I can promise you that much. (*She checks herself.*) Oh, what's it matter anyway? He can have them all. Who cares? He can have the whole Girl Guide movement, I don't care. (*Feeling her face*) I must look worse than ever, now, don't I?

HENRY: (*Totally in love with her*) You look . . . beautiful.
(IMOGEN *stares at him.*)
Quite beautiful. Honestly.

IMOGEN: I warn you, if you say things like that, I shall start crying again.

HENRY: Please. Be my guest.

IMOGEN: If you're pitying me, forget it.

HENRY: (*Hastily*) Oh, no. Don't worry about that. I'm not the sort to do that. I never pity people. Not in my nature.

IMOGEN: Really? You surprise me.

HENRY: I kick children. I jostle old-age pensioners. I knock over flag-sellers for the blind. And I go out of my way to run over hedgehogs in the road.

IMOGEN: You don't even drive, you told me.

HENRY: With my bare feet.

IMOGEN: (*Smiling*) God. One of those tough sort of men? I see.

HENRY: You bet.

IMOGEN: Heavens. I'd better watch my step then.

HENRY: Unless you want to feel the back of my hand.

IMOGEN: Oh, I don't know. (*Taking his hand in hers*) It looks a very gentle sort of hand really.

(*She kisses it lightly.* HENRY *moves in to return the kiss on her mouth.* IMOGEN *evades him gently and easily.*)

Now. My husband's car is even now roaring up the drive and I don't know about you but everything's moving a little bit too fast and I need a breather.

HENRY: OK.

IMOGEN: Sorry. So, to bring you down to earth again, would you help me to put my sock on?

HENRY: Well . . . It'll have to do instead, won't it?

(*He takes up the sock and starts to help her on with it.*)

IMOGEN: I'll leave the boot, I'll never get that on again. Lucky I got it off.

HENRY: Tell me if I'm hurting you.

IMOGEN: It's OK. I think the worst thing is the frostbite from that wretched girl's ice.

HENRY: You have a beautiful foot.

IMOGEN: You should meet the other one, it's half the size.

HENRY: Maybe I will. One day.

(*He kisses her foot, gently.*)

IMOGEN: (*Sternly*) Stop that! Pull! (*It hurts.*) Ah!

HENRY: Sorry.

IMOGEN: It's all right. Keep going. Aaah!

HENRY: (*Alarmed*) Sorry. I must be hurting you.

IMOGEN: It doesn't matter. I can do with the pain. I'm enjoying it. Go on, don't mind me. Ah! Ah! AAAAH!

(*As this is occurring,* ANTHONY *enters and stands in the doorway, watching them.* WINNIE *hovers behind him.* HENRY *manages to get Imogen's sock back on.*)

Thank you. (*Seeing* ANTHONY, *coolly*) Oh, hallo.

ANTHONY: Hallo. Sorry to interrupt things . . .

HENRY: (*Getting up guiltily*) I was just putting your wife's sock on.

ANTHONY: (*To* IMOGEN) You coming, then? Only I'm mid-mouthful through my lunch.

IMOGEN: (*Drily*) Yes, darling, I just have this little trouble walking, you see.

ANTHONY: Serve you right. I told you to sell him ages ago.

IMOGEN: I am not selling Silas.

ANTHONY: He's far too strong for you. You want to buy yourself a nice, placid, fat old mare. Something you can handle.

IMOGEN: Well, I won't argue with you, you're the expert on placid mares, aren't you, darling . . .? (*She hobbles to the door and turns.*) Goodbye, Henry. And thank you very much.

HENRY: Goodbye, Mrs –

IMOGEN: Imogen.

HENRY: Imogen.

(IMOGEN *goes out.* ANTHONY *gives* HENRY *a look and then follows her.* WINNIE *makes to follow them.*)
Er, Winnie, just a second . . .

WINNIE: Sir?

HENRY: (*Fumbling in his pocket*) This phone message you took from Miss Karen . . .
(*He produces the piece of paper.*)

WINNIE: Yes, sir?

HENRY: I can't quite make it out. Is this – Miss Karen's conditioning rods . . .?

WINNIE: I think she said condition red, sir.

HENRY: Oh, condition *red*. I see. Thank you, Winnie.

WINNIE: Sir.

(WINNIE *goes out.*)

HENRY: Condition *red*. My God . . .
(*The lights fade on him as* HENRY *follows* WINNIE *out and the scene changes back to –*)

SCENE 5
4.15 p.m.

The Lembridge Tennit Building. The outer area of Bruce Tick's office.
KAREN *is sitting at her desk filling in time by trying to master her electric typewriter. Unfortunately, even the first principles seem to elude her.*
KAREN: (*Glaring at it*) Stupid machine.
(LYDIA *sticks her head round the door. She carries a large envelope.*)

69

LYDIA: Hello.

KAREN: (*Rather forgetting herself*) Oh, hi! (*Remembering*) Hello.

LYDIA: Had a good day?

KAREN: Wonderful. So exciting.

LYDIA: Get on all right with old Tick?

KAREN: Oh yes, he's a very stimulating man. Full of ideas.

LYDIA: Yes, well. Just watch him. Especially after lunch. He's got the old roving hands, I'm afraid. Mind you, I shouldn't think you'll . . . (*Checking herself in time*) I shouldn't think you'll be the sort of person who won't be able to cope with him.

KAREN: Oh, no. Men never try that sort of thing with me. Well, never more than once anyway.
(*She smiles.*)

LYDIA: Oh, this just came by messenger for you. (*She holds up the envelope.*) It was at the front desk. If it's something you urgently need, then it's best to collect it yourself. They do bring things round but in their own sweet time.

KAREN: Thank you. I'll give it to Bruce when he comes back from lunch.

LYDIA: Oh, yes. Only four fifteen, isn't it? It's all right for some people, eh?

KAREN: (*Laughing*) Oh, yes.

LYDIA: See you tomorrow.

KAREN: 'Night.

(*LYDIA goes. As soon as she's gone, KAREN swiftly opens the envelope and removes a sheaf of letters and their envelopes all neatly typed and ready for signature. Also the original tape cassette which she puts straight in her bag. She drops the main envelope in the bin and arranges the letters neatly by her machine. She starts to put the cover back on her typewriter.*)
Oh, dearie me, what a day.
(*At this moment, BRUCE rolls in. He has wined and dined well, as he does every day. His manner is more expansive than ever.*)

BRUCE: Good afternoon, my little sweetie. My little petal. How are we coping, then? Keeping our little noses above the water, are we . . .?

KAREN: (*Playfully*) Just about, Bruce. Just about.

BRUCE: Phone messages?

KAREN: Nothing urgent. I left them on your desk.

BRUCE: (*Coming round the back of her*) Splendid, they can keep till tomorrow. Did you finish my letters, then?

KAREN: Just done the last one.

BRUCE: (*Patting her on the shoulders*) Good. Clever girl. Right, I'll sign them before I go . . .

KAREN: Shall I bring them in to you?

BRUCE: No, it's all right, my sweet, I'll sign them here. Shift yourself, that's it.

(*He helps* KAREN *from the chair, somewhat unnecessarily. She moves rapidly out of his grip and allows* BRUCE *to sit.*)

Oh. lovely warm chair.

(KAREN *smiles at his playfulness.*)

(*Snapping his fingers*) Pen, pen, pen, sweetheart. Come along.

(KAREN *is forced to move in to the desk again and leans past* BRUCE *to find a pen for him. As she does this,* BRUCE *pats her bottom. He blows on his fingers as if they had been burnt.*)

Oooh! That's nice and warm too, eh?

KAREN: (*Handing him the pen and moving away again*) I'm very fortunate. I have excellent circulation . . .

BRUCE: Oh, oh, oh. Enough said.

(*He scans the letters cursorily, scrawling his signature on the bottom of each after he's done so. He burps softly.*)

KAREN: Did you have a pleasant lunch, Bruce?

BRUCE: (*Still engaged in his task*) Very good. Excellent. There's a first-rate steak house. Just opened round the corner. I'm afraid you'll find, Kieron, after you've been with me for a couple of days. You'll find I have one major weakness . . .

KAREN: Really, Bruce, you do surprise me . . .

BRUCE: You know what that is?

KAREN: I couldn't begin to hazard a guess, Bruce.

BRUCE: Food.

KAREN: Food?

BRUCE: I cannot resist it. Good food, I mean. French, Italian, Chinese, Greek, Indonesian . . . Plain basic English, even. I don't mind. So long as it's good. Do you know what I had today?

KAREN: No?

BRUCE: Want to hear?

KAREN: Oh yes, please.

BRUCE: We had mulligatawny soup to start with. Then fresh lobster. Then I had whole roast guinea-fowl, all the trimmings, of course, game chips, lovely home-made stuffing, breadcrumbs, beautiful firm Brussels sprouts, roast potatoes and fresh crispy *mange-tout*. I love *mange-tout* like that. Then to finish with, we had something I haven't tasted since I was a kid. Steamed treacle sponge. Moist. Plenty of treacle. Coffee. *Petits-fours*. And with that we had, what? A bottle of Chablis, a bottle of Nuits-Saint-Georges, and a glass of magnificent vintage port. That sound all right to you?

KAREN: Well, I must say the canteen here does a very tasty cheese salad but that's not quite in the same bracket . . .

BRUCE: No, but you see with my metabolism – I'm very fortunate – I can eat all that and within two hours, literally, I'm going to feel hungry again, you see. Because although I'm putting it in, I'm simultaneously burning it up. My wife hates me for that. She really hates me for it.

KAREN: Does she?

BRUCE: I mean, if she eats so much as a water biscuit she's immediately the size of a house. I mean, the kids are like me. They can eat anything, but Hilary – that's my wife – well, we call her Lettuce Leaf Lettie.

(KAREN *laughs merrily*.)

She can't drink either. Same reason.

KAREN: What a beastly life for her.

BRUCE: Oh, I don't know. She gets a few fringe benefits, don't worry. (*He winks at her.*) And the one thing she never has to worry about is me. You know what I mean? Because I'm there. She knows I work hard. She expects that, she married me knowing that. And she reaps the benefits of that. She's got a beautiful home, beautiful car, beautiful garden, beautiful kids . . .

KAREN: I bet she's beautiful, too.

BRUCE: She's not bad. I have to admit it. I've never kicked her out of bed yet, let's put it that way . . . (*He laughs.*)

KAREN: (*Laughing with him*) And even if you did I'm sure you have beautiful bedside rugs too, don't you . . .

BRUCE: What's that? – No, seriously, she knows – Hilary knows that she has got me one hundred per cent.

KAREN: She's a very lucky woman.

BRUCE: (*Tapping his chest*) No time-sharing with this one.

KAREN: Wonderful.

BRUCE: How many men can say that, hand on heart?

KAREN: Very, very, very few.

BRUCE: Exactly. I mean I kid around, sweetie, but . . . as I always tell her . . . every day when I leave home in the morning, I leave my balls back there with her in Sunningdale.

KAREN: What a wonderful gesture of loyalty.

BRUCE: So. (*Jokily*) Hands off, all right . . . (*Rising*) Oh, God . . . What's the time? Yes. Listen, sweetie. Can you phone my wife, can you phone Hilary for me now? I gave you the number, didn't I?

KAREN: Yes.

(*She takes an address book from her drawer and sits.*)

BRUCE: I promised to have a drink with this man from JCC, OK? Phone her and tell I'll be on the later train, if she can meet that. OK?

KAREN: Yes, I'll do that, Bruce.

BRUCE: See you in the morning, then. Good girl, you've done well. (*Waving at the letters*) Excellent work. Good.

KAREN: Thank you, Bruce.

BRUCE: (*As he goes*) Nine sharp, OK? I'll be waiting.

KAREN: Right-o, Bruce. You betcher.

BRUCE: (*Seeing someone in the corridor outside, as he goes*) Oh, Ted, Ted. I'm glad I caught you, sweetie. Just a quickie, love . . . (*He has gone.* KAREN *looks up the number. She pauses on the point of dialling. She goes into her bag, humming softly to herself as she produces her cassette recorder. She puts it on the table and finds a pre-recorded cassette in her bag. She loads the machine and tests it. A short burst of fairly funky pop.* KAREN *goes to the door and checks the coast is clear. She returns to the desk, sits and dials.*)

KAREN: (*Humming softly as she does so*) I left my balls in San Francisco . . .

(She listens. The phone the other end starts to ring. She starts up her cassette machine and lets it play near to the mouthpiece. She listens.)

(As someone answers, yelling to an imaginary person in an altogether younger, laid-back, sexier voice) Stop it, don't do that . . . Hallo, sorry about that. Hallo . . . Is that Mrs Tick? This is Karen. I'm Bruce's new sec. Hi! Sorry about the din. Hi! Look, Bruce said can you meet the later train? OK? Because he's been held up here. OK? Got that? Super. What's that? . . . No, I just started today. Yeah . . . If you don't mind my saying so, I think you're frightfully lucky. I think he's just completely fabulous. Yeah. Must dash. Sorry. Bye.

(She rings off and switches off the cassette player.)

(With a little secret cheer of malicious delight) Yeah!

(She sits savouring the moment as the lights change again to –)

SCENE 6
11.00 a.m.

The piggery at the Staxton-Billings' farm. A lot of appropriate sounds as IMOGEN, *still limping slightly, comes through with a bucket. She is, again, quite grubby, this time from mucking out. Wellington boots, old jeans and a sweater. Hair tied back with a scarf. Rather sweaty.*

IMOGEN: *(Shouting at a particularly insistent sow)* Not yet, not yet, you greedy girl. You wait till it's time.

(HENRY sticks his head round the door.)

(Continuing her conversation) It's not food, no. Does it look like food, you stupid thing? No. You know it's not. You just wait until . . .

(She is suddenly aware that she is being watched. She looks up at HENRY.)

Oh. God. Hallo, there.

HENRY: Hallo.

IMOGEN: I was just talking to Sarah.

74

(HENRY *looks around puzzled*.)

The sow, there.

HENRY: Oh, yes. Do all of them have names?

IMOGEN: Oh, Lord, no. Most of them come and go too quickly
for that. No, Sarah's a bit special. We've had her quite a
time. (*Indicating another sty*) Those over there, do you see . . .
Those are all hers.

(HENRY *looks into another sty*.)

HENRY: (*Smiling*) Oh, yes. (*To* SARAH) Congratulations.

IMOGEN: They're being slaughtered tomorrow.

HENRY: Oh, really?

IMOGEN: Somebody's breakfast.

HENRY: Oh, well. (*Philosophically*) That's life, I suppose.

IMOGEN: It is round here.

(*They stare at each other*.)

Well. This is a surprise.

HENRY: Yes. Well, I was out on a stroll. And I thought I'd – see
where you lived . . .

IMOGEN: Well, not in here.

HENRY: Oh no . . . Only I just happened to catch sight of you
coming in here. And I thought, well, it would be a bit rude of
me not to come and say hallo.

IMOGEN: Well, hallo. (*Slight pause. She self-consciously brushes her
face*.) We always seem to meet when I'm covered in
something.

HENRY: How's the ankle?

IMOGEN: Oh, perfectly fine. I woke up this morning, I'd
practically forgotten about it.

HENRY: Good.

(*He smiles at her*.)

IMOGEN: Anthony's just across the meadow somewhere, I think.

HENRY: Yes, I did happen to see him.

IMOGEN: I see.

HENRY: He had some sort of gun with him.

IMOGEN: Yes, I think he's after squirrels.

HENRY: Oh. You don't eat them as well, do you?

IMOGEN: (*Smiling*) No. Not yet, anyway.

(*Slight pause*.)

75

HENRY: I – I wanted to say – I wanted to tell you . . . I really did want to tell you . . . to say how . . .

IMOGEN: You don't have to say . . .

HENRY: No, I wanted to say just . . .

IMOGEN: I know what you wanted to say . . .

HENRY: You do . . . ?

IMOGEN: And you don't need to say it. Really.

HENRY: It's just I . . .

IMOGEN: All I want to say, from my side, is that I wanted to say that too.

HENRY: You did?

IMOGEN: Yes, I did.

HENRY: That's wonderful.

IMOGEN: No, it's not wonderful at all. It's terrible.

HENRY: Terrible?

IMOGEN: What are we going to do? It's awful. I never thought this would happen to me. It's appalling.

HENRY: I don't think falling in love is appalling.

IMOGEN: I went to bed last night hoping I'd sleep it off. You know, like a cold. Only I didn't. When I woke up this morning it was even worse. But you see, I don't want to fall in love. Don't you understand? Not with you. Not with anyone. I just want to get on with my life, feed the pigs and – grow old. If you must know, I'm very miserable. And I blame you entirely. It's nothing personal.

HENRY: (*Startled by this outburst*) I'm sorry.

IMOGEN: (*Fiercely*) Just go away. Go on. Stop bothering me.

HENRY: (*Retreating*) Right.

IMOGEN: (*Desperately*) No, don't go away. Please don't go away! Please!

HENRY: (*Moving back to her again*) No, I won't. I won't.

IMOGEN: Hold me. Just hold me.

HENRY: Right.

(HENRY *holds her. She clings to him. He thinks about kissing her.*)

IMOGEN: No, don't kiss me. I don't want kissing. I just want holding.

HENRY: OK. Fine. Fine. Say when.

76

(*He continues to hold her.*)

IMOGEN: (*Pushing him away*) What are we doing? What are we both doing?

HENRY: We're in love. That's what we're doing.

IMOGEN: No, we're not.

HENRY: We are.

IMOGEN: No.

HENRY: (*With some passion*) Of course we are. Do you think I'd be standing here holding you in a – pig shed – if I wasn't in love? I don't know about you but I'm in love. I'm forty-two years old so don't you – try and tell me how I feel, you – you stupid woman. I love you.

IMOGEN: (*Affectionately*) Oh. Oh, Henry.
(*She holds him again.*)

HENRY: (*Feeling this firm line is the one to follow*) That's better. Let's have less of that, please.
(*A distant gunshot from outside*)
Ah, well. RIP one squirrel.

IMOGEN: (*Drawing away from him, calmly*) Henry, we're going to have to be very adult about this.

HENRY: Yes. How do you mean?

IMOGEN: I mean, I don't want anybody hurt.

HENRY: Who's there to hurt?

IMOGEN: The children.

HENRY: Oh yes.

IMOGEN: And even Anthony. Though I don't know that he deserves all that consideration. Not after – how he's treated me. Is still treating me, come to that. But I've never believed that because one person behaves badly we all have to start.

HENRY: But surely if you're unhappy . . .

IMOGEN: But if I left him, I might be even more unhappy, I don't know . . .

HENRY: Sounds unlikely.

IMOGEN: Anthony'd never agree to let me go. He'd put up a hell of as fight.

HENRY: Would he?
(*Another gunshot.*)

IMOGEN: I know he would.

77

HENRY: Even though he doesn't love you?

IMOGEN: I'm afraid Anthony is not what you'd term one of the new men. The fact that he's been fooling around quite openly with Karen Knightly – has been for two years – doesn't automatically give me grounds for complaint. After all, what can I expect? He's a man. He's just pursuing his natural basic urges. I am merely a wife. A woman. No, not even a woman. An ex-woman.

HENRY: But surely most people would . . .

IMOGEN: Most people here would utterly take his side, I'm afraid. We're not in Earls Court, you know.

HENRY: (*Mystified*) Earls Court?

IMOGEN: Well, wherever. Highgate, then. Wherever it is that women behave as badly as men. I'm out of touch. Round here, women are women and men are men. And ever more shall be so. Sarah there and I – we are not altogether dissimilar.

HENRY: You're much prettier.

IMOGEN: Oh, do you think so? I think she's rather beautiful.
(*Two closer gunshots in quick succession.*)

HENRY: Grief, there can't be very much left alive out there. He must have slaughtered everything by now.

IMOGEN: Sounds as if he's on his way back. We haven't settled anything, have we?

HENRY: We're hardly going to. Not here. Not now. We've established we're both in love. That's a major step forward. That'll keep me going for – oh, hours.
(*Another gunshot.*)
Maybe he keeps missing them.

IMOGEN: Anthony's an excellent shot. He very rarely misses.

HENRY: Doesn't he? Well, maybe it's time I was . . .

IMOGEN: (*Smiling*) Maybe it is.

HENRY: Very – wonderful to have seen you.

IMOGEN: Yes. See you in the chicken run some time.

HENRY: Why not?
(*They kiss. Not for long but with conviction and enjoyment.*)
Whoo!

IMOGEN: Whoo!

78

HENRY: Good.

IMOGEN: Very.

(ANTHONY *enters suddenly. He is dressed for shooting and has a shotgun, broken open, over his arm. As usual, he barely seems to notice* HENRY *but addresses his remarks to* IMOGEN.)

ANTHONY: (*Without stopping*) Somebody's left the bottom gate open and there's about a dozen heifers wandering all over the lane. I thought you might like to know.

(ANTHONY *goes out of the door.*)

IMOGEN: Oh, God. Where's Clem? Can't Clem do it?

ANTHONY: (*Off*) Clem's doing the job he's being paid to do.

IMOGEN: All right. (*To* HENRY) Here we go then.

HENRY: I'm sorry, I think that may have been me. The gate. I had trouble with the string.

IMOGEN: (*As she goes*) Don't worry. Come on. You can give me a hand.

HENRY: (*Following her*) Well, I'll do my best. I'm not frightfully good with cows . . .

(*They both go out. A second and* ANTHONY *returns. He stands and watches them for a second as they disappear into the distance. He closes his shotgun abruptly and returns the way he came. As he does so, the lights change back to —*)

SCENE 7
4.45 p.m.

Lembridge Tennit again. The outer area of Bruce Tick's office. The end of another day. KAREN *is opening another envelope of letters for signature when* BRUCE *comes back from his lunch. He seems rather more subdued than usual. He also has indigestion.* KAREN, *as she sees him, hastily gets rid of the envelope in which the letters were returned.*

KAREN: Good evening, Bruce. Good lunch as usual?

BRUCE: (*Abstractedly*) Pretty good, pretty good. Thank you.

(*Seeing the letters*) These for me? Right.

(KAREN *rises, as before, and allows him to sit in her chair. She is adept now at avoiding his hands. Actually,* BRUCE *seems too*

79

abstracted this evening to grope. He starts to sign his letters.)
(*Burping quietly*) Excuse me. (*As he signs*) I have to get off home early tonight, sweetie – if you can hold the fort for me . . .

KAREN: Of course I will, Bruce. You and Hilary going out, are you?

BRUCE: Er, no, no. Just thought I'd better put in an appearance. Cool the atmosphere.

KAREN: Oh dear.

BRUCE: No, it's nothing. It's just . . .

KAREN: Do you want to talk about it, Bruce?

BRUCE: Well, it's mad. It's crazy. But she – seems to think I'm up to something.

KAREN: Up to something?

BRUCE: You know – I'm playing around. Nooky. You know.

KAREN: Oh really, Bruce, how can she think that?

BRUCE: I don't know, it's just a series of . . . (*He burps again.*) Excuse me.

KAREN: Who with?

BRUCE: Well . . . I hardly like to say this but – with you.

KAREN: (*Scandalized*) Me?

BRUCE: I know it's ridiculous.

KAREN: How on earth could she think that?

BRUCE: I know, she's just – you've obviously got a very . . . I think that your voice must sound different on the phone. That's all I can think.

KAREN: Really? I've always been told I have an excellent telephone manner but . . .

BRUCE: Hilary says you sound like a scrubber.

KAREN: (*Indignantly*) A scrubber?

BRUCE: A tart, you know. I'm sorry, perhaps I shouldn't have said that.

KAREN: Well . . .

BRUCE: It's other things as well, you see. Like, you know I was in Birmingham for that meeting – last weekend.

KAREN: I know. I booked your hotel . . .

BRUCE: Exactly. And now I can't find the bill. Did I not give the bill to you? Are you sure?

KAREN: No, Bruce. If you remember I asked you for it on
    Monday evening.
BRUCE: If I had that bill she might believe me.
KAREN: She doesn't believe you?
BRUCE: She thinks I was in Dorset for some reason.
KAREN: Dorset?
BRUCE: This hotel – I've never even heard of the place – they
    posted back this nightdress this morning . . .
KAREN: Nightdress?
BRUCE: I opened it over breakfast . . . With a note saying my wife
    had left it behind last weekend . . .
KAREN: What was your wife doing in Dorset?
BRUCE: She wasn't in Dorset. That's the point. Nobody was. But
    she thinks I was. That's the point. (*He burps.*) Excuse me.
KAREN: With me?
BRUCE: Probably. And then this nightdress turns up. Bright red
    frilly thing with bows on . . .
KAREN: (*Disapprovingly*) Oh, no . . . I think I'll stay with my
    thermals, thank you . . .
BRUCE: I could almost believe someone was doing it –
    deliberately, only . . . I can't think . . . (*A thought crosses his
    mind.*) No, he wouldn't do that sort of thing. No.
KAREN: Who's that?
BRUCE: No. Forget it. Anyway, you can cut it with a knife back
    home, I can tell you. At the moment. Here. (*He produces a
    small gift-wrapped parcel.*) Look at that. Peace offerings. Has
    it come to this, my sweet? Answer, yes it has. (*He burps.*)
    Excuse me.
KAREN: What is it?
BRUCE: Just a little pendant thing. Hilary likes to wear them.
KAREN: How lovely. That will cheer her up, I'm sure.
BRUCE: I hope to God it does. I'd better sign these and catch the
    early one.
KAREN: If you'll excuse me. I'll just pop to the loo . . .
BRUCE: Yes . . . Sure . . . (*He burps.*) Excuse me.
KAREN: Indigestion, Bruce?
BRUCE: Just a touch. (*He burps.*) Excuse me.
    (BRUCE *takes the phone off the hook. He signs the letters with*

81

one hand while punching a number with the other.)
Hallo – Is that you, Damien? . . . It's Daddy, sweetie . . .
Daddy . . . Now come on, Damien, it's Daddy. You want to
talk to Daddy, don't you . . . ? Yes, of course you do . . .
Damey darling, is Mummy there? . . . Well, is she crying at
the moment? . . . Well, when she's stopped talking to Mrs
Phillips, will you tell her Daddy's on the early train . . . Will
you do that . . . ? Damien . . . Dam . . . Oh God!
(*He hangs up.* KAREN *has returned, in time to hear the last.*)

KAREN: How are things at home?

BRUCE: I don't know. Everyone seems to be crying. Hilary's
crying, the kids are crying, I don't know.

KAREN: You promised you'd pop across the hall and have a quick
word with Mr East before you went home.

BRUCE: (*Glancing at his watch*) No, tomorrow. Tomorrow . . .

KAREN: You did promise.

BRUCE: All right. It will be quick, I can tell you. I miss that train,
I am dead. Get my coat and briefcase ready, will you?

KAREN: Yes, Bruce.
(KAREN *trots into Bruce's office.* BRUCE *goes out of the other
door.*)

BRUCE: (*As he goes, calling*) Ah, Raymond – this is going to have
to be a quickie, my sweet . . .
(KAREN *returns immediately. She has Bruce's coat and briefcase.
Seeing the room is empty she moves swiftly. Putting down the
items on the desk, she removes from her pocket a tiny pair of
(bright red) lacy briefs. She takes up the small gift package that*
BRUCE *has left on the desk and contrives to attach the lace
trimming of the garment to the parcel. She holds the parcel up to
inspect her handiwork. The briefs dangle from the wrapping as if
caught there by accident. She slips the items into the pocket of
Bruce's coat. She steps back behind the desk. As she does so,*
BRUCE *returns.*)
(*Calling behind him*) . . . yes, well, we'll talk again tomorrow,
sweetie. We'll have to talk tomorrow . . . God, that man
drives me insane. (*To* KAREN) Right. Coat! (*He burps.*)
Excuse me.

KAREN: Yes, Bruce.

(KAREN *springs forward and helps him into his coat.*)

BRUCE: (*While they do this*) Will you try ringing home again for me once more? I don't know if Damien understood that message at all . . . Tell her I'm on the early one . . .

KAREN: I will, Bruce, I will.

BRUCE: Briefcase!

KAREN: Here!

BRUCE: (*Moving to the door*) Goodnight, see you tomorrow. Wish me luck. (*He burps.*) Excuse me.

KAREN: I do, I do.

BRUCE: (*Stopping*) My God! The present. I forgot her bloody present.

KAREN: In your right-hand coat pocket, Bruce.

BRUCE: (*Patting his pocket to confirm this*) Clever girl. Well remembered.

KAREN: If I were you, I should just whip it out the minute you're through the front door.

BRUCE: (*Patting her bottom*) Brilliant. What would I do without you, eh? 'Night! (*He burps.*) Excuse me.

KAREN: 'Night!

(BRUCE *goes. As soon as he has gone,* KAREN *does her disgusted routine.*)

Yeeerrrrkkk!

(*Purposefully now, she goes to the desk and dials a number, taking out her cassette recorder as she does so. As someone answers, she switches it on as before.*)

Hallo? Who's that speaking? . . . Oh, you're Damien . . .

(*She switches off her cassette player.*) Hallo, Damien . . . this is someone from Daddy's office . . . yes . . . that's right . . . yes, he does . . . Damien, have you got a pencil there? Well, yes, a pen will do . . . Are you big enough to write with a pen? . . . Of course you are, yes . . . Write down this number . . . (*She reaches into her bag and pulls out her radio phone as she speaks.*) Are you ready? 0836-213661. All right? Have you got that . . . ? Clever boy. Tell Mummy it's very, very important, will you? Right. Bye . . . Bye bye . . . Bye.

(*She rings off. She swaps the tape on her cassette player and takes a quick look out of the main door to make sure she'll be*

83

uninterrupted. She has barely had time to do this when her portable phone rings. KAREN *switches on the cassette player and holds it close to the mouthpiece. The music is slightly more slushy and romantic than before. She then answers her phone.*)

(*In a suburban sing-song*) 213661 Paradise . . . Can I help you? . . . What? . . . I really couldn't say, love . . . I'm sorry, this is a private club, madam, we can't give that sort of information, not to strangers . . . What? . . . Oh, well, just a minute, I'll ask . . . (*Calling to someone*) Maureen . . . is Bruce Tick upstairs still? . . . What? . . . Well, are they still here? . . . Did they? . . . (*Back into phone*) Sorry, love, they both left about half an hour ago . . . I don't know, love, I should ask him . . . well, try where he works . . . he must work sometimes . . . Goodbye. Please call Paradise again, thank you.

(KAREN *rings off. She switches off the cassette machine and puts both it and the mobile phone away in her bag. The phone on her desk starts ringing as she does so. She answers it in her sexy secretary's voice.*)

Hallo. Mr Tick's secretary, can I help you . . . ? (*Surprised*) Oh hallo, Mrs Tick . . . no . . . he left about half an hour ago . . . no, I've been here at my desk all the time . . . yes . . . you did? . . . well, I don't know where that number came from, I'm sure . . . Paradise? . . . no, I'm afraid I don't at all . . . No, all he wanted you to know was that he'll be on the early train . . . yes. Bye-ee.

(KAREN *is now very cheerful. She sings to herself as she punches up another number. She wanders round and sits on her desk to make the next call. She shivers suddenly and brings her knees together.*)

Brrr! Draughty.

(*She waits while the number engages. As the phone is answered, a separate light comes up on* HENRY.)

HENRY: Hallo.

KAREN: HenryBell . . . it's me.

HENRY: Oh, hallo. Where are you?

KAREN: In my office on the fourteenth floor . . . HenryBell, I had to ring you . . . I am near to gold . . .

HENRY: To what?

KAREN: Gold. Gold, HenryBell, gold. I have him on the run. The fall of the house of Tick is imminent.

HENRY: Karen, what are you doing?

KAREN: HenryBell. It's brilliant. Brilliant. I am brilliant. You're going to be so pleased with me. They're all so stupid, HenryBell. They're fools . . .

HENRY: Yes, well, some of them . . .

KAREN: All of them. I could take over this whole place tomorrow if I wanted to . . . I've got them all running in circles . . . None of them has a clue . . .

HENRY: Yes, Karen, Karen, listen. They may just be pretty busy getting on with their jobs, you see. They wouldn't necessarily be expecting machiavellian plots from their temporary secretaries . . .

KAREN: Exactly. That's the brilliance of the whole scheme. How are you getting on, tell me? What stage are you at?

HENRY: Er . . . oh, quite well. Pretty well.

KAREN: Are you anywhere near gold?

HENRY: No . . .

KAREN: Condition red though, surely?

HENRY: Yes, sort of – pinkish . . .

KAREN: (*Suspicious*) You are making some progress?

HENRY: Oh yes.

KAREN: I don't have to remind you, HenryBell, that this scheme is up and running. You are now committed.

HENRY: Oh yes . . .

KAREN: How close have you managed to get to the Pedigree Friesian?

HENRY: Who?

KAREN: The cow, HenryBell. The scheming cow.

HENRY: Oh yes, yes . . . I'm getting closer all the time.

KAREN: Make her suffer, HenryBell. Punish her and leave her for dead.

(*She hangs up. The lights go out on* KAREN *but remain on* HENRY.)

HENRY: Karen . . . Karen . . .

(*He realizes she has gone and hangs up. As he does so –*)

85

SCENE 8
5.00 p.m.

The lights spread around HENRY *and we see he is in the hall at Furtherfield House. He is deeply worried.* WINNIE *comes through.* NORMA *follows her carrying some logs in her arms.*

WINNIE: Supper'll be ready in a few minutes, sir.

HENRY: Winnie . . .

WINNIE: Yes, sir. (*To* NORMA) Stop there.
(NORMA *stops patiently.*)

HENRY: Can you remember the last time Mr Staxton-Billing came to this house?

WINNIE: Well, he was here the other day, sir, to collect his wife . . .

HENRY: Yes, before that?

WINNIE: And then he was here for that meeting a couple of Sundays back . . .

HENRY: Yes, but before that when was he here?

WINNIE: (*Straining to remember*) Ohh . . .

HENRY: When did he last visit Miss Karen . . . ?

WINNIE: Oh, you mean when did they last stop seeing each other romantically, you mean, sir?

HENRY: Yes – that's what I meant. Yes.

WINNIE: Well, that would have been – six months back.

HENRY: Six months?

WINNIE: Yes, they had a great bust-up right here in the hall. She threw everything at him. Then she went at him with one of them duelling pikelets . . .

HENRY: Pikelets?

WINNIE: Up there on the wall there, see. The bent one. Caught him a cracker.

HENRY: Good God.

WINNIE: We got that off her. Then she was in with her fists, like. Took four of us to hold her down. Temper like a tea-kettle, she has. Not one to get on the wrong side of is Miss Karen, if you take my meaning.

HENRY: No, I do see that. And she hasn't seen Mr Staxton-Billing since?

86

WINNIE: Not to my knowledge, sir. Hardly likely after that, wouldn't you think?

HENRY: Yes, I would, I would. Winnie, do you – happen to know if – I mean, do you happen to have heard rumours about Mr Staxton-Billing perhaps taking up with anyone else? Another woman, I mean?

(OLIVER *enters. He is in evening dress.* WINNIE *gives a glance at* NORMA *who still stands, patiently and uncomplainingly, sagging slightly under the weight of the logs.*)

WINNIE: (*Tight-lipped*) I wouldn't know about that, sir, I'm sure. I'm not one for gossip.

HENRY: No, quite. Quite right.

OLIVER: Hi!

HENRY: Good evening.

WINNIE: Excuse me, sir. (*To* NORMA) Come on, then. In here with them. Follow me.

(NORMA *follows* WINNIE *off.*)

HENRY: How long's Norma been here now?

OLIVER: Oh. Months. I don't know.

HENRY: She seems to be taking a long time to get the hang of the job, doesn't she?

OLIVER: (*Vaguely*) Does she? I suppose so. Still I believe it is fairly complicated. Well, I'm all ready for the hop. You really not going to come?

HENRY: No, no. I'd . . .

OLIVER: I don't know why you're not taking my partner instead of me. You seem to get on better.

HENRY: No, I don't think that would be a good idea at all.

OLIVER: No. See what you mean. Hunt Ball. Small village. What do you expect? Her husband really ought to be taking her, oughtn't he?

HENRY: Why isn't he?

OLIVER: No idea. Off with somebody else probably, knowing him.

HENRY: Who?

OLIVER: Haven't the foggiest. Well, I'd better get the car out. See you later.

HENRY: Possibly.

(OLIVER *strolls to the front door. As he does so, the bell rings.*)

OLIVER: Who the hell's that?

(*He opens the door.* IMOGEN *steps inside. For once, she is done up to the nines for the dance. She is the most beautiful vision that* HENRY *has ever seen.*)

Oh hi, come in.

IMOGEN: Thank you.

HENRY: (*Incapable of speech*) Ah!

IMOGEN: (*Softly*) Hallo.

HENRY: Hallo.

OLIVER: I thought I was supposed to be collecting you.

IMOGEN: I thought I'd collect you instead.

OLIVER: Great. That's the modern way. Yah. Why not?

(HENRY *continues to gape at* IMOGEN *adoringly. A pause.*)

Right. I'll go and sit in your car then.

IMOGEN: Thank you.

(OLIVER *goes out. The two continue to stare at each other.* WINNIE *comes out, followed by* NORMA.)

WINNIE: Now who could that – (*She stops and takes in the scene immediately.*) Ah. Right. (*To* NORMA) Back in here then. Come along.

(WINNIE *and* NORMA *exit again.*)

HENRY: This is a nice surprise. I didn't expect to see you tonight. I'd resigned myself to a good book.

IMOGEN: I thought you might just like to see that I can look reasonably presentable, when I want to.

HENRY: You look – stunning.

IMOGEN: Not always covered in half the countryside.

HENRY: Just so – so beautiful.

IMOGEN: (*Rocking self-consciously from one foot to the other*) Oh, well. I don't know about that exactly.

HENRY: You're just the most beautiful woman I've ever seen in my life. Really.

IMOGEN: (*Faintly tearful*) Oh, Henry, you say such lovely things.

HENRY: I love you, Imogen . . .

IMOGEN: Oh, please don't make me cry now. I'll just run. I'll run all over the place, I always do. I must go. I just had to see you first.

HENRY: I'll think of you dancing with all those men . . . think of me.
IMOGEN: I'll only be dancing with you really, Henry. You know that, don't you?
(*She kisses him lightly.*)
Goodnight, my darling.
HENRY: Goodnight.
(IMOGEN *goes.* HENRY *watches her leave. He turns in the doorway.*)
(*A little cry, half pain, half pleasure*) Ah!
(*As he stands there, the lights cross-fade to –*)

SCENE 9
10.00 a.m.

Lembridge Tennit. KAREN *at her desk.* BRUCE *comes in, he looks ashen and unkempt.*

KAREN: (*Brightly*) Good morning, Bruce.
BRUCE: Morning.
(*He burps.*)
KAREN: Miss the train, did we?
BRUCE: Yes, I . . . yes. It sounds ridiculous but I fell asleep on the platform. At Sunningdale.
KAREN: Oh dear . . .
BRUCE: Probably because I didn't sleep at all last night. We had a . . . she had a . . .
(*He grips the desk unsteadily.*)
KAREN: Would you like to sit down?
BRUCE: Thank you. Nobody had the decency to wake me. You'd think British Rail would have the decency to wake me up. I mean, what are we paying for, that's what I want to know.
(*He burps.* KAREN *gets up. He sits in her chair.*)
Someone's doing this to me . . . I know they are . . . this is a conspiracy . . . you've no idea what's happening, Kieron . . . you've no idea . . . strange women ringing up . . . nighties . . . knickers in my pocket . . . you name it . . . (*He burps.*)

89

I've got this terrible indigestion . . . and I haven't even eaten anything.

KAREN: Do calm down, Bruce . . .

BRUCE: We had this ferocious row last night, Hilary and I. Really terrible. And right in the middle of it, this girl in suspenders turns up with a kissogram . . . I mean, who'd do a thing like that? What bastard would do a thing like that to me . . . ?

KAREN: Is there anything I can do to help, Bruce?

BRUCE: Help? (*He burps.*) How? She's leaving me. She's taking the kids and she's leaving me. I'll be going home tonight to an empty house. No supper.
(*He burps.*)

KAREN: If there's anything I can do . . .

BRUCE: (*With a burst of gratitude, grasping her bottom*) Oh, Kieron – sweetie . . .

KAREN: (*Removing his hand firmly*) Don't do that, Bruce, that isn't going to help, is it . . . ?

BRUCE: Sorry. I just needed – reassurance. I don't know how you can help. The trouble is she thinks you're –

KAREN: I'm responsible?

BRUCE: I think she does. It's ridiculous.

KAREN: Ridiculous. What if I talked to her . . .

BRUCE: No, she wouldn't listen – she's obsessed . . . She has this image of you. Beautiful, sexy. You know.

KAREN: Yes, would that I were . . .

BRUCE: I mean, you know what I mean?

KAREN: Bruce, if you were to invite her somewhere. For a talk. To thrash things out. And I was to – just happen to wander in . . .

BRUCE: What, you mean here in the office? I couldn't –

KAREN: No, no. Somewhere nearby. A quiet wine bar, say. And you could meet her. And then I could just stroll in and say, 'Oh, Bruce, I'm so glad I caught up with you . . .'

BRUCE: 'Mr Tick.' Better make it 'Mr Tick'. Not 'Bruce'.

KAREN: 'Oh, Mr Tick, I'm so glad I caught up with you. These urgent papers do need your signature tonight.' You see?

BRUCE: (*A man grasping at straws*) Yes, yes . . .

KAREN: And then she could meet me, face to face. You could say,

'By the way, Hilary, have you met . . . Kieron?' And she'd see right away what sort of person I was.

BRUCE: Maybe. Maybe.

(*He burps.*)

KAREN: She'd see straight away there was nothing between us.

BRUCE: It might work, you know, it might. I mean, if she saw you as you are. I mean . . . don't take me the wrong way . . .

KAREN: Oh no, Bruce, I'd never take you the wrong way . . .

BRUCE: The point is, will Hilary agree to meet me? Will she come?

KAREN: Well, phone her.

BRUCE: Phone her?

KAREN: Now.

BRUCE: Now? Yes. I will. She won't have left yet. (*Rising*) What's my number? No, I know I know my number. It's all right. I'll phone in here.

(*He burps.*)

KAREN: You do that. Good luck.

BRUCE: Thank you.

(*He goes into his office.*)

KAREN: (*To herself*) You're going to need it.

(*She takes out her own mobile phone, humming as she does so.*)

(*Getting through, normal voice*) Hallo, is that Jean? It's Miss Knightly. Hallo, darling. I want to make a hair appointment for tomorrow, please. With Martin, yes. Just a wash and blow-dry. Five o'clock-ish? Super. Bye. (*She rings off.*)

BRUCE: (*His voice from his office, angrily*) Look don't start on that again, Hilary, for God's sake, sweetie . . . What are you talking about? The woman's about as sexy as a sand bucket . . .

(KAREN *sits at her desk, humming to herself and smiling. As she does so, the scene changes to –*)

SCENE 10
4.00 p.m.

The same day. A hen house. Chicken noises. IMOGEN, *now back in her farm clothes, and* HENRY *crawl inside. The place apparently has quite*

91

*a low ceiling. From now on the action accelerates and the scenes begin
to cross-cut faster and faster.*

HENRY: How long do we have?

IMOGEN: About six and a half minutes, that's all.

HENRY: God, I want you so much, Imogen . . .

IMOGEN: Well, we can't make love in a hen house, Henry, it's
    impossible.

HENRY: (*Desperately*) Why not? Why not?

IMOGEN: Well – it's not . . . conducive. And it would probably
    stop them laying. And all sorts of things.

HENRY: I love you.

IMOGEN: I love you. So what?
    (*A motor horn sounds.*)
    Oh, that's Betty bringing back the kids. (*Moving out*) She's
    early. I must go . . .

HENRY: (*Despairingly*) Imogen . . .
    (*Cross-fade quickly to –*)

SCENE 11
6.00 p.m.

The same day. A wine bar. Muzak behind. BRUCE *approaches and
sits at a table for two. He has a glass of white wine and a bowl of
appetizers which he starts to devour compulsively, almost desperately.
He burps as he devours them. His health is deteriorating fast. He looks
about him anxiously. In a moment,* HILARY TICK *appears. In her
thirties, normally quite attractive, at present she is drawn, tired and
angry.*

BRUCE: (*Calling to her*) Hilary!
    (HILARY *approaches the table.*)
    Thank you for coming, darling. Thank you. Thank you.

HILARY: One drink, Bruce, that's all I'm having.

BRUCE: Yes, yes. OK, sweetie.

HILARY: Please don't call me sweetie. You know I hate it.

BRUCE: I'm sorry. I'm sorry, love.

HILARY: I don't think we've anything more to say, have we?

BRUCE: I hope we have. I hope we have, Hilly.

HILARY: Well, I don't know what to say. I'm still stunned. That's all. Stunned. I phoned my mother. She was stunned, too. I phoned your father. He was totally stunned.

BRUCE: I only wish I could . . . I could . . .

HILARY: (Cutting him short) I'll have a white wine, thank you.

BRUCE: (Indicating his own glass) Would you like a glass of this? It's very . . .

HILARY: I honestly don't care, Bruce. Just anything . . .

BRUCE: Right, right. (He crams the rest of the appetizers into his mouth.) I'll get some more of these.

(He goes, leaving HILARY hunched and tense in her chair. A quick cross-fade to –)

SCENE 12
3.00 p.m.

The village green. We see only HENRY and IMOGEN in coats standing formally side by side, not touching because they are in public. They seem to be watching some morris dancing. At least, the music suggests they are.

HENRY: (Fairly irritably) What is all this prancing about?

IMOGEN: (Also rather tetchily) It's morris dancing. You must have heard of morris dancing.

HENRY: Never heard of it.

IMOGEN: Don't be so ridiculous. Everyone's heard of morris dancing.

HENRY: Well, I haven't. And I think it's awful and I wish they'd go home. I want to touch you.

IMOGEN: Well, you can't. I don't know what you're doing here. (Calling to a child) Simon, don't stand there, you'll trip them up. Now come back, outside the ropes. Outside! That's better. (To HENRY, fiercely) What are you doing here, Henry?

HENRY: (Sulkily) What do you think I'm doing? I'm watching this terrific morris dancing.

IMOGEN: You just said you didn't like it.

HENRY: Yes, I do. I've got the hang of it now, it's tremendous. (*Shouting at the dancers*) Oooh – lay!

IMOGEN: Henry! Anthony is watching, the entire village is watching, now stop it or I'll never speak to you again.

HENRY: I don't care. I love you . . .

IMOGEN: Oh, this is impossible! What am I going to do . . . (*Sound and lights cross-fade back to* –)

SCENE 13
6.15 p.m.

The wine bar again. HILARY *is still sitting where she was.* BRUCE *returns with her wine and another bowl of nibbles.*

BRUCE: Here we are. Not a bad wine this. It's actually German but it tastes not unlike a white burgundy. It's got that same . . .

HILARY: I really don't give a damn, Bruce, I really don't.

BRUCE: Yes, yes. Fair enough, love. Fair enough. (*He burps.*) Excuse me.
(*He takes a handful of nibbles from the bowl. Hilary's glass remains untouched.*)
(*His mouth full*) Some of these?

HILARY: No. What did you want to say to me? I don't want to be here long. Mother's with the children on her own . . .

BRUCE: (*Affectionately*) Oh, bless her. How is Mary?

HILARY: She's livid, Bruce. She thinks you're a shit. So do I. Now, what did you want to say?

BRUCE: That this has all been – a conspiracy . . .

HILARY: Oh, not again . . .

BRUCE: Someone has deliberately broken up my marriage . . .

HILARY: Bruce . . .

BRUCE: It's true.

HILARY: But who, Bruce? Who would want to do that?

BRUCE: (*Shouting*) I don't know, do I? Somebody wants to, that's all I know. Them. I don't know. The government. The KGB. The FBI. The CIA.

94

HILARY: Bruce!

BRUCE: MI5! How the hell do I know? (*Looking round accusingly*) Somebody here.

(*He burps.*)

HILARY: BRUCE!

(*A silence.* BRUCE *crams some more food into his mouth.*) I think you ought to see someone, I really do. I think you're going mad.

BRUCE: I probably am.

HILARY: And if you eat many more of those, you'll drop dead anyway.

BRUCE: I don't care.

(*He burps.*)

HILARY: Look, I'm going. There's obviously nothing new to be said, is there?

BRUCE: (*Glancing anxiously at his watch*) No. Hang on. Hang on. Just one minute.

HILARY: Why? What for?

BRUCE: Just for a minute.

HILARY: Are you expecting someone?

BRUCE: No. No. (*Pause.*) No.

(HILARY *looks at him suspiciously. They continue to sit there as the lights cross-fade back to –*)

SCENE 14
11.00 a.m.

A cowshed. Appropriate noises. HENRY *stands miserably. Apart from him stands* IMOGEN, *penitent.*

IMOGEN: I'm sorry. I'm trying my best.

HENRY: Well, it's not good enough.

IMOGEN: Don't be angry with me.

HENRY: I'm going.

IMOGEN: Where?

HENRY: Back to London. I've had it with the country. I'm sick to death of all these pigs and chickens and squirrels and cows all

95

happily having each other while we're both standing about.

IMOGEN: Henry . . .

HENRY: . . . waiting to be shot, or made into bacon . . .

IMOGEN: Henry!

HENRY: What?

IMOGEN: This weekend.

HENRY: What about it?

IMOGEN: Anthony's going to be away . . .

HENRY: Where?

IMOGEN: I don't know. There's a meeting or something in London. Something to do with Uncle's firm. So he says, anyway. The point is I'll be on my own. I think I can get someone to look after the kids . . .

HENRY: You could?

IMOGEN: I think so.

HENRY: Can you come and stay up at the house?

IMOGEN: Do you think that's wise?

HENRY: Why not?

IMOGEN: Won't she be there?

HENRY: No, of course she won't be there . . .

IMOGEN: It would mean I'd be near the kids, wouldn't it? If anything happened. I could tell Betty where I was. She'd never say anything. All right then. Yes.

HENRY: That's wonderful.

IMOGEN: I thought you'd be pleased.

HENRY: (*Embracing her*) God, that's wonderful . . .

IMOGEN: Careful, I'm covered in cow muck . . .

HENRY: (*Still holding her*) I love you, I love you, I love you . . .
(*They cling to each other. The cows moo in approval as the lights change again to –*)

SCENE 15
6.30 p.m.

The wine bar again. As before. BRUCE *has nearly finished the second bowl of nibbles.* HILARY *sits stiffly.*

96

HILARY: Right, that's it, I'm afraid. I'm going.

BRUCE: (*Alarmed*) Don't you want your wine?

HILARY: No, I don't. You drink it. I'm going. Goodbye, Bruce. I'll talk to Arnold about the divorce. It's all right, I won't be vindictive. I think we can settle it all quite quietly . . .

BRUCE: Hilly! What are you saying? This is Bruce. This is Brucie baby. (*He burps.*) Excuse me.
(HILARY *gets up.*)
(*Shouting in desperation*) Remember my promise. I always left them with you, sweetie. I always left them with you, I swear it . . .

HILARY: (*Icily*) Well, congratulations. All I can say is, you must have a second pair, Bruce.

BRUCE: (*Tearfully*) Hilary. Hilly, Hilly baby, please don't go!
(*He clings to her.*)

HILARY: Bruce, everyone is staring at us. Come along.

BRUCE: Don't leave me!

HILARY: Bruce!

BRUCE: You have to stay and meet her. You have to meet her, Hilly. Please.

HILARY: What are you talking about?

BRUCE: You've got to meet her . . .

HILARY: Meet who?
(KAREN *appears. She has made a very special effort with her appearance. She looks sensational.*)

KAREN: Yoo! Hoo! Bruce! Hi!

HILARY: Who is that?

BRUCE: That's Miss . . . (*Looking at her*) Oh, my God. That's Miss . . .

KAREN: (*Reaching them*) Hi! Sorry to trouble you. You forgot to sign these . . . (*To* HILARY) Hallo, you must be Hilary, I'm Karen. Bruce's little helper. (*She smiles fondly at* BRUCE.)

HILARY: (*To* BRUCE) You bastard! Is this why you got me here?

BRUCE: (*Staring at* KAREN *in horror*) I don't know what she's . . . why is she . . . ?
(*He burps.*)

HILARY: That's it, Bruce. Forget it. Gloves off now, darling. Total war. All right? (*To* KAREN) You're welcome to him,

dear. From the look of you, you thoroughly deserve each
other.

(HILARY *goes.* BRUCE *stares after her.*)

HILARY: Are you going to sign the letters for me, Bruce?

BRUCE: (*Staring at her with horrified realization*) You little . . . (*He
burps.*) It was you, wasn't it? It was you all the time. Who are
you working for, eh? Who's been paying you to do this to
me . . .

(*He burps. His indigestion is getting worse.*)

KAREN: Come along, Bruce, calm down . . .

BRUCE: (*Rising*) I'm going to kill you. You know that? I'm going
to kill you right here for what you've done to me. You
scheming tart, you . . . (*He doubles up in pain and sits again.*)
Ah!

KAREN: Bruce?

BRUCE: (*Gasping for air*) My God! She's poisoned the crisps as
well. Help me someone, she's poisoned my crisps.

KAREN: Will someone get a doctor, please? I think this man isn't
well . . .

BRUCE: (*Weakly*) Who are you working for? I have to know.
Please tell me . . . The CIA? No? The FBI? The CBI? The
EEC? Please tell me. You must tell me.

KAREN: Very well, I'll tell you.

(*She leans forward and whispers the name in his ear.* BRUCE
stares at her. Then he starts to laugh.)

BRUCE: I don't believe it? Him? You did this for . . . *him*? I don't
believe you. (*A convulsive burp.*) Now that's what I call . . .
That's what I call . . .

(*He gives a couple more chuckles and a burp. His eyes glaze over.
He slides off his chair.* KAREN *moves to catch him.*)

KAREN: Somebody! Please. Help me, please. I think my boss has
just dropped dead . . .

(*The lights change again to –*)

*The hall in Furtherfield House. As the lights come up, the front
doorbell rings.* WINNIE *comes to answer it.* HENRY *rushes on in rather
indecent haste. He has on a smoking jacket and has made an effort for
this weekend. He sees* WINNIE *has beaten him to the door and stands
waiting while she opens it.* WINNIE *does so.* IMOGEN *steps into the
hall. She has her coat on and has also made an effort. She carries a
small overnight case. She stops as she sees* HENRY. *They stare at each
other. She smiles at him. He smiles. It's the moment they've both
dreamt of.* WINNIE *senses she is in the way. She tiptoes out and leaves
them.* HENRY *and* IMOGEN *move together. They touch each other,
almost incredulously.*

IMOGEN: (*In a whisper*) I can't believe this is happening.
HENRY: (*In a whisper*) Nor can I.
IMOGEN: (*In a whisper*) Oh, my darling . . .
HENRY: (*In a whisper*) My darling . . .
   (*They move to go into the longest kiss ever. Their lips brush. The
   front door opens.* KAREN *stands there.* HENRY *and* IMOGEN
   spring apart.)
KAREN: Hi!
   (*They stare at her.*)
   Sorry. Did I . . . ? (*Pause.*) Carry on. Don't mind me.
IMOGEN: (*Recovering*) I'd better . . . I'd better be . . .
HENRY: Please, no. Don't . . .
IMOGEN: (*Hurriedly*) No. Please. Sorry. I have to . . . I have
   animals to feed. Excuse me.
   (IMOGEN *grabs her suitcase and rushes out into the night.*)
KAREN: 'Night.
   (HENRY *stands crestfallen.*)
   Sorry, HenryBell, you were obviously on the brink of
   something major. I should have phoned, but I just had to get
   out of that dreadful place for a bit. Get some fresh air.
   (*Throwing herself down*) God, I feel better already. I'll have a
   bath and then I'll feel really clean. I haven't felt clean for
   days. You never can in London, can you?

(HENRY *continues to stare at her dully*.)

Well, HenryBell. First, the news in brief. Mission accomplished. Mr Bruce Tick. RIP.

HENRY: (*Dully*) What?

KAREN: RIP. Deceased. No more. Dropped dead in a wine bar. What more suitable way to go? Leaving behind him a widow and two children all of whom seem totally unaffected.

HENRY: How did he . . . How did he – die?

KAREN: Cholesterol. And overexcitement, I think. Don't worry. He died with your name on his lips.

HENRY: This is . . . I can't believe it. You killed him? You murdered Bruck Tick?

KAREN: No. I – just nudged him in the general direction of – death, that's all. He was already well on the road.

HENRY: (*Sitting*) I don't know what to say. What are we going to do?

KAREN: Nothing.

HENRY: Nothing?

KAREN: Nothing. Anyway, how about you? You seem to be progressing. You doing all right?

HENRY: (*Still dazed*) What?

KAREN: Softening her up, I take it. And then ththutt! (*She makes a chopping motion with her hand*.) Yes? That the plan? Brilliant. She looked as if she was cooking nicely to me. (*Getting up*) I'll have that bath . . . (*Yelling*) Winnie! (*As she moves off*) Tell you something. I think I'll hang on with that firm for a bit. I'm rather enjoying it. Be fun to see how far I can get before they rumble me. Bet I can make Managing Director's sec. A bet? Yes?

(WINNIE *enters*.)

Winnie! Bath!

WINNIE: Yes, Miss Karen.

(WINNIE *goes off*. KAREN *looks at* HENRY, *who sits motionless*.)

KAREN: What's the matter, HenryBell? You look really depressed. You should be celebrating. You've won. We've won. Tell you what, I'll get in my bath. And then you come on up to the bathroom and I'll teach you some water sports

you never dreamt of. Have you ever played Dive, Dive,
Dive . . . ?
(HENRY *shakes his head*.)
No? Sailors and Mermaids?
(HENRY *shakes his head again*.)
Hot Lobsters? No? HenryBell, you've never been in a bath
till you've played Lobsters . . .
HENRY: No, I have to . . . I couldn't, Karen.
KAREN: What?
HENRY: I'm a bit . . . I'm very . . . I'm sorry.
KAREN: (*Cooling*) OK. Suit yourself. (*She studies him.*) I do hope
you're intending to keep your side of the bargain, HenryBell.
You're not getting seriously involved with the Friesian, are
you? Because that's not our deal. Not at all it isn't and you
know it. So don't try and double-cross me, HenryBell, will
you, because although I'm a loyal friend, I'm also a very bad
enemy. Very bad. Awful. Believe me.
(HENRY *stares at her*.)
(*Softly*) Do you know what I do to people who try to double-
cross me, HenryBell? (*In a whisper almost jokily, but not quite*)
I take revenge! Revenge!
(*She puts her finger to her lips and tiptoes off. Off along the
passage we hear her shout 'Revenge' once again. Then the sound
of her receding laughter.*)
HENRY: (*To himself, in dawning horror*) My God, she's mad! She's
completely mad. What am I going to do?
(*As he stands there, the lights fade to blackout.*)

PART TWO

ACT III

Darkness. A single spot comes up on KAREN *with her mobile phone.
She is in a passageway at Lembridge Tennit. She is back in her
secretarial outfit, although this has gone slightly up-market since we
last saw her. In fact, chameleon-like, she subtly alters to suit whoever
she's working for or with.*

KAREN: HenryBell . . .
  (*A single spot comes up immediately on* HENRY *on the phone at
  Furtherfield House.*)
HENRY: Karen?
KAREN: Wonderful news, HenryBell . . .
HENRY: Karen, good. I needed to talk to you –
KAREN: (*Excitedly*) . . . listen, listen, I haven't got much time.
  I've been promoted. What do you think of that? I've got a
  new boss. Up four floors, two grades and a thousand a year.
HENRY: (*Dismayed*) Really? You really intend to carry on at
  Lembridge Tennit, do you?
KAREN: Of course I do. I'm a mobilely upward special secretarial
  temp. I'm a MUSST, HenryBell. An absolute MUSST. Isn't
  it exciting?
HENRY: Yes, congratulations. Who's the – who's the lucky man
  this time?
KAREN: (*Consulting a piece of paper*) Er. A Mr Seeds. Graham
  Seeds. Head of Transportation – Brackets South East. Did
  you know him?
HENRY: No, I was North West.
KAREN: I'm just going to meet him. I'll report back . . . Wish me
  luck. I must go. Bye . . .
HENRY: (*Urgently*) Karen, wait . . .
KAREN: What?
HENRY: Listen, I have to ask you this – I wanted to ask you at the
  weekend only I – I didn't really get a chance – with being so
  . . . so . . .

(*He falters.*)

KAREN: Tied up is the phrase I think you're looking for,
   HenryBell . . .

HENRY: Yes . . .

KAREN: Wasn't that fun?

HENRY: Yes, an absolute hoot.

KAREN: Did someone eventually find you?

HENRY: Yes. Eventually. Winnie, this morning. Listen, Karen –

KAREN: Never mind, your turn next weekend . . .

HENRY: Listen, about Anthony –

KAREN: In the Red Room. Do your worst, O master . . .

HENRY: Anthony Staxton-Billing . . .

KAREN: (*Rather impatiently*) Yes? What about Anthony Staxton-
   Billing?

HENRY: Are you absolutely certain that he left you to go back to
   his wife? Back to Imogen?

KAREN: Of course I'm certain, how many more times?

HENRY: There couldn't possibly – even remotely – just ever so
   obliquely and distantly – have been, say – another woman.
   That he went to? Instead?

KAREN: Who?

HENRY: Anthony.

KAREN: To another woman?

HENRY: Yes.

KAREN: No. No. No.

HENRY: You're sure?

KAREN: Yes. Yes. Yes.

HENRY: Would you – would you object very strongly if I made
   some enquiries . . .?

KAREN: Look, do what you like. I don't care what you do as long
   as you keep to our bargain, all right? Keep to that. Or else.
   OK?

HENRY: Yes, only if there was another woman, then maybe
   you're trying to take revenge against the wrong one, you
   see . . .

KAREN: Third and final warning. Beep – beep – beep. Bye.
   (*She switches off her phone. The light goes out on* HENRY, *before
   he can say any more.* KAREN *frowns slightly and puts away the*

phone. As she does so, LYDIA *scurries into view.*)

LYDIA: Oh, there you are. Sorry to keep you. There was a slight crisis in the – How are you?

KAREN: Oh, much better. I had a long lie-down over the weekend.

LYDIA: Oh, how sensible.

KAREN: Got waited on hand and foot.

LYDIA: Quite right. Poor you. Poor Mr Tick. Dreadful.

KAREN: Shocking.

LYDIA: Poor Mrs Tick.

KAREN: Indeed.

KAREN: Were there any . . . ?

KAREN: Yes, two little Ticks too, apparently.

LYDIA: Appalling. Was there any prior warning that that might happen?

KAREN: Well, Bruce had had digestive problems, it has to be said.

LYDIA: Ah. Yes, I did hear that . . .

KAREN: But no real warning, no. I'd taken his letters into the wine bar just along the road there for late signature and Bruce just toppled over at the table.

LYDIA: (*Shaking her head*) Well . . .

KAREN: So.

LYDIA: It could happen to any of us, I suppose.

KAREN: Very true.

(*They reflect for a second on the uncertainty of existence.*)

LYDIA: Well, are you ready to meet the new boss? Mr Seeds?

KAREN: Rather.

LYDIA: I hope this works out well. I'd hate it if you – I mean frankly, as Mrs Bulley was saying at the meeting only this morning, you're too valuable to lose, Karen.

KAREN: (*Modestly*) Thank you.

LYDIA: Now, just a word of warning, between the two of us. Mr Seeds is only just back at work. He's been off sick for – oh, nearly five months.

KAREN: Oh dear, was it serious?

LYDIA: I understand it was something very nearly approaching a – (*dropping down to near inaudibility*) nervous breakdown.

KAREN: No?

LYDIA: Well, Mr Seeds is . . . he's a rather nervy man. Absolutely
    brilliant, of course –
KAREN: Of course. Thank you for telling me. These things are so
    useful to know in advance.
LYDIA: I thought you should know. I don't like telling tales but I
    felt you should be prepared. By the way, I love your new
    image, I never said. You're looking – decidedly chic, Karen.
KAREN: (*Blushing*) Thank you, Lydia.
LYDIA: Right-o. Are we ready? Let me introduce you to Mr
    Seeds.
    (LYDIA *knocks gently on the office door. They wait. She knocks
    again, louder.*)
    (*Calling as she does so*) Mr Seeds! Mr Seeds!
MR SEEDS: (*A thin, startled voice*) Who is that? Who's there?
LYDIA: Excuse me, Mr Seeds. It's Lydia, Mr Seeds. Mrs Bulley's
    Lydia.
MR SEEDS: Well, there's no need to knock the door down, is
    there?
LYDIA: (*Pulling a face at* KAREN *and then ushering her in ahead of
    her*) I want to introduce you to Karen, Mr Seeds. Whom we
    feel sure you'll find a little gift from heaven . . .
KAREN: (*Gushing, as she enters*) Hallo, Mr Seeds. How nice to
    meet you . . .
    (*As both women go off, the lights change to –*)

SCENE 2
9.15 a.m.

The dining room at Furtherfield House. HENRY *is finishing his
breakfast. The sound of the motor bike racing around indoors in the
house.* NORMA *enters with an empty tray, shadowed, as usual, by*
WINNIE.

WINNIE: (*To* NORMA, *in the usual undertone*) Ask the gentleman if
    he'd care for more toast, then.
HENRY: (*Attempting to anticipate her*) No, thank you, Norma.
NORMA: Would you care for more toast, sir?

HENRY: No, thank you, Norma.

NORMA: Thank you, sir.

WINNIE: (*Indicating the breakfast debris*) Clear that away then.

(NORMA *starts to clear the table.* WINNIE *watches her.*)

HENRY: (*Rising from the table*) Delicious. As always.

WINNIE: Thank you, sir.

NORMA: Thank you, sir.

(HENRY *moves away to the windows to look out. A bird flutters above his head. He ducks. In the other room, the motor bike stalls and stops.*)

OLIVER: (*Off, angrily*) Oh, knickers.

HENRY: Pity they never had that building replaced.

WINNIE: Pardon, sir?

HENRY: That summer-house on the other side of the lawn, there. It's a shame they've never replaced it, isn't it?

WINNIE: Oh no, sir. That building'll never be replaced. Not in our lifetime. Those charred remains are there as a reminder to all.

HENRY: A reminder of what?

WINNIE: (*Darkly*) A reminder of the fire.

HENRY: Ah.

WINNIE: This rain'll be good.

HENRY: Will it?

WINNIE: Oh, yes. We need the rain.

HENRY: Winnie, don't you think . . . I don't want to interfere but . . . don't you feel that Norma is probably up to coping on her own now?

WINNIE: On her own?

HENRY: Yes.

WINNIE: Oh no, sir. She's a long way to go yet, sir.

HENRY: Really? She seems to have more or less the hang of things. I mean, as I say, it's none of my business . . .

WINNIE: You see, young Norma, sir, she's being like groomed to replace me. You see. When I retire, then Norma steps in. So she's got to know it all.

HENRY: I see.

WINNIE: (*Pointedly*) Because once she takes over, I won't be here no more. I'll be retired. With just my pension.

HENRY: Oh yes, I see.

WINNIE: So I agreed with Master Oliver, I'd go when I'd got her good and ready. And not before, you see. And with a girl like Norma there, that could take years if you get my meaning.

HENRY: (*Tactfully*) Say no more. I quite understand.

(*The bird flutters over his head. He ducks.* OLIVER *enters. He wears motor-cycle boots, pyjamas, dressing-gown and his crash helmet, which he is in the act of removing.*)

OLIVER: (*Seeing* HENRY) Ah! Hi!

HENRY: Good morning. Have a good ride?

OLIVER: So-so. I've got quite a circuit laid out now.

HENRY: Yes, I noticed.

WINNIE: (*To* NORMA) Take that out now.

(NORMA *goes out with the tray during the next.* WINNIE *hovers in the doorway, waiting for a word.*)

OLIVER: Hope I didn't wake you. Filthy day, so I'm afraid it's the wet-weather circuit. Billiard room, through the ballroom, then along the passageway, chicane into the library, hairpin round the cabinets, then it's straight all the way to the east study where you can really open up and then you're back in the billiard room – and into lap two.

HENRY: Terrific.

OLIVER: Want a go?

HENRY: No, thank you.

OLIVER: No? Well, probably wise. It's not as simple as it looks, I can tell you.

HENRY: I bet it isn't.

(*The bird flutters over their heads.* HENRY *ducks.* OLIVER *glances at it.*)

OLIVER: Blue tit.

HENRY: Oh, yes?

WINNIE: Would you care for some breakfast, Master Oliver?

OLIVER: No, I ate. Out of the fridge. Earlier.

WINNIE: Very good, sir.

OLIVER: (*Holding out his crash helmet*) Here, you can take this, though.

(WINNIE, *taking the helmet, goes.*)

Of course, if it wasn't for this rain, I could be out of doors.

HENRY: Do you ever feel the urge to wander?

OLIVER: Wander? How do you mean? In the garden?

HENRY: No, somewhere else? Get away? To new places?

OLIVER: Where?

HENRY: Anywhere.

OLIVER: No. (*A pause.*) I can't think of anywhere. (*Pause.*) I like it here, actually. It's rather good.

HENRY: It is. Yes, it is, I agree. Only . . . (*Deciding this is not a fruitful avenue for discussion*) Well, I think I'll brave the rain, anyway. Go for a stroll.

OLIVER: Why not?

HENRY: I was just saying to Winnie that it's a pity you've never had that place rebuilt.

OLIVER: The summer-house?

HENRY: Yes. It's a bit of an eyesore, isn't it?

OLIVER: (*Frowning*) Yes. (*Pause.*) It's . . . it's difficult really.

HENRY: How do you mean?

OLIVER: That's – that's where the parents both died, you see. In the fire.

HENRY: Oh, I'm sorry. I had no idea.

OLIVER: They were both keen lepidopterists, you know. Moths, mainly. Always chasing about in the middle of the night together. Smearing trees with treacle and so on. To catch the things, you know. Bunging them in jars, pinning them on boards. They had quite a collection. Really pretty famous. Amongst other lepidopterists, you understand.

HENRY: Of course.

OLIVER: I must say they all looked a bit the same to me. A moth's a moth, isn't it? Anyway, one night we all woke up and there was this fire. That whole summer-house was blazing like a beacon. Moths everywhere. No one could get anywhere near it. They both must have died almost instantly.

HENRY: How terrible.

OLIVER: It was. Yes. They were awfully decent people, actually. I mean, I know you're always supposed to think that about your parents but I know a lot of people who loathe the sight of theirs. But I rather rated ours. I thought they were something a bit special.

HENRY: What did Karen think of them?

OLIVER: (*Evasively*) Karen? No idea. I should ask her. We're both very different, you see. I can't speak for her.

HENRY: What caused the fire? Do they know?

OLIVER: No. Oil lamp possibly, they think. There was no electricity out there. Not in the summer-house.

HENRY: Was Karen – here at the time?

OLIVER: (*Troubled*) Oh, yes. Karen was here. We were both home on school holiday. Why?

HENRY: (*Avoiding this question*) How old were you both?

OLIVER: Well, I was about nine or ten. So she'd have been about thirteen. Difficult age.

HENRY: Thirteen?

OLIVER: No, ten.

HENRY: Oh, yes. The tragedy must have affected you both?

OLIVER: I suppose it did. Fortunately there was Winnie and the others to look after us. We coped. (*He's not enjoying this conversation.*) Look, don't let me keep you from your walk, will you . . .

HENRY: No. No, I'll . . .

(*He makes to move away.* NORMA *enters again, with a tin of furniture polish and a duster. She is followed by* WINNIE.)

WINNIE: Excuse me, Master Oliver, is it all right if we do the table . . .?

OLIVER: Yeah. Sure. Do it away.

(*He makes to move off.*)

WINNIE: (*To* NORMA) Start on the table, then.

NORMA: Right.

(NORMA *starts polishing the dining table, while* WINNIE *watches her and pretends not to be listening to the following conversation.*)

HENRY: (*Calling him back*) Oliver . . . Sorry. Just one other small question . . .

OLIVER: Yah?

HENRY: (*Confidentially, drawing* OLIVER *aside*) Look, this may seem like none of my business again – but I do have a reason for asking it . . . There was, I know, a certain friendship between Karen and Anthony Staxton-Billing, wasn't there?

OLIVER: Oh, sure. Way back, there was.

HENRY: How long is way back?

OLIVER: Well. Nine months. A year. I don't know. Karen moped about for ages. Muttering.

HENRY: Muttering what?

OLIVER: I don't know. I couldn't hear. Breaking things.

HENRY: But then – did Anthony Staxton-Billing take up with someone else? Or did he leave her in order to go back to his wife?

OLIVER: No idea.

HENRY: Has he got another woman, do you think?

OLIVER: 'Fraid I couldn't tell you. I really hardly know him. Matter of fact, I don't actually like him very much.

HENRY: Why not?

OLIVER: I don't know. I think he's rather stupid. I don't know how he gets all these women. They must be even more stupid than he is. (*Pause.*) Sorry. I didn't mean that about . . .

HENRY: Love can make all of us a bit stupid.

OLIVER: Really? Don't know. I've never done it. Don't fancy it.

HENRY: No? It can be – quite a good feeling, sometimes.

OLIVER: Can it? It always seems to end up with a lot of crying and people trying to kill each other. At least it does in this family. Look, it's clearing up. I should get that walk in. See you later.

HENRY: Yes, indeed.

(OLIVER *goes out.* NORMA *has finished the table.*)

WINNIE: (*To* NORMA) Let's do the table in the hall now.

NORMA: Right.

(NORMA *goes out.* HENRY *is still staring thoughtfully in the direction of the summer-house.* WINNIE *stops in the doorway.*)

WINNIE: If you're looking for the other woman . . .

HENRY: (*Startled*) What?

WINNIE: I say, if you're hunting for this other woman, sir . . .

HENRY: Mr Staxton-Billing's other woman? Then there is one, Winnie? She exists?

WINNIE: Maybe she does. Maybe she doesn't. I'm not one for spreading rumour. All I'm saying is – if she does exist – and I'm not saying she does – then you could do worse than start by talking to Norma out there.

HENRY: Norma?

WINNIE: I'm saying no more.

HENRY: Norma?

WINNIE: Excuse me, sir.

(*She makes to leave.*)

HENRY: Then I must talk to Norma . . .

WINNIE: She's rather busy, sir, just at the . . .

HENRY: Please, Winnie. I must talk to her. Now. Send her in here now.

WINNIE: Very well, sir. But don't you frighten her, mind.

HENRY: I wouldn't dream of frightening her.

(WINNIE *goes out.* HENRY *waits. The bird flutters past his head. He ducks.*)

(*Incredulously, to himself*) Norma? Anthony Staxton-Billing and Norma?

(NORMA *enters nervously.* WINNIE *follows.*)

Would you leave us alone for a moment, Winnie?

WINNIE: I don't think I should –

HENRY: Please.

WINNIE: I don't care to leave her unsupervised.

HENRY: Please, Winnie. I do insist.

WINNIE: (*Reluctantly*) Very good, sir. (*To* NORMA, *in an undertone*) You just answer the gentleman's questions, all right?

NORMA: Yes.

(WINNIE *goes out.* NORMA *is trembling with nerves.*)

HENRY: (*Aware of this*) Now don't be frightened, Norma. You mustn't be nervous. I just want a little personal talk with you. Would you like to sit down?

NORMA: (*Inaudibly*) No, I can't sit down, sir.

HENRY: (*Straining to hear*) What? What's that?

NORMA: I can't sit down, sir.

HENRY: (*Rather alarmed*) You can't sit down? Why can't you sit down? Don't be afraid to answer, Norma, I'm a friend. Why can't you sit down?

NORMA: I'm not allowed to sit down, sir. Not in here.

HENRY: Oh, I see. Well, you can sit down if I ask you to sit down, though. Sit down, Norma.

NORMA: No, sir, I can't sit down, sir. Don't make me sit down, sir . . .

HENRY: (*Rather losing patience*) All right! Stand up then, I don't care.

NORMA: Yes, sir.

HENRY: (*Controlling himself*) How old are you, Norma?

NORMA: Sixteen and a half, sir.

HENRY: Sixteen and a half. (*Gently*) Well now, Norma . . . I want you to tell me about Mr Staxton-Billing. Do you know who I mean?

NORMA: Yes, sir . . .

HENRY: I want you to answer me honestly, Norma. And don't worry, this will go no further than this room, I promise. It's a secret just between us two, you see? Tell me truthfully, Norma, are you sleeping with Mr Staxton-Billing?
(NORMA *opens and closes her mouth. She makes little squeaks that grow swiftly into a wail of misery. Before* HENRY *can stop her, she rushes from the room. Her voice is heard receding through the house.* HENRY *stands alarmed.* WINNIE *comes in.*)

WINNIE: (*Looking at* HENRY *reproachfully*) Now there was no cause for that, sir, was there?
(*As they stand there, the lights cross-fade to –*)

SCENE 3
Noon.

Lembridge Tennit. The outer area of Mrs Bulley's office. LYDIA *enters with* KAREN, *who is clearly distressed.*

LYDIA: How awful for you. How absolutely awful. You poor thing. Sit down.

KAREN: Thank you.
(*She sits.*)

LYDIA: Now, look, you really must take the rest of today off, Mrs Bulley insists on that . . .

KAREN: That's very good of her.

LYDIA: Well, dear girl, that's the least . . . Now, look, she just

wants a quick word before you go off, just to say in person
how sorry she is about all this . . .

KAREN: Thank you.

LYDIA: I mean, gosh, it's absolutely horrid luck for you – losing
two bosses in less than a week . . .

KAREN: Yes. Poor Mr Seeds . . .

LYDIA: Poor man. Now, let me get it absolutely clear, because I
don't want you to have to go through the story over and over
again needlessly . . . You say that there was the fire drill –

KAREN: Yes, first thing this morning . . .

LYDIA: Yes. I remember it. And somehow Mr Seeds got the
impression that it wasn't a practice but the real thing . . .

KAREN: Yes, he just started running up the corridor. Shouting. I
tried to run after him to stop him but . . .

LYDIA: Yes, I'm sure. So then what happened?

KAREN: Well, I saw him open the door to the emergency
staircase . . .

LYDIA: Yes. Well, he acted perfectly correctly. He was right to
avoid the lifts . . . But why do you think, when he'd taken
the stairs, he ran up them, rather than down them?

KAREN: I think he somehow got the idea that the fire was
downstairs . . .

LYDIA: Oh, I see. So he ran upstairs on to the roof?

KAREN: Yes. And then jumped.
    (*She sobs.*)

LYDIA: And then jumped. How awful. Thirty-two floors.

KAREN: Yes.

LYDIA: I suppose he wouldn't have known much.

KAREN: Well, so they say.

LYDIA: Anyway, not after the first twenty or so.

MRS BULLEY: (*Off*) What are you chattering about out there,
Lydia?

LYDIA: Sorry, Mrs Bulley, I was just talking to Miss Knightly.

MRS BULLEY: (*Off*) Well, bring her in here, Lydia. Bring her in
here. I can't talk to the woman out there, can I?

LYDIA: No, Mrs Bulley. (*To* KAREN) Come on in.

MRS BULLEY: (*Off*) I think you're going gently potty, Lydia, do
you know that?

LYDIA: (*Laughing, as she ushers* KAREN *in*) Yes, Mrs Bulley.
Here's Miss Knightly, Mrs Bulley.
(KAREN *goes off, followed by* LYDIA.)
MRS BULLEY: (*Off, jokingly*) Now, Karen, my dear girl, what on
earth have you been doing to half our middle management,
eh?
(*She laughs heartily. The door closes, cutting off her laugh. The
lights cross-fade to –*)

SCENE 4
3.00 p.m.

A junior gymkhana. IMOGEN *is tense and pale. Dressed sensibly for
chilly outdoors, she feigns great interest in the riding events which we
hear but don't see. The galloping of occasional hoofs, crowd reaction
and an indecipherable PA system commentating cheerfully on the
events.* HENRY *hovers, a little apart from* IMOGEN. *He, too, is
tense.*

HENRY: I say again, you didn't really mean it.
IMOGEN: Oh yes I did. I meant every word of it. (*Calling out*)
Well done, Lucy! She's a good little rider, that kid.
HENRY: What? You never loved me, you found our whole
relationship boring . . . ?
IMOGEN: I never said boring. I never said it was boring.
HENRY: Boring. I have the letter.
IMOGEN: Fruitless. That's what I said.
HENRY: Boring. That's what you said.
IMOGEN: I said fruitless. I know what I wrote.
HENRY: So do I, so do I . . .
IMOGEN: It took me hours to write that letter. Do you think it
was easy for me? It was agony.
HENRY: What do you think it was like to get it? (*Pause.*) Through
the common or garden postal service. (*Pause. Bitterly*)
Second class.
IMOGEN: Well, you're only living half a mile away, there was
hardly any point in wasting money on stamps.

HENRY: It still took three days. You were that close, why couldn't you deliver it by hand, for God's sake? If you had to write.

(*Applause from the crowd as someone wins.*)

IMOGEN: (*Calling out*) Well done.

HENRY: Or didn't you have the courage to do that?

IMOGEN: No, I didn't. You're quite right.

HENRY: Why not?

IMOGEN: Because I knew if I faced you, I'd . . .

HENRY: You wouldn't have been able to say all that, would you?

IMOGEN: (*A small voice*) No.

HENRY: Can you say it to me now?

IMOGEN: I can't remember what I said.

HENRY: You just said you could.

IMOGEN: Not every word. I can remember words like fruitless. But not all of them.

HENRY: Just the cruel ones, eh? Well, come on, do your best. Improvise.

IMOGEN: I can't.

HENRY: Go on. Of course you can.

IMOGEN: (*Yelling*) Well jumped, Simon. I wish I could ride like that. I wish I could do anything.

HENRY: Don't you think you owe me that, at least? To tell me to my face? Live?

IMOGEN: Go away, Henry.

HENRY: Come on. Let's hear it, then. 'Dear Henry . . . '

IMOGEN: (*Utterly miserably*) Oh, leave me alone . . .

HENRY: 'Dear Henry . . . ' How did it go . . . ? 'I'm afraid this is goodbye . . . ?' There you are, I can remember it. 'Dear Henry . . . ?' Come on . . .

IMOGEN: Why are you doing this to me?

HENRY: Because I want to hear it. I still love you and I think you love me. And I want to hear it from you. And not from a second-class letter that came via Exeter.

(IMOGEN *is now crying openly. But* HENRY *is angry and desperate.*)

Come on. 'Dear Henry . . . '

(*Another whimper from* IMOGEN.)

(*Relentlessly*) 'Dear Henry . . . ' Why can't you say it?

IMOGEN: (*Weakly*) 'Dear Henry . . . '

HENRY: That's it. Go on. Dear Henry, what?

IMOGEN: Dear Henry . . . Dear Henry . . . (*Softly*) Dear, dear, dear Henry. . .

HENRY: (*Gently*) Imogen . . .

(*With a sudden wail,* IMOGEN *rushes from him.* HENRY *looks in alarm. A horse whinnies.*)

My God! Look out. (*He sighs with relief as some sort of accident is averted.*) Whew! That was close.

(HENRY *watches* IMOGEN *out of sight.* ANTHONY *appears. He is also dressed for the occasion with a steward's badge and a pair of binoculars.*)

ANTHONY: Hoy! I say . . .

HENRY: (*Alarmed*) Hallo?

ANTHONY: Just a quick word, old boy . . . If you can spare a moment.

HENRY: (*Bracing himself*) Yes, of course.

ANTHONY: From now on, I'm afraid I'm going to have to rule that little number out of bounds as far as you're concerned, old boy.

HENRY: (*Irritated*) What little number are you talking about?

ANTHONY: That one there who's just tried to throw herself under the hoofs of the Under-Thirteens' Selling Plate. She's my wife and she's off-limits, OK?

HENRY: That's up to her, isn't it?

ANTHONY: No, it isn't. It isn't up to her, at all. It's up to me. And I'm telling you, OK?

HENRY: I suppose you're going to tell me she's your property?

ANTHONY: Since you ask, yes, she bloody well is. So hands off.

HENRY: God, you're a nasty piece of work, aren't you?

ANTHONY: Now listen, chummy, I'm being fairly civil to you, all things considered . . .

HENRY: Civil?

ANTHONY: Fairly civil . . .

HENRY: You couldn't be more unpleasant if you tried –

ANTHONY: Oh yes, I could be. I could be a lot more unpleasant than this if I tried, I warn you. I can be deeply, deeply unpleasant, chummy, if I choose to be – believe me, so far as

119

you're concerned, at this moment in time, I'm being as charming as you're ever likely to know me, so I should make the best of it. Because I'm not going to be made a public laughing stock by some poncified townie with a hideous taste in suits coming down here and bonking my wife in my own chicken sheds, all right? Now bugger off. Is that loud and clear enough for you?

HENRY: (*Taking a deep breath*) You don't perhaps consider your own behaviour has anything to do with this?

ANTHONY: What behaviour?

HENRY: Your behaviour with – with Karen Knightly, for one thing.

ANTHONY: Karen Knightly?

HENRY: Yes, Karen Knightly. I presume you remember her?

ANTHONY: What the hell's she been telling you?

HENRY: That you had an affair with her . . .

(ANTHONY *laughs humorously*.)

Yes. And then chucked her over, when you'd had enough of her.

ANTHONY: Is that what she told you?

HENRY: More or less, yes.

ANTHONY: Karen Knightly and I had – well, you could hardly term it an affair – had a bit of sex together, let's say – for all of a month. Well, quite a lot of sex, really. We tried out all twenty-five of the bedrooms in that house of hers over the course of about a fortnight, starting in the attic and finishing up in the master suite. She insisted we dressed in suitable clothes to suit different locations. I remember our night in the nursery as particularly bizarre. When we'd completed the course, she declared that according to ancient law we were now legally engaged. And that at the next full moon I had to sacrifice my existing wife Imogen and change my name to Alric the Awesome. At which point, I realized she was stark staring mad and I broke off the relationship. She then plagued us both for months. Writing anonymous letters, drawing strange runes on our front door, phoning up claiming to be a midwife delivering my illegitimate child. You name it, she did it. Culminating, finally, in a phone call

demanding that I be on Chelsea Bridge at eight thirty sharp
or she would throw herself in the Thames.

HENRY: (*Suspecting a ring of truth in all this*) My God. And did you
go?

ANTHONY: Yes, I did. I stood on that bloody bridge for an hour
and a half hoping to see her jump. No such luck. Not so
much as a ripple. So I went home again.

HENRY: She was on Albert Bridge, actually.

ANTHONY: (*Uninterested*) Was she? Oh well, that figures.
Anyway, that's beside the point. Karen Knightly is totally
immaterial. I've forgotten her. We're talking about Imogen.
And that one you can forget. You keep out of my chickens.
Away from my cows. Off my pigs. And well clear of my wife,
all right?

(ANTHONY *moves away*.)

HENRY: I'm afraid you won't get rid of me that easily.

ANTHONY: Really? Then I'll have to do it the hard way, won't I?

(ANTHONY *strides off, leaving* HENRY *brooding and scheming.
The gymkhana goes on remorselessly as the lights cross-fade to –*)

SCENE 5
9.00 a.m.

Lembridge Tennit. LYDIA *is leading* KAREN *into the outer area of
Jeremy Pride's office.*

LYDIA: (*Looking around*) No, I think they're probably both in the
meeting at present. What day is it? Wednesday. Yes. Right.
Just time for a quick run down, then. (*Rapidly*) Mr Pride.
Mr Jeremy Pride, he's the younger of our two Mr Prides –
our other one's Stuart Pride – they're not actually related but
they're both directors and it can get rather confusing – but
they loathe it if you get them muddled up so try not to.
Anyway, Mr Jeremy Pride, whom you'll be working for, is
mainly concerned with our building operations in the
domestic sphere. Obviously, we've got an overseas building
side as well but that's on a completely different floor and

really won't bother you and is run by a man called John Hatch, whom you'll probably never meet, nobody ever does. Now, as I said, this is only just a temporary filler for you until we can find you another more permanent job but it will give you a chance to see a whole operation globally, rather than just bits of it – which I think should be really quite fascinating for you, don't you agree? Strictly, of course, you won't be working for Mr Pride but technically you'll be assisting Mr Pride's assistant who's been screaming for help because apparently their paperwork has just got beyond a joke. That all make sense? Great. Can I leave you to introduce yourself then? Only we've got a crisis. It's the flu season come round again, I'm afraid. Always seems to coincide with Wimbledon fortnight for some inexplicable reason. May see you at lunch. I think that'll be your desk there . . . Bye!

KAREN: Bye . . .

(LYDIA *hurries out.* KAREN *explores the office a little. She examines the other desk. She idly opens one of the drawers.* VERONICA WEBB *enters. She sees* KAREN *and stops.* VERONICA *is a woman in her late forties. She is an abrupt, matter-of-fact, no-nonsense sort of woman. She stares at* KAREN *suspiciously.*)

VERONICA: What the hell do you think you're doing?

KAREN: (*Jumping guiltily*) Oh, hallo.

VERONICA: Who are you? What are you doing in here?

KAREN: I'm Karen Knightly.

VERONICA: Who?

KAREN: Karen Knightly. I've been sent here by Mrs Bulley's office. I understand they wanted assistance.

VERONICA: You got a staff card?

KAREN: Er, yes.

(KAREN *produces her card.* VERONICA *studies it and her with deep suspicion.*)

VERONICA: (*Studying* KAREN'*s picture*) This meant to be you?

KAREN: Yes.

VERONICA: Not a very good picture, is it?

KAREN: No, I'm afraid I'm not very photogenic.

VERONICA: You can say that again, you look like a sheepdog. What did you say you wanted?

KAREN: I'm here to help out, apparently.

VERONICA: Help who?

KAREN: Mr Pride's assistant. He apparently wanted some help. Is he around, by any chance?

VERONICA: (*Returning* KAREN's *card*) He certainly is. She's here. I'm Mr Pride's assistant.

KAREN: (*Taken a little aback*) Ah!

VERONICA: About time. I've been yelling for someone for days. (*Looks* KAREN *up and down*.) Well, I suppose you'll do. You're better than nothing. Where do you come from? The pool?

KAREN: No, I was Mr Seeds' secretary. But unfortunately . . .

VERONICA: You mean the one who fell off the roof?

KAREN: That's right.

VERONICA: Stupid ass. Right. Well, if you're working for me, let's get the ground rules absolutely clear. I work for Mr Pride and I work very hard indeed. You'll be working for me and you're going to work even harder. Up till now I've no doubt you've wiggled your rear end at your boss and got away with murder. Well, that won't cut any ice round here, girl, so forget it. I don't lust after your body and I don't want to listen to your vacuous conversation. You just get your nose down and keep it there, all right? You do that, we'll get along just fine. First hint of trouble and I'll personally boot you straight downstairs again, is that clear?

KAREN: Yes, Miss . . . Mrs . . .

VERONICA: Webb. Miss Webb. If you're still here on Wednesday, you can call me Veronica. If you make it till next Christmas you can call me Ronny. That's your desk there.

KAREN: Yes.

VERONICA: This is mine. Don't touch it again.

KAREN: No, Miss Webb.

(*She prepares to sit.*)

VERONICA: (*Gathering an armload of folders*) Here you are. Start with these. Can you read?

KAREN: Yes, I have shorthand and typing . . .

VERONICA: So long as you can read that's all that matters.

Alphabetical by name. All of these, all right? Anything pre-1980 – bin it. OK? When you've finished these, there's a room full of them next door. As you finish each folder, take it along to Janey in the computer room at the end of the corridor there. Too complicated for you?

KAREN: No, I'm sure I'll manage that, Miss Webb. It looks a real challenge.

VERONICA: (*Looking at her suspiciously*) Yes. Butter wouldn't melt in your in-tray, would it? I bet you're a load of trouble given the chance, aren't you?

(*Their eyes meet.* KAREN *merely smiles at her sweetly.* JEREMY *enters. A pleasant, rather shy man in his fifties.*)

JEREMY: (*As he enters*) Ronny, I've been wondering whether we shouldn't be – (*Seeing* KAREN) Ah. Good morning. Who have we here?

VERONICA: (*Her manner subtly changing*) Oh, Jeremy, this is Miss Knightly . . .

KAREN: Karen Knightly . . .

VERONICA: Karen Knightly, who's been sent upstairs to help us out. Karen, this is Mr Pride . . .

JEREMY: Hallo. Jeremy Pride. Welcome aboard the madhouse.

(*He laughs.* VERONICA *laughs.*)

KAREN: (*Smiling*) Thank you.

JEREMY: Good, right-o then. Anything you want, Ronny will . . . Miss Webb will sort you out, I expect. Give me five minutes, Ronny, and then can we have a chat.

VERONICA: Yes, right. I put that letter for Taylor's on your desk . . .

JEREMY: Oh, Lord, yes. OK.

(JEREMY *goes into his office.* KAREN *has been watching* VERONICA. *The latter is aware of the look and readjusts her face, which has been smiling nonstop since* JEREMY *first came in.*)

KAREN: He seems very nice.

VERONICA: (*Shortly*) Yes, he is.

KAREN: I should imagine he's very intelligent, too.

VERONICA: He's brilliant. Utterly brilliant. This whole place would fall apart without him. He's the only one of the directors with any . . .

KAREN: Is he married?

VERONICA: (*Sharply*) Why?

KAREN: I was just curious, that's all.

VERONICA: Well, you can forget that straight away.

KAREN: I beg your pardon?

VERONICA: If I catch you making eyes at him, you'll be straight downstairs, I can tell you.

KAREN: I'm sure I'd no intention . . .

VERONICA: Mr Pride only has eyes for his work. He's there at his desk long before anyone else in this building arrives and he's usually the last to leave. He is a happy contented bachelor and that is how he prefers to remain. I should know, I've been with him for twelve years and I know him better than anyone.

KAREN: (*Mildly offended*) I'm sorry, I'm sure. I won't ask again.

VERONICA: As long as that's clear.

KAREN: I won't say another word.

VERONICA: Just – get on with your work, girl. And forget about him, all right?

KAREN: Yes, Miss Webb.

(*She opens a folder.*)

JEREMY: (*Off*) Ronny, here a second. Do you mind?

VERONICA: Coming, Jeremy. (*She hurries to the door. To* KAREN) And by the way, no smoking and no strong perfumes, OK? I can't stand the smell and they bring on Mr Pride's asthma . . .

KAREN: Yes, Miss Webb . . .

(*She starts to hum to herself, thoughtfully.*)

VERONICA: (*Turning in the doorway*) And we can do without the musical refrain, too, thank you very much.

KAREN: Yes, Miss Webb.

(VERONICA *goes out.* KAREN *looks up from her work as soon as she has gone. She smiles secretively to herself. A scheme is hatching somewhere. Slowly she begins to rock to and fro and starts to hum softly again. As this happens, the lights cross-fade to –*)

The lounge of Daphne Teale's bungalow. Bright and tasteless.
From above, the distant bass thud of pop music from a record player.
DAPHNE *leads* HENRY *into the room.*

DAPHNE: Come in, please . . .

HENRY: Thank you. (*Taking in the room*) Oh, ah.

DAPHNE: (*Proudly*) Like it?

HENRY: (*Who can't think what to say*) Very much. Very much.

DAPHNE: It's partly the lighting.

HENRY: Yes, yes.

DAPHNE: You can do a lot with coloured bulbs.

HENRY: Yes. (*He searches for words.*) Yes, they give the place a lot
of . . . light and . . .

DAPHNE: Colour.

HENRY: Colour. Yes. Very interesting.

DAPHNE: Like a drink, Mr –

HENRY: Henry, please, Henry. No thank you –

DAPHNE: Daphne, then.

HENRY: Daphne.

DAPHNE: Sure?

HENRY: Absolutely.

DAPHNE: Take a seat, then.

HENRY: Thank you. (*Noticing a photograph*) Oh look, this is . . .
Is this you in all your . . .

DAPHNE: That's when I was mayor.

HENRY: Heavens!

DAPHNE: Fourteen years ago that was.

HENRY: Ah. And this is – who's this with you? Surely its the –
Princess . . . ?

DAPHNE: (*Proud*) Yes. The Duchess of Kent.

HENRY: The Duchess of Kent, yes, of course it is.

DAPHNE: Opening the new wing of the hospital.

HENRY: Oh, yes. Must have been an – occasion.

DAPHNE: Oh, yes. She made a speech. I made a speech.

HENRY: But you're not mayor now?

DAPHNE: Oh no, I served my term.

HENRY: But you're still a councillor, of course?

DAPHNE: Oh, yes. But I have the business to run as well.

HENRY: What's that?

DAPHNE: The Beauty Salon. I'm a beautician by profession.

HENRY: Yes, of course. I think I've passed your – shop . . . ?

DAPHNE: Salon.

HENRY: Salon. The one with the pink curtains?

DAPHNE: Ruched. Right. Well, what is it I can do for you? I take it you don't want a facial, do you?
(*She laughs.*)

HENRY: (*Laughing heartily*) No, no . . . (*A slight pause.*) This is very awkward really, but . . . Is Norma at home at the moment?

DAPHNE: She's upstairs, listening to her music. Why?

HENRY: Well, I've come to talk to you. As her mother.

DAPHNE: I'm not her mother.

HENRY: (*Taken aback*) Oh. I'm sorry, I understood –

DAPHNE: She's my sister's child.

HENRY: Oh, I see. And your sister . . . . ?

DAPHNE: Dead. Died when Norma was three.

HENRY: And her father?

DAPHNE: (*Dry laugh*) What father?

HENRY: Oh, I see.

DAPHNE: Could have been any one of a dozen.

HENRY: Oh. A bit flighty, your sister, was she?

DAPHNE: She was a whore.

HENRY: Ah.

DAPHNE: (*With satisfaction*) She'll be suffering now, wherever she is.

HENRY: Well . . .

DAPHNE: Red-hot coals heaped on her navel.

HENRY: Ah.

DAPHNE: What about Norma? I mean, I'm responsible for her, if that's what you want to know.

HENRY: Well, it's just that . . . she is, I think you'll agree – at an impressionable age.

DAPHNE: She's only half there, isn't she?

HENRY: Well, let's say she's yet to develop her personality fully.

DAPHNE: I'd have had her working for me in the Beauty Salon. Only she'd have been a liability. She can't tell face cream from floor polish, that one. Been rubbing all sorts of things into people, wouldn't she? Better off working up there with that old layabout, that's what I say.

HENRY: You mean Winnie?

DAPHNE: And those two, her and her brother, they just about suit Norma. All about the same level. They make a good household. I don't know what you're doing up there, I'm sure.

HENRY: No. Nor do I. Altogether.

DAPHNE: That girl – that Karen . . . When we opened that hospital wing, she was a patient in the new ward. Ten years old. She stood up on her bed and sang 'The Red Flag'.

HENRY: Heavens . . .

DAPHNE: This was with royalty coming round, mark you. Right in front of the Duchess. Should have drowned that child at birth, her parents. But they never . . . Too busy with their butterflies. They paid for it dearly later though, didn't they?

HENRY: How do you mean?

DAPHNE: (*Changing the subject sharply*) What about Norma, then? What's she done? Do you want to see her?

HENRY: No, no. She hasn't done anything. It's what's being done to her. In a sense. I think she's in danger of being . . . well, to use an old-fashioned phrase . . . corrupted.

DAPHNE: Corrupted?

HENRY: I don't think it's her fault. Please. In fact, I'm certain it isn't. The man, whom I've been told it is – is . . . well, he's a notorious womanizer. And I think Norma is just another of his – conquests.

DAPHNE: (*Rising, grimly*) Who is it?

HENRY: Now you must promise –

DAPHNE: Who is it?

HENRY: You mustn't take it out on –

DAPHNE: Tell me his name.

HENRY: Well, all right. It's Anthony Staxton-Billing.

(DAPHNE *stares at him, her face a mixture of emotions*.)

128

DAPHNE: (*At length, softly*) Anthony Staxton-Billing?

HENRY: Yes.

DAPHNE: With Norma?

HENRY: Yes.

DAPHNE: Anthony. Staxton. Billing. (*Crossing to the door, fiercely*) NORMA! NORMA!

NORMA: (*Off*) Hallo?

DAPHNE: (*Yelling*) Come down here. Now.

NORMA: (*Off*) Just a minute.

DAPHNE: (*Yelling*) Now. Do you hear? Now.
(*Upstairs, the music stops.*)

HENRY: Look, I must ask you not . . .

DAPHNE: It's all right, thank you. You can leave this to me now, thank you.

HENRY: But you mustn't take it out on Norma because . . .

DAPHNE: This is a family matter, thank you so much. Now, would you leave, please.
(*Before* HENRY *can do so,* NORMA *comes down. Out of her maid's outfit and dressed in jeans and a T-shirt, she looks a rather different sight. She also has make-up on and probably plans to go out.*)

NORMA: What is it then? (*Seeing* HENRY) Oh. Evening, Mr Bell.
(*She does an involuntary little bob. To* DAPHNE) What you want then?

DAPHNE: (*Softly*) You just had to have him, didn't you? Couldn't resist him. Somebody else's and you just had to have him.

NORMA: Have who?

DAPHNE: You know bloody well who. Don't you stand there, madam, like that. I can see the lust steaming off you from here. You cheap little Jezebel. Look at you, coated in tart's make-up and your bust hanging half out, in your tight trousers so you can see every brazen bump that God gave you, you filthy little trollop – why don't you just stick a price tag on it and have done with it, eh?

NORMA: (*Alarmed*) What have I done?

DAPHNE: It just had to be him, didn't it? I knew this was going on. I knew it. It had to be Tony Staxton-Billing, didn't it? Not anybody else? Not someone your own age, oh no. It had to be him –

NORMA: (*Totally bemused*) Mr Staxton-Billing?
DAPHNE: (*Approaching her*) I'm going to give you a facial, my girl, you won't forget in a hurry –
(DAPHNE *swats* NORMA *across the face. The force of the blow sends the unprepared girl flying. She falls backwards into a chair.* DAPHNE *follows up the attack by falling on top of her. A brawl ensues.* NORMA *recovers enough to make the contest slightly more evenly matched.* HENRY, *once he's recovered from the shock of this, attempts to separate them.*)
(*As this ensues*) You tart . . . you whore . . . you hussy . . . you trollop . . . you bitch . . .
NORMA: (*Simultaneously*) Look, why are you . . . don't you . . . you've gone mad, you've . . . someone get her off me . . . she's bloody off her head . . .
HENRY: (*Simultaneously, getting vocally rather stuck in a groove*) Now, come on. Come on. Come on. Come on – come on – come on. Come on, come on. Come on. Comeoncomeoncomeon.
(*At last the antagonists separate. Probably thanks to exhaustion, rather than to* HENRY's *efforts. They are all on the floor.*)
That's it. That's it.
(NORMA *is crying softly.* DAPHNE *recovers her breath and then starts to get to her feet.*)
(*Alarmed*) Now, just a minute, don't –
DAPHNE: It's all right. I've finished with her.
HENRY: Where are you going?
DAPHNE: I'm going to have a word with him. I know just where Mr Staxton-Billing will be at this time of night. In the saloon bar of the Fox and Hounds, drinking with all the other so-called young farmers. I'll just go and have a little word with him in public. Excuse me.
(*She marches out.*)
HENRY: (*Vainly*) Don't you think you ought to . . .
NORMA: (*Muttering*) I haven't had him, what's she going on about?
HENRY: (*Bringing his attention round to* NORMA) What?
NORMA: What she think I want her feller for? I wouldn't want her old feller, anyway.

HENRY: Her old feller?

NORMA: Her old feller.

HENRY: Whose old feller?

NORMA: Her old feller. Why should I want her old feller? I got my own young feller. I don't even like her feller, I think he's horrible. I don't want her feller, do I? What's my feller going to say if he thinks I've been with her feller?

HENRY: Wait a minute, Norma. This old feller. Are we talking about Anthony Staxton-Billing? That old feller?

NORMA: Yes, her feller.

HENRY: (*Dully*) Her feller? He's her feller?

NORMA: Yes. Who else are we talking about?

HENRY: Yes. (*Thoughtfully*) Right. Right. I'd better go and try and – (*Turning in the doorway*) Sorry about this. I really am. Oh, God.

(HENRY *goes after* DAPHNE. *He doesn't seem to be in much of a hurry to catch her up.*)

NORMA: (*Miserably*) What's my feller going to say? That's what I want to know . . .

(*The lights fade on* NORMA *and cross-fade to* –

SCENE 7
9.10 a.m.

Lembridge Tennit. The outer area of Jeremy Pride's office. It is empty. JEREMY's *and* VERONICA's *voices are heard from his office.*

VERONICA: . . . I think you'll find, Jeremy, they wanted twenty. I'm sure that's what they said in their letter. If you like I'll go and check.

(*During this,* KAREN *sticks her head cautiously round the outer door. She listens and, seeing the coast is clear, nips in and places a gift-wrapped single red rose on one side of Veronica's desk. She darts out again.*)

JEREMY: (*During this*) No, you're invariably correct on these matters, Ronny. I'm certainly not going to argue with you. I must say, though, twenty does seem an awful lot.

131

VERONICA: Well, I thought so at the time but I didn't like to say anything. I heard you agreeing to twenty and I remember saying to myself, is this wise? Aren't we perhaps going to regret this by June?

JEREMY: Yes, the answer to that is we certainly are. Well, it's done now. I'll sort it out, don't worry.

VERONICA: Anything else, Jeremy?

JEREMY: No, thanks. I'll give you a yell.

VERONICA: Right-o.

(VERONICA *comes out of the inner office. She has scarcely done so when* KAREN *comes rushing in through the outer door*.)

KAREN: (*Breathlessly*) Miss Webb, I'm so sorry. The trains have gone mad this morning . . .

VERONICA: (*Coolly*) Good morning.

KAREN: You feel so helpless. Just sitting there on that tube. And they never bother to tell you, do they? I –

VERONICA: (*Cutting her off, rather brusquely*) Karen, I'm really not at all interested in your travelling saga. If the journey's that complicated, you'd better set off earlier, hadn't you, dear? And it would be a nice gesture if you paid me back the ten minutes you owe me at the end of the day. That I would appreciate.

KAREN: (*Sitting, suitably mortified*) Yes, course. Of course, Miss Webb.

(*Without further ado,* KAREN *opens her file and continues with her seemingly endless task.* VERONICA *also sits. In a moment, she comes across the rose. She stares at it, mystified*.)

VERONICA: (*Holding the box at arm's length*) What on earth's this?

KAREN: (*Looking up*) Sorry?

VERONICA: Where on earth did this come from?

KAREN: No idea. What is it?

VERONICA: (*Inspecting the box cautiously*) Looks like a flower. Yes, it's a rose.

KAREN: How nice.

VERONICA: A red rose.

KAREN: Oh-ho.

VERONICA: (*Slightly irritably*) What do you mean, 'Oh-ho'?

KAREN: Single red rose. You know what that means? An admirer.

VERONICA: (*Putting the box down again, irritably*) Oh, rubbish.

KAREN: Who's it from?

VERONICA: I don't know. It doesn't say.

KAREN: An anonymous admirer!

VERONICA: I don't even know how it got there.

KAREN: Was it there when you arrived?

VERONICA: I don't think so. It may have been. I never noticed. I went straight in to see Jeremy. Like I always do.

KAREN: The mystery thickens.

VERONICA: It's a joke by someone.

KAREN: Lovely joke. I wish someone would play jokes like that on me.

VERONICA: You can have it. I don't want it.

KAREN: No, it's yours. Keep it.

VERONICA: What am I supposed to do with it? Put it behind my ear?

KAREN: Take it home.

VERONICA: No point. The cats will eat it.

KAREN: Do you have cats?

VERONICA: Four. And they all eat flowers for some reason.

KAREN: Ah, well. That's because they live in a city.

VERONICA: Is it?

KAREN: Well, my father was a vet – well, both my parents were actually . . .

VERONICA: Were they really, how lovely.

KAREN: They were in practice together. And he always said, my father, that cats who lived in cities always tried to re-create their natural habitat. And if they couldn't find the real thing – real trees, real grass, real flowers and so on – they'd start to invent them.

VERONICA: How interesting. How very interesting. I think that might be right.

KAREN: Cats apparently have tremendous imaginations.

VERONICA: Oh, I know. They do. They do. Do you keep cats?

KAREN: Not now, alas, not now. But when I was a child our cottage was just swarming with animals – and there must have been – oh – about ten cats at any one time . . .

VERONICA: How lovely. Where was this?

KAREN: Cumbria.

VERONICA: Cumbria. Oh, beautiful. Well, I must bring you in my pictures. Would you like to see my cats?

KAREN: I'd love to. Thank you so much, Miss Webb.

VERONICA: (*Smiling*) Please. Veronica.

KAREN: Veronica.
(*She smiles back.*)

VERONICA: (*Admonishingly*) Ah well. Down to work.

KAREN: You don't think that rose could have been from . . . (*She indicates* JEREMY's *office.*)

VERONICA: (*In a whisper*) No! Of course not. (*She looks at the rose.*) No. He never has done in twelve years, I don't know why he should start now. (*Another look.*) No.

KAREN: Aren't you going to put it in water?

VERONICA: I haven't got time to put it in water.

KAREN: You know what they say, Veronica?

VERONICA: (*Irritably*) What do they say?

KAREN: If you let it wither, then his love will die . . .

VERONICA: Absolute poppycock. (*She laughs self-consciously.*) I've never heard anything so infantile. Romantic twaddle.
(*A silence. They work.*)
(*Crossly*) Oh, well, I suppose there's no point in sitting here watching all the petals fall off it. (*Rising*) I'll get a jug or something. This is all a very silly joke by someone. I'm sure it is.
(VERONICA *goes out, slightly flustered.* KAREN *watches her, smiling. She starts to hum to herself again. As she does so the lights cross-fade to* –)

SCENE 8
9.30 a.m.

The dining room at Furtherfield House. HENRY *sits finishing his breakfast. A bird flutters past and divebombs him.* HENRY *ducks.* WINNIE *comes in, alone, carrying an empty tray. There is a slight atmosphere between her and* HENRY.

WINNIE: Finished, sir?

HENRY: Yes, thank you.

WINNIE: Anything more, sir?

HENRY: No, thank you.

WINNIE: May I clear then, sir?

HENRY: You may, Winnie, thank you.

WINNIE: Thank you, sir.

    (*A silence.* HENRY *rises and thinks about leaving the room.*
    WINNIE *clears the table.*)

HENRY: (*Unable to avoid the topic*) Winnie . . .

WINNIE: Yes, sir?

HENRY: I'm afraid I got – You may have misled me rather badly
    yesterday.

WINNIE: Me, sir?

HENRY: Yes. You see, I clearly had the impression from you that
    Norma was having some sort of relationship with Mr
    Staxton-Billing.

WINNIE: I'm sure I never said that, sir.

HENRY: Well, you certainly gave that impression, Winnie. To me
    at any rate. With the result that the fur is now flying.

WINNIE: It certainly is, sir.

HENRY: Oh, you've already heard?

WINNIE: Norma telephoned me earlier. To say she wasn't coming
    in on account of her injury.

HENRY: Injury?

WINNIE: Her black eye, sir.

HENRY: Oh . . .

WINNIE: Nothing to the injuries down at the Fox and Hounds, so
    I've heard.

HENRY: Well, I arrived too late to stop any of that.

WINNIE: Five young farmers with broken limbs.

HENRY: Yes, all right . . .

WINNIE: I don't know how you ever thought to get that
    impression from me, sir.

HENRY: (*Angrily*) Well, I did. And it's too late now, isn't it? The
    damage is done.

    (*The doorbell rings.*)

WINNIE: (*Huffily*) Excuse me, sir.

    (WINNIE *goes out to the hall.* HENRY *paces about agitatedly.*

The bird divebombs him again. He ducks. In a moment,
WINNIE *returns with* IMOGEN.)
Mrs Staxton-Billing, sir.

IMOGEN: Henry, what have you been doing?

HENRY: Oh, don't start, please . . .

(*During the next,* WINNIE *gathers up the laden tray and goes off
to the kitchen.*)

IMOGEN: The whole village was in pandemonium. Ambulances
rushing to and fro, the pub's got half its windows boarded
up. What on earth did you do?

HENRY: (*Wretchedly*) I was trying to . . . I was . . . getting hold of
entirely the wrong end of the stick. That's what I was doing,
if you must know. (*Angrily, after* WINNIE) And it wasn't
totally my fault.

IMOGEN: (*Tenderly*) Did you do all that because of me?

HENRY: How do you mean?

IMOGEN: You did. Didn't you?

HENRY: (*Slightly guiltily*) In a – in a way. Possibly.

IMOGEN: That's very touching. (*She smiles.*) Well – don't I even
get a kiss?

HENRY: I thought you'd broken off our relationship.

IMOGEN: When?

HENRY: On Tuesday? At the junior gymkhana? We can't go on,
you said.

IMOGEN: Well. I was in one of my moods. Forget it.

HENRY: I can't keep up with your moods.

IMOGEN: Look who's talking. Look who's got moods.

HENRY: I'm entitled to moods.

IMOGEN: (*Pleading*) Kiss. Please?

(HENRY *kisses her, lightly and without a great deal of
commitment. The bird flutters past.*)
My God. What was that?

HENRY: Just a bird.

IMOGEN: Oh. I thought it was a bat. Knowing this house, it could
easily have been. I'm sorry if I get moody sometimes, Henry.
You must see, it's not easy for me.

HENRY: No. Nor is it for me.

IMOGEN: No. I realize that. And I'm afraid it's going to get even

136

harder for you soon.

HENRY: How do you mean?

IMOGEN: Well, you don't suppose there aren't going to be repercussions to all this, do you?

HENRY: Who from?

IMOGEN: God knows. Mrs Teale? Who apparently has fractured her knuckles. Norma? Who may have a chipped cheekbone. Assorted young farmers. Or Anthony, who has mild concussion and a very dented reputation.

HENRY: Is that all he's got? Pity.

IMOGEN: You can't go around saying things like that about people.

HENRY: But the man was having an affair after all.

IMOGEN: Yes, but with Mrs Teale. Not with her daughter.

HENRY: Not much difference, is there?

IMOGEN: There's a hell of a difference. Besides, everyone knew about him and Mrs Teale. It was above board. It's quite another thing to accuse him of being a cradle-snatcher. Mud sticks.

HENRY: Did you know about him and Mrs Teale?

IMOGEN: No. But then I didn't want to. I didn't want to know he was having a good time with Mrs Teale. I preferred to believe that he was still with Karen. At least if he was with her, I knew she'd be giving him a terrible time.

HENRY: You think there'll be a backlash, then?

IMOGEN: Didn't you expect one when you started all this?

HENRY: I – I don't know. I just wanted you – to see what sort of man you were married to –

IMOGEN: (*Calmly*) I know what sort of man I'm married to, Henry, you didn't have to tell me –

HENRY: It might have done the trick and tipped you over.

IMOGEN: Tipped me over where?

HENRY: Tipped you over in my direction. Made you leave the wretched man, finally and for ever.

IMOGEN: Henry, I'm sorry, I can't go away and live with you in a bedsit. Not with two children. I love my home, too, actually. So do the kids. It's paradise for them. What's more, it's mine. I don't see why I should just give it all up and leave it

137

for Anthony. If anyone's going, it's him. So there.

HENRY: Then what's keeping him there? He obviously doesn't love you any more. Why doesn't he just buzz off and make room for someone who does?

IMOGEN: I know, I know. It's a dead marriage. The last rites have long been read. I know that. You know that. But unfortunately Anthony doesn't. He will not let go. He doesn't really want me any more but he won't let me go. Why? I don't know. The children, of course. He's fond of them. And, whatever else, I'm very useful to him and he'd find it extremely hard to get another woman to run things the way I do for absolutely no thanks at all. I don't think either Karen Knightly or Daphne Teale would do what I do for him.

HENRY: Then why do it? Why make yourself so invaluable? I don't see why you bother.

IMOGEN: (*Sighing*) I don't know. Because I'm me, I suppose. You're right. I should just let the whole place go to pot. Let the pigs starve, the chickens get bunged up with eggs, the cows fill up with milk and burst . . . I don't know. Why do I clean the kitchen floor every single evening once the kids have gone to bed? I don't know . . . Yes, I do know, actually. Because I can't bear wading through filth, that's why. I can't bear bits of old bread and Marmite glued to my instep. God, I loathe Marmite. (*Pause.*) I'm sorry. I don't make it very easy, do I? (*Pause.*) Do you want to pack it in? Us, I mean?

HENRY: No.

IMOGEN: I'd quite understand, really. I wouldn't be hurt. I'd cry for weeks on end, but I'd quite understand.

HENRY: (*Gently*) I don't want you to cry any more. Ever.
(IMOGEN *smiles at him.*)

IMOGEN: Well, if you don't, you'd better not say things like that to me for a kick off, had you? That makes me cry immediately. (*Dabbing at her eyes with her fingers*) God, I'm in such an *awful* state, I don't know what's the matter with me. It's much too early for the change, isn't it? I do hope so. I went to the children's concert the other day, you know. It was absolutely God-awful. I mean *frightful*. You've no idea.

And our two were just so embarrassingly bad, it wasn't true.
And I sat there crying my eyes out. As if I was watching
some wonderful, brilliant opera. Or *King Lear* or something.
There they were, all standing in a line singing 'Nick-nack
Paddiwack' and me in floods of tears. God, it was so
dreadful . . .

(*She trails off, unable to continue.* HENRY *holds her gently.*)
I'm sorry. I'm such a dreary person to be with. I wouldn't
blame you if you went and found someone terribly fat and
jolly . . .

HENRY: (*Softly*) It's OK. It's OK. I'll think of something.

(*The doorbell rings.*)
Oh God, who's that now?

(WINNIE *comes through to answer it.*)

WINNIE: (*Eyeing them both disapprovingly*) Excuse me, please.

IMOGEN: (*Weakly*) I must go.

HENRY: Yes, all right.

(IMOGEN *gets to her feet.* HENRY *kisses her lightly on the cheek.
She moves to the door. Before she can reach it,* WINNIE *ushers in*
MARCUS. *He stops as he sees* IMOGEN.)

WINNIE: (*With some satisfaction*) Colonel Lipscott, sir.

MARCUS: Ah!

IMOGEN: Hallo, Uncle.

MARCUS: Hallo, Imogen.

(*He stares at her intently.*)

IMOGEN: (*Avoiding his stare*) Excuse me, I was just off, I have to
. . . Excuse me.

(IMOGEN *hurries out, followed by* WINNIE.)

HENRY: Hallo.

MARCUS: We have met.

HENRY: Yes.

MARCUS: You had a different suit on, I remember.

HENRY: That's right.

MARCUS: (*Extending a hand*) Marcus Lipscott.

HENRY: Henry Bell.

(*They shake hands.*)
Would you prefer to move into the –

MARCUS: No, here's fine. Here's absolutely fine.

HENRY: Fine.

MARCUS: How are things in Strewth Street?

HENRY: Oh, pretty brisk.

(*A pause.*)

MARCUS: I couldn't help noticing she'd been crying. My niece.

HENRY: Oh, yes . . .

MARCUS: Not really fair on her. All this, you know.

HENRY: I agree.

MARCUS: She's a nice girl. A damn nice girl.

HENRY: She is.

MARCUS: In a country which, in my humble opinion, is running pretty short of nice girls just at present.

HENRY: (*Intrigued by this theory*) Really?

MARCUS: I haven't met any. All too busy taking their clothes off and selling cornflakes. Anyway. Imogen means a lot to me.

HENRY: And to me.

MARCUS: Maybe. Maybe. We shall see.

HENRY: (*Defiantly*) We certainly shall.

(*A pause.* MARCUS *is evidently impressed by Henry's vehemence. The bird flutters overhead.*)

MARCUS: (*Momentarily startled*) Good God . . .

HENRY: (*Apologetically*) Sorry.

MARCUS: That's a green woodpecker, isn't it?

HENRY: Is it?

MARCUS: Shouldn't keep it indoors. He'll have your panelling for breakfast. Anyway. Why I'm here. You're probably aware you've stirred up a hornets' nest?

HENRY: Yes.

MARCUS: Managed to slander half the neighbourhood. Including my – nephew-in-law. Anthony.

HENRY: Most of what I said was true. I may have got the wrong woman. But the principle remains. It was essentially, give or take a few details, the truth.

MARCUS: I don't give a tinker's whether it was true or not. You still can't go around saying things like that. Not in this village.

HENRY: Why not if it's true?

MARCUS: For the love of Mike, man, if we all went around

shouting out the truth every time we felt like it there wouldn't be a building left standing in the county. It's just not on. It really isn't. You've spread accusations about a chap, some of which were as it happens entirely false and now he's demanding some sort of satisfaction from you.

HENRY: What sort of satisfaction? Money?

MARCUS: Have you got any money?

HENRY: Not much.

MARCUS: Then don't be ridiculous.

HENRY: What does he want then? An apology?

MARCUS: He wants a bit more than that, old chap.

HENRY: What, then?

MARCUS: What do you suppose? He wants to fight you.

HENRY: Fight me?

MARCUS: A duel, man, a duel.

HENRY: A duel? What sort of duel?

MARCUS: He suggests guns.

HENRY: Guns? He wants to fight with guns?

MARCUS: Have you another preference?

HENRY: Well . . . swords . . . ?

MARCUS: Can you use a sword?

HENRY: No.

MARCUS: Then don't be so ridiculous. Neither can he. Both of you waving swords about indiscriminately – you'd be an absolute liability to everyone. No, guns are safer. They're also cleaner. Take my tip.

HENRY: Don't be absurd. We can't fight a duel. Not in this day and age.

MARCUS: Why not?

HENRY: People just don't do it any more.

MARCUS: They do round here. You know when the last duel was fought around here?

HENRY: No idea.

MARCUS: Go on. Have a guess.

HENRY: Seventeen fifty.

MARCUS: Last June.

HENRY: Good God. What did the police have to say?

MARCUS: They said what we wanted them to say. Accidental death.

HENRY: You mean you bribed the police?

MARCUS: Of course not. No need to. Listen. A group of like-minded chaps arrange a shooting party. Amongst them are the two protagonists and their seconds. They set off at dawn to shoot a few rabbits, grouse, whatever. Depending on the season. They even bag a brace or two, just to make it look above board. They reach a quiet spot – say, a clearing in the middle of a wood – and the two rivals get on with it. Ten paces, turn and fire and the slowest man buys it . . .

HENRY: I'm having a spot of trouble with this . . .

MARCUS: One of the party, an innocent member, rushes for help. Officer! Officer! So-and-so – blithering idiot – just ran right in front of the guns . . . killed instantly. Terrible tragedy, sir. Happens all the time. Flowers to the widow. Rest in peace.

HENRY: You've actually done this?

MARCUS: When things reach a certain stage between two chaps, it becomes more or less inevitable. I don't know, I expect women will be doing it, too, before long.

HENRY: There must be another way.

MARCUS: What way's that?

HENRY: Well, lawyers . . .

MARCUS: Lawyers? Good God, man, you're better off taking a chance with both barrels.

HENRY: I'm sorry, I can't accept this. I'm sorry. Besides, Anthony Staxton-Billing's an experienced – gunsman. I've never fired a shot in my life. What sort of contest is that?

MARCUS: You never know. You might have beginner's luck.

HENRY: Thank you. That's very reassuring.

MARCUS: You're within your rights to refuse, of course. So long as you don't care what people think of you.

HENRY: I don't give a damn. They don't think much of me round here, anyway.

MARCUS: You presumably care what Imogen thinks of you?

HENRY: I don't honestly think that my not fighting a duel is going to alter her view of me.

MARCUS: Not fighting it mightn't. But fighting it might.

HENRY: Sorry?

MARCUS: Look at it this way. If you win, that makes her a widow.

The way's clear to marry her. A free idyllic farmhouse.
Built-in family. There'll even be a vacancy on the board of my
company if you fancy it. So there's a job promised, as well.
What more could you want?

HENRY: This is monstrous. Do you think I'd risk getting killed just
for that?

MARCUS: People have done it for a damn sight less than that. Come
on. Do you want the girl or don't you?

HENRY: Yes.

MARCUS: Well, then. Where's your problem?

HENRY: What if I lose?

MARCUS: You've got no problem at all then, have you?

HENRY: And what if I refuse?

MARCUS: Then I suggest you leave the district immediately.
Because you won't be welcome here, I can tell you.

HENRY: I could take Imogen with me.

MARCUS: Always providing she'd agree to go.

(*A silence.*)

Well, you don't have to answer straightaway. Twenty-four
hours will do. (*Producing his wallet*) Here's my card. Better do
things correctly. You can generally get hold of me at one or
other of those numbers. It's all right, I can find my way out.

(MARCUS *moves to the door.*)

HENRY: (*With sudden determination*) Colonel . . .

MARCUS: Yes?

HENRY: Tell Mr Staxton-Billing that I accept his challenge. And
that I retract nothing.

MARCUS: Splendid. Good man. I take it firearms are acceptable?

HENRY: (*Bravely*) Yes. Firearms are perfectly acceptable.

MARCUS: Excellent. Good day to you, sir.

HENRY: Good day, sir.

(MARCUS, *just before he leaves, turns in the doorway.*)

MARCUS: (*Almost as an afterthought*) Oh, by the way, if you take my
tip you'll get yourself a second who can teach you how to fire
the thing.

(MARCUS *goes out.* HENRY *takes a deep breath and looks rather
worried. The bird swoops. He ducks nervously. As he does so, the
lights cross-fade to –*

Lembridge Tennit. The outer area of Jeremy Pride's office. KAREN *is at her desk going idly through her folders. After a second,* VERONICA *enters, looking rather flushed.*

VERONICA: Oh, I'm so sorry I'm late . . . I mean, I've never been as late as this, I mean *ever* . . . I am sorry, I . . .

KAREN: (*Reassuringly*) Don't worry, Veronica; no flap, really.

VERONICA: (*Anxiously*) Is Jeremy . . . ?

KAREN: He's at the finance meeting . . .

VERONICA: Oh yes, of course, that's today, isn't it? I should have been there, too. Honestly, I don't know if I'm coming or going . . .

KAREN: Sit and get your breath. Don't worry.

VERONICA: Yes, I'll . . .
    (VERONICA *sits. There is another red rose in the middle of her desk.*)
    Oh, look! Another . . .

KAREN: Yes. I noticed.

VERONICA: That's – five days in a row. This is getting beyond a joke, isn't it? And do you know, when I got home last night, the woman in the flat next door – she sometimes feeds the cats if I'm away – she's very helpful – she'd taken in this parcel. And guess what it was?

KAREN: I've no idea.

VERONICA: (*In a whisper*) Chocolates.

KAREN: Really?

VERONICA: A beautiful, beautiful huge box of chocolates. I mean huge. I was quite overwhelmed. I mean, I've never ever – in my life . . .

KAREN: Who do you think they were from?

VERONICA: It didn't say. No note, nothing. Posted locally. That I did see.

KAREN: Must be the rose man again.

VERONICA: It could be, couldn't it? Oh, and wait. That's not all. The reason I was late in this morning. I was just leaving and there's this Interflora man. With a huge bunch. Huge. For me. The woman next door must wonder what's going on.

KAREN: Flowers?

VERONICA: Roses.

KAREN: Red?

VERONICA: A dozen.

KAREN: Oh. Well. You're as good as engaged then, aren't you?

VERONICA: Oh, really . . .

KAREN: If you only knew who he was.

VERONICA: Well, I do have one small clue . . .

KAREN: You do?

VERONICA: Whoever it was certainly knows me. It's not a complete stranger, anyway. Not some crank who's just picked me out of the phone book.

KAREN: That's a relief.

VERONICA: No, I was thinking on the bus . . . He knew exactly the sort of chocolates I liked.

KAREN: Ah-ha!

VERONICA: Remember, I was telling you the other day over lunch . . .

KAREN: Were you? I don't remember.

VERONICA: Dark chocolates with soft centres. I'm very particular. Now who would have known that? Eh? Tell me that.

KAREN: Well . . . (*She indicates Jeremy's office.*) You know who? Would he have known?

VERONICA: Yes. I think it has to be . . . I think it really has to be . . . (*She indicates Jeremy's office.*)

KAREN: Oh, well.

(*She shakes her head.*)

VERONICA: What is it?

KAREN: Nothing.

VERONICA: What? Tell me.

KAREN: Oh, well . . . Since you've guessed already, I suppose it doesn't matter . . .

VERONICA: What are you saying?

KAREN: Promise you won't let on? You must promise.

VERONICA: What? (*Pause.*) Come on. What?

KAREN: All right. I got here a little early this morning, anyway. And – of course Jeremy was here – and he came in and asked where you were – and we conjectured that you'd probably been held up . . .

VERONICA: (*Agitated*) Oh, he did notice? He did notice, then?

KAREN: It didn't matter. Anyway, I happened to remark on that rose on your desk . . .

VERONICA: Oh, you shouldn't have done that . . .

KAREN: Well, he was sort of standing there looking at it . . .

VERONICA: Was he? I see. I see.

KAREN: So I said something like, 'Oh, isn't that lovely, she's got another rose.' And before I knew, he sat down there where you are now . . .

VERONICA: (*Touching the chair*) Jeremy did? Here?

KAREN: Yes. And he just poured his heart out to me. Went on and on and on.

VERONICA: (*Suspiciously*) What about?

KAREN: You.

VERONICA: Me?

KAREN: Veronica, he's absolutely besotted with you.

VERONICA: Jeremy is?

KAREN: Yes. It's very worrying. I don't know what you're going to do . . .

VERONICA: Worrying?

KAREN: He's quite obsessive.

VERONICA: (*Frowning*) Yes, that is worrying, isn't it?

KAREN: What are you going to do?

VERONICA: I don't know. I don't know.

KAREN: You won't say anything, will you? He begged me not to tell you.

VERONICA: Why on earth should he do that?

KAREN: He's obviously terrified of openly declaring himself. You know how some men fear rejection . . . ?

VERONICA: Yes. Do they? Yes . . .

KAREN: I think it depends what *you* want to happen. You could confront him and frighten him off. That's often a good way.

VERONICA: (*Unenthusiastically*) Yes . . .

KAREN: Or you could ignore him. Hope it dies out naturally . . .

VERONICA: Yes . . .
  (*She considers this option.*)
KAREN: It depends really what you want, doesn't it?
VERONICA: Yes.
KAREN: I think those are your safest options.
VERONICA: Yes.
KAREN: That is unless you want to start gently encouraging the
  wretched man . . . (*She laughs.*)
VERONICA: (*Laughing*) Yes . . .
KAREN: (*Laughing*) Maybe you do?
VERONICA: (*Laughing*) No, no, no, no, no, no no . . .
KAREN: Well.
VERONICA: Heavens.
  (*They stop laughing.*)
  What did you mean by gentle encouragement?
KAREN: Oh, you know – little signals a woman gives off to a man
  – message received and understood, you know. Safe to
  proceed into harbour. Standard stuff.
VERONICA: Oh yes. (*Pause.*) What sort of little signals? I mean –
  I'm sorry – I haven't, I've never – well, certainly not for . . .
  not since . . . Oh, dear, it's very hot . . . it's this dreadful
  air-conditioning . . . What are these signals one's supposed to
  give off?
KAREN: Well, you know, you smile at him a lot. That tells him
  you're happy in his company . . .
VERONICA: Yes, yes . . .
KAREN: You get a little girlish occasionally . . .
VERONICA: Girlish?
KAREN: Make him feel masterful . . .
VERONICA: Do you think I could get away with being girlish?
KAREN: There's a little girl inside every woman, Veronica.
VERONICA: Possibly.
KAREN: You wear your prettiest clothes.
VERONICA: I don't know that I've . . .
KAREN: Or you buy pretty clothes. Just for him. A little perfume.
VERONICA: No, no. Jeremy's asthma . . .
KAREN: Oh, yes. Well, slap on a bit of make-up . . .
VERONICA: Oh, I never wear make-up.

147

KAREN: Well, men appreciate it. It says to him – 'See, I have made the effort for you.'

VERONICA: Oh, I don't know about all this . . .

KAREN: Well, otherwise where's the signal, Veronica? Where's your signal?

VERONICA: Oh yes, I see, I see. Of course. No signal. But I haven't worn make-up since I was seventeen . . .

KAREN: Excuse me. May I . . . ?

(KAREN *dives into her bag and produces a very large bulging make-up bag. She places the bag in front of* VERONICA.)

VERONICA: Heavens! What's all this?

KAREN: Discovered! My secret weakness. I'm afraid I buy make-up by the ton. Take that lot home with you and experiment – it's the only way . . .

VERONICA: Well, I – er – I . . . Are you sure you can spare it?

KAREN: That's just my emergency kit . . .

VERONICA: (*Opening the bag and looking inside*) Well, I don't know . . . Some of this is very vivid . . .

KAREN: Experiment. Have fun.

VERONICA: I'll have to get up at three in the morning to put all this on.

KAREN: (*Coyly*) Many women do to please the man they love.

VERONICA: The cats aren't going to be very happy – being woken up at that hour. Still, I suppose if I –

KAREN: (*Hearing someone approaching*) Shh!

VERONICA: What? Oh!

(*She hastily conceals the make-up bag.* JEREMY *comes in, rubbing his eyes. He is rather tired this morning.*)

KAREN: (*Mouthing to* VERONICA) Smile . . .

VERONICA: (*Flashing him a deep smile*) Morning, Jeremy.

JEREMY: (*Without so much as a glance at her*) Oh. Morning, Ronny. Give me five minutes, will you?

VERONICA: (*Holding her smile, gamely*) Right-o, Jeremy.

(JEREMY *goes into his office.* VERONICA *seems a little disconcerted.*)

KAREN: (*In a whisper*) Don't give up. If at first you don't succeed . . .

VERONICA: (*Whispering eagerly*) Try, try again . . .

(They smile at each other. As they do so, the lights cross-fade again to –)

SCENE 10
Noon.

A drawing room at Furtherfield House. OLIVER *sits in a chair staring thoughtfully at the wall.* HENRY *enters.*

HENRY: Ah. Oliver . . .
OLIVER: (*Thoughtfully*) Mmmm?
HENRY: Could you spare a minute?
OLIVER: (*Not moving*) Yah.
 (HENRY *waits for a second but* OLIVER *still remains deep in thought.*)
HENRY: (*Plunging in*) I was just wondering if you –
OLIVER: (*Cutting over him*) You see, if that wall came down. If we bashed that one out . . .
HENRY: Sorry?
OLIVER: I don't think that wall's important, do you? That one there?
HENRY: Well. It depends what you mean by important. I suppose that, in so far as it separates this room from the next, it's fairly vital.
OLIVER: (*Impatiently*) No, no, no, no, no. Structurally.
HENRY: Structurally? I've no idea.
OLIVER: I had a look upstairs, briefly. It doesn't appear to be holding anything up. Not that I could see.
HENRY: Except the roof, perhaps?
OLIVER: No. That'll be the wall on the floor above the floor above this one that'll support the roof.
HENRY: (*Accompanying this with a few unhelpful hand gestures*) Yes, but something must in turn be supporting the floor that's supporting the wall – that's – supporting the floor – that's supporting the – wall above that – which in turn is supporting the roof.
 (HENRY *pauses.* OLIVER *considers.*)
If you follow me.

149

OLIVER: (*Nodding appreciatively*) Good point. You've studied architecture, then?

HENRY: No. Only from the street. What were you planning on doing then?

OLIVER: I was wondering, if I knocked that wall down there, whether I could combine these two rooms to make a squash court. But that's shot that idea in the head.

HENRY: Pity. Do you play squash?

OLIVER: Not at all. But I was thinking, if I had my own private court here on the premises there'd be no more excuse not to learn, would there?

HENRY: True. (*Looking about*) If you did that, you wouldn't leave yourself anywhere much to sit down though, would you?

OLIVER: (*Irritably*) I wouldn't want to sit down, would I? I'd be playing squash, for God's sake?

HENRY: (*Giving up*) Yes. Absolutely true. (*Trying again*) I wondered if I could . . . ?

OLIVER: Oh yes, sure. What was it you wanted?

HENRY: Do you have . . . ? I wondered if you had anything in the house like a gun?

OLIVER: A gun?

HENRY: Yes.

OLIVER: A shotgun? That sort of thing?

HENRY: Exactly.

OLIVER: Got a whole room full of them, why? Want to shoot something, do you?

HENRY: Yes. Yes, I do.

OLIVER: What you after? Rabbit? Pheasant? Partridge?

HENRY: Actually. No. A person.

OLIVER: A person?

HENRY: Yes.

OLIVER: You mean a person as in people?

HENRY: Yes.

OLIVER: You mean generally? I mean, are you simply planning on blazing away at the public in general or at someone specific?

HENRY: Oh, someone specific.

OLIVER: Oh, that's OK, then. Sure. I hope you didn't mind my asking?

HENRY: No, no.

OLIVER: Only obviously you can't hand out guns willy-nilly just like that, can you?

HENRY: Absolutely not.

OLIVER: The gun room's along the back there. Past the kitchen, about the third door along. Help yourself.

HENRY: Thank you.

OLIVER: Who were you planning on shooting?

HENRY: Anthony Staxton-Billing.

OLIVER: Bloody good idea. Good luck. Does he know you're planning to?

HENRY: Oh, yes, yes. We're actually – we're going to be actually fighting a sort of duel. Actually.

OLIVER: A duel? With Anthony Staxton-Billing?

HENRY: Yes.

OLIVER: He's a pretty good shot, you know.

HENRY: Yes, so I've heard.

OLIVER: Are you?

HENRY: I've never fired a gun in my life.

OLIVER: I see. (*He reflects.*) Look, I don't want to stick my nose in but do you think you've settled on the right choice of weapons?

HENRY: I don't really think it matters a damn. Swords, pistols, blowpipes, pointed sticks, what's the difference? I've never fought with anything more dangerous than a school ruler in my life.

OLIVER: Perhaps you'd like me to give you a few tips. On guns. Loading and aiming and that sort of thing. I mean, if you didn't think I was interfering.

HENRY: I was secretly hoping you'd offer. I really need someone to help me rather a lot. And possibly even come with me. See fair play and so on.

OLIVER: You mean a second? You'd like a second?

HENRY: Yes. Oh, yes.

OLIVER: Why didn't you say so before?

HENRY: Would you mind?

OLIVER: Absolutely delighted. I'm your man.

(*They shake hands.*)

(*Enthusiastically*) Right. Let's get cracking, then. When is this duel, do you know?

HENRY: It hasn't yet been decided.

OLIVER: Good. Well, we'll try and get you in a bit of practice. To the gun room. (*Remembering*) Oh, it'll be locked, won't it? We'll have to get the key from Winnie. I have to keep it locked. Prowlers and servants and so on. Follow me.

HENRY: Lead on.

(HENRY *follows* OLIVER *out as the lights cross-fade to –*)

SCENE 11
9.45 a.m.

Lembridge Tennit. The outer area of Jeremy Pride's office. KAREN *at her desk.* JEREMY *comes out of his office.*

JEREMY: No?

KAREN: Not yet, Mr Pride.

JEREMY: Dear, oh dear. This is getting to be rather a habit, isn't it?

KAREN: (*Shrugging*) Well . . .

JEREMY: I've known her – what? – over ten years. She's never been late like this before.

KAREN: No?

JEREMY: Mind you, she's . . . No, I mustn't talk about her. I mustn't talk about her behind her back. Ronny's been absolutely first rate, I couldn't have done without her. A pillar of strength. A rock. An absolute foundation. An ally, a loyal friend and a colleague. (*Pause.*) She is behaving very oddly, though. Very, very oddly. Have you noticed?

KAREN: Well, I haven't been here that long, Mr Pride . . .

JEREMY: No, no . . .

KAREN: . . . so I don't really know what might be termed her norm.

JEREMY: She's growing increasingly . . . kittenish. I think that's the word.

KAREN: (*Sympathetically*) Yes, yes . . .

152

JEREMY: Do you think it's . . . something to do with women? You know . . . glands? That sort of thing?

KAREN: Glands?

JEREMY: Yes, you know . . .

KAREN: Well, I don't really know Veronica well enough to pass judgement on her glands, Mr Pride . . .

JEREMY: No, no, no. I'm sorry. I mustn't involve you, Karen. Very naughty of me. Oh, look at the time. This is ridiculous. What are we going to do? I want to read my letters.

KAREN: Can't you read your letters?

JEREMY: No, you see. I can't open them. Unless Veronica's here, I can't open them.

KAREN: Are they tricky to open?

JEREMY: Well, yes, you wouldn't think so, but they are. Very. Apparently whenever I do try to open them on my own, I put envelopes in the wrong bins and letters in the wrong trays and that confuses the system. I don't quite understand it – all these bins and trays – but Ronny made me promise never to open my letters personally, so I never do.
(*He has moved to Veronica's desk. He picks up the boxed rose that is waiting here, as usual.*)
Here's another of these flowers. Where does she get all these flowers? She seems to get them every morning.

KAREN: I think she does.

JEREMY: Has she some admirer, do you think? It doesn't sound very likely. I asked her the other day if she had one. She just sort of winked at me. At least, I think it was a wink. She's putting so much stuff on her eyelashes these days, they seem to be in danger of getting glued together permanently. (*Still holding the rose*) Who do you think these can be from?

KAREN: Well, I hate telling tales but I have a sneaking feeling that she may be sending them herself.

JEREMY: Herself?

KAREN: Yes. Though I loathe telling tales.

JEREMY: To herself? (*Gravely*) Oh dear. Oh dear. That doesn't sound so good, does it?

KAREN: No.

JEREMY: What do you think we should do?

KAREN: I don't really know. Humour her? Hope it will pass?

JEREMY: Yes. That's the best course to take perhaps.

KAREN: Oh, I despise and detest telling tales.

JEREMY: You're a very sensible young person – Karen.

KAREN: Thank you, Mr Pride.

JEREMY: Jeremy.

KAREN: (*Smiling*) Jeremy.

(VERONICA *enters in a rush. She has on a rather too bright dress and is vividly made up. While the result is far short of plain ludicrous, it has to be said that it doesn't really work.*)

VERONICA: Good morning. Good morning. Oh . . .

(*She looks at* JEREMY *and* KAREN *suspiciously.* JEREMY, *who has still been holding the rose in its box, puts it down, absent-mindedly on Karen's desk and moves away from her.*)

JEREMY: Really, Ronny. It's ten to, you know. This really isn't . . .

VERONICA: I'm sorry. (*Looking at the rose*) What's that doing on there?

JEREMY: I beg your pardon?

VERONICA: My rose. What's it doing on her desk?

JEREMY: Oh, I'm sorry. I must have put it there.

VERONICA: (*Tense*) Why did you put it on her desk?

JEREMY: I'm sorry, I put it there accidentally.

VERONICA: Why isn't it on my desk?

JEREMY: It was on your desk. I just picked it up and put it on her desk . . .

VERONICA: Why? Simply because I was late? Is that why?

KAREN: Look, I'll put it back on your desk . . .

VERONICA: I don't want it back on my desk. If he wants to put it on your desk, I don't care.

KAREN: (*Crossing with the rose*) I'm putting it back on your desk, all right?

(*She puts it on Veronica's desk.*)

JEREMY: I don't see what the fuss is about. I picked it up from your desk and I walked over here with it –

VERONICA: (*Snatching the flower off her desk*) Don't put it on my desk. I don't want the thing on my desk. You can have it on your desk . . .

154

(*She slams it down on Karen's desk.*)

KAREN: I don't want it on my desk, honestly.

(*She picks it up and plans to return it again.*)

VERONICA: (*Shouting*) Don't you dare, don't you *dare* to put that *thing* back on my desk . . .

KAREN: (*Also raising her voice*) Well, what am I supposed to do with it?

JEREMY: (*With sudden, uncharacteristic anger*) Right. That's it. That's enough. (*He takes the rose from* KAREN.) I don't want another word from either of you. This – (*he brandishes the rose*) – is going in – here. (*He drops it into the waste bin.*) And that is where it will stay. We all have a good deal of work to do, I suggest we get on with it. Ronny, as soon you've pulled yourself together, I'd like you in here, opening my letters. Thank you.

(JEREMY *stalks back into his office. A silence.*)

VERONICA: (*At length*) Well, what a lot of stupid fuss about nothing. (*Pause.*) I got up rather early. (*Pause. Anxiously*) Do you think this is really working, Karen. Are you sure it's working?

KAREN: Oh yes, Veronica.

VERONICA: Well, he does look at me slightly more than he used to, I suppose.

KAREN: Believe me, Veronica, it's working like a dream.

VERONICA: (*Softening*) Please. Ronny. I think it's time for 'Ronny', don't you?

KAREN: Thank you, Ronny.

(VERONICA *goes into Jeremy's office, rather brighter.* KAREN *gets out her mobile phone and dials. A bright laugh from the next office from* VERONICA.)

Hallo. It's Karen Knightly again . . . Yes, that's right . . . Absolutely fine . . . thank you . . . yes, I wanted to order some more flowers . . . yes . . . no . . . two dozen . . . yes, it's a very special occasion . . .

(*As she speaks, the lights cross-fade to –*)

SCENE 12
Dawn.

A clearing in the wood. Birdsong. A group of men arrive together. First,
MARCUS *with* ANTHONY *and* PERCY CUTTING. *Following them,*
HENRY *and* OLIVER. *All carry guns.* PERCY *also carries a couple of*
dead rabbits. They stop.

MARCUS: Right you are, gentlemen, this looks an ideal spot. Will
this suit you both?

ANTHONY: (*Grimly*) Perfect.

MARCUS: Mr Bell?

(HENRY *opens and shuts his mouth but manages to make no sound.*)

OLIVER: Fine. Absolutely perfect.

MARCUS: Splendid. Well, just to go over the rules once again. Both
seconds will load the combatants' weapons to ensure they're
using the correct cartridges. The seconds will retire, the
combatants will stand, traditionally, back to back. Mr Cutting
here, as the neutral observer, will count out the regulation ten
paces, at which point, gentlemen, you will turn and fire. Is
that clear? Any questions?

ANTHONY: Perfectly clear.

OLIVER: (*For* HENRY) Crystal.

MARCUS: Very well, gentlemen. Mr Cutting, will you take up your
position?

PERCY: Yes, Colonel.

(*He stands to one side, at a central vantage point.*)

MARCUS: Seconds will now prepare the combatants.

(MARCUS, PERCY *and* OLIVER *set aside their own weapons.*
MARCUS *takes Anthony's gun and loads it.* OLIVER *does the same*
for HENRY. ANTHONY *makes to take his coat off.*)

I'm afraid you'll have to keep your coats on, gentlemen. For
all our sakes, this needs to look like a fatal accident . . .

(HENRY *gives an involuntary whimper of fear.*)

OLIVER: You all right?

(HENRY *makes another little noise.*)

(*Quietly, to* HENRY) Better with your coats on. It'll slow him
down.

HENRY: What about me?

OLIVER: Ah yes, but you're slow anyway. It'll make it more even. Incidentally, just a tip . . .

HENRY: (*Eagerly*) Yes?

OLIVER: I appreciate I haven't been an awful lot of help to you these past couple of days . . .

HENRY: You've been splendid . . .

OLIVER: I'm afraid I wasn't able to teach you as much as I'd hoped but – well, if I were you when you shoot – I should keep your eyes closed –

HENRY: Closed?

OLIVER: It's just that you seem to be a lot more accurate when you shut them.

MARCUS: (*Calling to them*) Ready, gentlemen?

OLIVER: (*Calling*) Ready.

MARCUS: Then take your places, please.

OLIVER: (*Handing* HENRY *his gun*) Incidentally, I had a fiddle with this trigger mechanism – it's pretty responsive. So don't, for God's sake, touch it unless you mean business. Good luck.

(HENRY *and* ANTHONY *take up their back-to-back stance.* MARCUS *and* OLIVER *retire to their corners.*)

MARCUS: Are we prepared? Good luck to you both. Mr Cutting, please proceed.

PERCY: Ready, gentlemen? And . . . one . . . two . . . three . . . four . . . five . . . six . . . seven . . . eight . . . nine . . . ten . . . (HENRY *and* ANTHONY *turn together. Their faces are left in single spots as the rest of the lights fade. A swift freeze and then a quick blackout.*)

ACT IV

SCENE I

The same. A few seconds earlier. We hear PERCY's *voice as the lights come up. Soon we see* HENRY *and* ANTHONY *are in their back-to-back stance.* MARCUS *and* OLIVER *have retired to their corners.*

PERCY: Ready, gentlemen? And . . . one . . . two . . . three . . . four . . . five . . . six . . . seven . . . eight . . . nine . . . ten . . .
(HENRY *and* ANTHONY *turn together.*)

HENRY: (*Suddenly, lowering his gun*) Just a minute. I'm sorry, just a minute. This is totally mad.
(ANTHONY *stares at him in amazement, uncertain whether he should fire or not.*)

MARCUS: (*To* HENRY) Shoot, man, shoot . . .

HENRY: (*Exploding with pent-up, nervous fury*) No, I'm sorry this is totally – totally ludicrous – this is stupid and foolish and crass and – insane . . . And this is the twentieth century and not the Dark Ages and we are grown up and we should know a damn sight better and I'm having nothing to do with it, so there!
(*He hurls his gun down on the ground in anger. There is a loud bang which startles everybody, especially* HENRY. ANTHONY *spins and falls to the ground with a cry. A stunned silence.* ANTHONY *moans.*)

OLIVER: Good shot.

HENRY: I'm – I'm – that was a complete – accident. I'm . . .
(MARCUS *and* PERCY *move to* ANTHONY. ANTHONY *tries to sit up. They support him.*)

MARCUS: You all right, old chap? (*To* PERCY) How is he?
(PERCY *gives a slight shake of his head.*)

HENRY: (*To* ANTHONY) It was an accident. I'm really most dreadfully sorry. Do you hear me? It was an accident. Honestly . . .
(ANTHONY *makes a strange croaking sound.*)

MARCUS: What's he saying?

PERCY: I think – I think he's laughing . . .

ANTHONY: (*With his last breath, still laughing*) Some . . . bloody
. . . accident . . .

(*He dies laughing. They lower him to the ground.*)

PERCY: May he rest in peace . . .

MARCUS: Hear! Hear!

(*A moment's respectful silence.* HENRY *is in a state of shock.*)
Well, I think we all witnessed that, didn't we? A clearer
accidental death than that I never saw . . .

HENRY: (*Dazed*) It was an accident . . .

MARCUS: Absolutely. My very words. (*To* HENRY) It's all right,
old man. You've absolutely no worries. We three witnessed
the whole shooting match. Between us, you've got a
landowner, a JP and a member of Rotary. You can't get more
reliable witnesses than that.

HENRY: It was an accident . . .

MARCUS: Oliver, old chap, take him home and give him a brandy
– try and persuade him to lie down . . .

OLIVER: OK. Will do. Come on, Henry.

(*He takes Henry's arm.*)

MARCUS: Leave his gun there. It's evidence. You'll both need to
have a word with the police later on – but it's a sheer
formality. Absolutely open and shut case.

OLIVER: Come on, Henry. Cheer up. (*As they go*) Look at it this
way. It could have been you, old boy, it could have been
you . . .

HENRY: It should have been me . . .

(HENRY *and* OLIVER *leave.* MARCUS *picks up Anthony's gun,
which has fallen by him.*)

MARCUS: Chap's taken it rather badly, I'm afraid . . .

PERCY: Yes.

MARCUS: I thought for one ghastly moment he wasn't going to
fire.

PERCY: That crossed my mind . . .

MARCUS: Nice enough chap, though.

PERCY: Very pleasant.

MARCUS: Don't think I'll take him shooting with me, though, not
on a regular basis . . . Still, he'll suit Imogen down to the

159

ground. Don't imagine he'll give her such a bad time as this monkey did, anyway.

(MARCUS *holds Anthony's gun up to the sky as he is speaking, squinting along the barrel. He pulls both triggers. There is a double click but no explosion.*)

(*Unsurprised.*) Good Lord, Percy, what do you think are the chances of that? Two dud cartridges at once. What are the odds on that happening?

PERCY: (*Smiling*) Almost astronomic, I should imagine . . .

(MARCUS *opens the gun, removes the dud cartridges and slips them into his pocket.*)

MARCUS: (*Producing two more cartridges from his other pocket*) Better give the poor fellow some decent ones then, hadn't we?

(*During the next,* MARCUS *reloads Anthony's gun and replaces it where it was.*)

PERCY: Would you like me to go on ahead and telephone, Colonel?

MARCUS: Oh yes, would you, Percy, that's a good chap. I'd better hang on here with the remains. Try and get Chief Inspector Rogers, if he's there. He tends to deal with these sorts of things rather tactfully . . .

PERCY: Chief Inspector Rogers. I'll do my best . . .

(PERCY *goes off, carrying both their guns with him.* MARCUS, *on his own, wanders over to inspect the body.*)

MARCUS: (*Jabbing the body with his foot*) Well, that ought to keep you in your own bed for a bit, anyway . . .

(*He wanders away from the body. As he does so, the lights cross-fade to –*)

SCENE 2
11.00 a.m.

A churchyard. A bell tolls. MARCUS *is joined by* IMOGEN, *dressed in black. He takes her arm to comfort her. Others, also sombrely dressed, join them. They gather in a circle. There is no dialogue, merely the bell and maybe a few birds. It is as though we are watching the scene in*

long shot. OLIVER *stands with* HENRY. PERCY *stands with* DAPHNE
and NORMA. WINNIE *stands alone. As from a distance,* KAREN
*appears and watches them. She is dramatically dressed in a long black
coat and a big black hat. She looks rather like a ghost. The mourners
start to disperse, without noticing* KAREN. *Last to leave is* HENRY,
who takes one rather apologetic glance back at the grave. He sees
KAREN *and is startled.* KAREN *puts one black-gloved hand
dramatically to her lips and blows* HENRY *a silent kiss. Then she is
gone.* HENRY *is rather alarmed by this. He looks round nervously and
then hurries after the others. As he does so, the lights cross-fade again
to –*)

SCENE 3
8.50 a.m.

Lembridge Tennit. The outer area of Jeremy Pride's office. It is empty.
JEREMY *comes out of his office. He is looking for something. He routs
about on Veronica's desk and finds what he is looking for – a pencil.*

JEREMY: (*Slightly irritably, to himself*) There was once a time
   when I was supplied with pencils . . . I didn't used to have to
   go grubbing about for them . . .
   (*He goes back in to his office. A slight pause.* KAREN *comes in
   through the other door, having just arrived for work. She carries a
   huge bunch of red roses wrapped in Cellophane. She is humming
   loudly. Seeing no one is in there she stops and listens. She looks
   cautiously through the door of Jeremy's office. Contenting herself
   that he is indeed in there, she starts humming again even more
   loudly. She makes another entrance from the doorway.*)
   (*Coming out of his office again, crossly*) Who's that? Who on
   earth is that? Oh – Karen, good morning. Do we really need
   the musical overture first thing?
KAREN: (*Irrepressibly cheerful*) Mr Pride, I'm so sorry . . . Good
   morning.
   (*She holds the flowers in front of her rather conspicuously.*)
JEREMY: Good morning. You're especially bright and early.
KAREN: Yes.
   (*She rattles the flowers slightly.*)

161

JEREMY: Let's hope one or two of your colleagues will follow suit, eh?
(*He laughs.*)
KAREN: Yes. I believe I saw Ronny just behind me on her way up.
(*She rattles the flowers again.* JEREMY *still fails to notice them.*)
JEREMY: Well, I must . . . I've got a mountain to get through in there . . .
KAREN: Yes, right . . . (*Sniffing her flowers vigorously through the Cellophane*) Ooo! Ooo! Ooo!
JEREMY: (*Genuinely seeing the flowers for the first time*) Good heavens above. What on earth have you got there?
KAREN: Oh – just some – roses . . .
JEREMY: Ah. A special occasion?
KAREN: Actually – it's my birthday . . .
(*She smiles modestly.*)
JEREMY: Well . . . Many happy returns.
KAREN: Thank you.
JEREMY: (*Playfully*) I won't ask how old . . .
KAREN: (*Equally playfully*) No. Better not.
JEREMY: A secret admirer?
KAREN: No, I think I know who they're from. I'm not completely sure. It could be one of three boys but I'm pretty sure it's Johnny. This is a typical Johnny gesture.
JEREMY: Well, you'd better be sure. You don't want to get them mixed up, do you?
(*He laughs.* KAREN *laughs.*)
Start saying thank you to the wrong one.
(*He laughs.*)
KAREN: (*Laughing*) No.
JEREMY: Oh, look. (*Indicating the flowers*) There's a card with them. See, here's a card.
(*He indicates the slightly larger than average card attached to the wrapping.*)
KAREN: Oh, yes. I never noticed that. We can find out. Could you possibly . . . ?
JEREMY: What?
KAREN: (*With a glance towards the door*) Could you possibly read it to me . . . ?

JEREMY: Oh, I don't think I should read it, should I?

KAREN: No, it's quite all right, I'm sure . . . It's just that I have my hands full and –

JEREMY: (*Doubtfully*) Well . . .

KAREN: If it's Johnny, I promise you it'll be perfectly clean . . . (*She laughs.*)

JEREMY: (*Enjoying this*) Well, I hope so, I hope so. (*Opening the card and reading the message*) Ah! Ah! Well, it's very – well, sort of personal but . . . very sweet . . .

(*He chuckles romantically. It is round about now that VERONICA, unseen by either of them, arrives in the doorway. She stops and stares at the tableau, thunderstruck.*)

KAREN: Well, read it, then. Go on.

JEREMY: I'll do my best. Oh dear.

(*He is still giggling a lot with embarrassment.*)

> Just to say
> Happy day
> And to pray
> You will stay
> Just the way
> You are today
> From Great Big J
> To Special K

KAREN: Oh, that's lovely. How lovely. Thank you.

JEREMY: Don't thank me.

KAREN: You read it so beautifully.

JEREMY: Thank you.

KAREN: (*Seeing* VERONICA) Oh, good morning, Ronny.

JEREMY: Ah, Ronny.

VERONICA: (*Coldly*) Good morning. Sorry I'm early.

JEREMY: No, no. You're not early . . . It's Karen's birthday, Ronny. Someone's sent her these flowers. Look.

VERONICA: Yes, I heard. From Great Big J, apparently. Whoever he may be.

JEREMY: What's his name? Johnny, did you say?

KAREN: That's right. Johnny. John – Bell, really.

VERONICA: Well, that's the first we've heard of him, isn't it? And where did John Bell spring from all of a sudden, I wonder?

163

KAREN: (*Smiling at her*) Croydon.

JEREMY: Oh, Croydon? That's quite near us.

VERONICA: Well, let me put these in water for you.

(*She takes the flowers from* KAREN.)

KAREN: No, I can do it . . .

VERONICA: No, I insist. You can't waste your day putting flowers in water, can you? Mustn't ruin your little hands on your birthday.

(VERONICA *sweeps out with the flowers*.)

JEREMY: She really is in the most extraordinary state, isn't she? I have to say it. I think I'm going to have to have a quiet word with her. Privately.

(LYDIA *appears in the doorway. She has a loosely wrapped parcel in her hand*.)

LYDIA: Excuse me, Mr Pride – Karen, dear, is this yours? I think you left it on my desk when you were with me this morning.

KAREN: (*Mortified*) Oh, how awful. I completely forgot them. Isn't that awful? I'm sorry. Thank you.

LYDIA: Well, we forgive you. Seeing it's your birthday. Here.

KAREN: Thank you. I wish they wouldn't send them to the office. It's so embarrassing. I've told them . . .

JEREMY: What's this, then? Another gift from Johnny?

KAREN: No – if I'm not mistaken – if it's what I think it is . . .

(*She opens the parcel*.) Oh, it is. It's chocolates. My favourites. Yes, it must be from him.

JEREMY: Johnny?

KAREN: No. These are from Jimmy.

JEREMY: Jimmy?

KAREN: Yes.

JEREMY: (*Laughing*) Johnny and Jimmy. All the Js, eh?

KAREN: Yes, so they are.

JEREMY: I'd better watch out, eh? I could be next on the list.

(*He laughs*.)

KAREN: (*Laughing*) Yes, of course. Jeremy! Of course.

LYDIA: (*Enjoying the joke*) Oh, Mr Pride . . .

(*All three laugh*)

JEREMY: (*Enjoying the joke enormously*) Oh, this is much, much better than working . . . Where are your flowers? I hope she hasn't walked off with them. (*He laughs.*) Karen had this lovely bunch of flowers, Lydia –

LYDIA: Yes, I saw them earlier . . .

JEREMY: Beautiful red . . . What were they? Roses? (*A sudden thought.*) I say – I've just had a thought. Do you think Ronny may have got hold of the wrong end of the stick?

KAREN: How do you mean?

JEREMY: It just occurred to me – Ronny's been getting all these anonymous flowers sent to her, Lydia . . .

LYDIA: Yes, I'd heard she had . . .

JEREMY: I'm wondering. Perhaps they weren't meant for her at all. Perhaps they were intended for you, Karen. What do you think?

KAREN: Well, it's possible, I suppose. I'd never thought of that. How stupid of me. Of course. It's just the sort of thing Johnny would do . . .

JEREMY: Sounds like Johnny's work to me.

KAREN: Either him or Jason, that's for sure.

JEREMY: (*Roaring with laughter*) Jason! Did you hear that, Lydia? She's got a Jason as well. The girl's incorrigible. I don't know when she finds time to come to work . . .

LYDIA: (*Laughing at this*) Oh, Mr Pride . . .

(JEREMY *playfully chucks* KAREN *under the chin. As he does so,* VERONICA *enters and takes in this jolly scene, frostily. She has the flowers. Or what's left of them. She has separated the heads from the stalks. The heads she has saved and wrapped in the original Cellophane. The stalks she has stuck into an impromptu 'vase' – the bottom half of a lavatory-brush holder.*)

VERONICA: I'm sorry to have taken so long. I'm afraid I had a disaster with your flowers, Karen, and all the heads fell off. But I'm sure you'd still like to sniff the stalks, though, wouldn't you? There.

(*She thumps the 'vase' down on Karen's desk.*)

LYDIA: Oh, dear . . .

JEREMY: (*Shocked*) Oh, good Lord.

VERONICA: Never mind, I saved you the heads. You can float them in your bath. If you ever take one.

KAREN: (*Hurt*) Oh.

JEREMY: What on earth has come over you, Veronica? Look what you've done to Johnny's flowers. What on earth is the matter? I demand an explanation . . .

KAREN: It doesn't matter, Jeremy . . .

JEREMY: Oh, yes, it does. I'm afraid I don't believe your story about an accident, Ronny . . .

KAREN: Jeremy, please. It is my birthday. Chocolate, anyone? (*Offering the box*) Lydia?

LYDIA: (*Wrestling briefly with temptation*) Well . . . (*She dithers over which one to take.*)

JEREMY: And quite apart from the damage you've done to these blooms, Ronny, you may care to know that for several weeks you've been appropriating flowers that were intended for someone else . . .

KAREN: Oh, Jeremy, please, don't tell her that . . .

VERONICA: (*Dangerously quiet*) What?

JEREMY: Those roses that were arriving every day, I think you might have realized that they weren't meant for you . . .

KAREN: It really doesn't matter, Jeremy . . .

JEREMY: They were obviously intended for Karen here. Only she was too kind to say anything.

KAREN: (*Offering him a chocolate*) Chocolate, Jeremy?

JEREMY: No, no, thank you. Not just at present.

KAREN: Oh, go on. They're lovely . . .

JEREMY: No, I can only cope with soft centres, Karen, I don't think I'll risk . . .

VERONICA: (*Taking the box from* KAREN) Please. Allow me . . . (*Before anyone can stop her, she walks a little way away from them, carefully replacing the lid of the box as she does so. Then she puts the chocolates on the floor and calmly jumps up and down on them a couple of times. The others watch her, dumbfounded.* VERONICA *picks up the box and prises it open again.*) (*Offering the box to* JEREMY) There you are. Now they're all soft centres . . . (*Icily*) Help yourself. (JEREMY *stands looking at her as though hypnotized.*)

JEREMY: I . . . I . . . I . . .

VERONICA: (*Suddenly screaming*) COME ON! EAT THEM, YOU LECHEROUS BASTARD!

(She makes to squash his face between both halves of the chocolate box. He retreats in terror. LYDIA *attempts to restrain her.)*

JEREMY: Get away, get away. Someone get her away. She's gone mad. She's gone completely mad . . .

LYDIA: *(Simultaneously)* Miss Webb! For heaven's sake! What do you think you're doing? What's come over you? Miss Webb!

VERONICA: *(Simultaneously)* I'll make you eat every one of these and your filthy flowers. Do you think I want your flowers? I don't want your revolting flowers . . .

*(*JEREMY *is driven back so he is lying across a desk.* KAREN *sits on her desk and watches, amused.* LYDIA, *who seems to have some rudimentary grasp of self-defence, finally manages to restrain* VERONICA.)*

LYDIA: It's all right, I've got her. I've got her. Don't hurt her, Mr Pride, there's no need to hurt her . . .

JEREMY: I wasn't going to hurt her . . .

LYDIA: All right. I can take her now . . .

*(*VERONICA *is making low growling noises in her throat.)*
I'll take her down to the nurse. She may be able to give her a sedative. *(Indicating* JEREMY, *who is still sprawled across the desk)* Karen, will you see to Mr Pride . . .

KAREN: Yes, of course. You bet . . .

*(*LYDIA *goes out with* VERONICA. JEREMY *tries to stand but is unable to do so. He is breathing noisily.* KAREN *has picked up the chocolates. She watches him. As she does so, she dips her fingers in the squashed chocolates and licks the cream fillings off them.)*

JEREMY: I'm afraid I can't . . . I can't . . . Karen, would you . . . ?

KAREN: *(Unmoving)* Just a tick, Jeremy.

JEREMY: There's an – an inhaler – an inhaler in the – bottom right – hand – drawer of my desk in there . . . would you mind . . . ?

KAREN: *(Still not moving)* Of course I will, Jeremy . . .

JEREMY: I think I'm having one of my – a little trouble breathing . . . Karen . . . please . . . *(He slips down behind the desk.)* Karen, are you there . . . ? Where are you?

KAREN: Yes, I'm looking for it, Jeremy. Hold on. Won't be a sec. Coming up.
(The phone rings.)
(Answering it) Hallo, B.E.S.U.K. Department. Mr Pride's

assistant. How can I help you? No, I'm sorry, Mr Pride is unavailable at this time. I'm presently in charge, can I help you at all . . . Yes . . . yes, of course . . . (*Laughing*) No problem . . . Karen Knightly . . . What's your name? . . . Hey . . .

(*As she laughs and chatters on,* JEREMY's *laboured breathing continues from behind the desk. The lights cross-fade to –*)

SCENE 4
3.45 p.m.

Imogen's farmhouse kitchen. A room that obviously serves as the main living area. Cosy and a little untidy. Evidence of children. IMOGEN *comes in with some washing that has evidently been drying. During the next, she folds it roughly for ironing later.* HENRY *follows her in. He has clearly been trailing about after her. He seems troubled.* IMOGEN *seems determined and practical.*

IMOGEN: (*After a silence*) So. What do you say?
HENRY: You don't feel it's a bit soon?
IMOGEN: Soon for what?
HENRY: For . . . respect. For Anthony.
IMOGEN: Why should I respect Anthony? He never respected me.
HENRY: No, but he's dead and it's usual to wait a proper . . . a respectful time . . .
IMOGEN: But that's only if you're in mourning . . .
HENRY: But you are in mourning. If we were in the Mediterranean you'd be walking around in a black sack . . .
IMOGEN: Well, thank God we're not, that's all I can say. How can I possibly mourn a man I didn't like?
HENRY: You did, though. At one time, presumably . . .
IMOGEN: Yes. I did. And if he'd dropped dead then, I would have mourned him. I'd have worn endless black sacks. But he's died too late for that, hasn't he? Hard cheese.
HENRY: You're very – tough, aren't you? I never realized you were quite so tough.

168

IMOGEN: Does that put you off me?

HENRY: No. It's just I have to reassess you.

IMOGEN: I'm going to have to be tough, aren't I? No point in lying around looking helpless, is there, with a farm to run, two children to feed and no husband? (*Slightly beadily*) No prospect of one, either.

HENRY: What makes you say that?

IMOGEN: You've just said no.

HENRY: I didn't say no.

IMOGEN: You did. I said, what about it then? And you said, no thanks.

HENRY: I didn't say no thanks, I said – Anyway, I'm supposed to be doing the proposing, not you. What are you doing proposing? You just wait till you're asked.

IMOGEN: Right. Sorry I spoke.

(*A silence.* IMOGEN *huffily continues with her tasks. She looks out of the window as she does so.*)

(*In her Snow White voice*) Goodness! It is nearly dark and still he hasn't returned to propose to me. Will my Prince ever come? What do you think, Sneezy? Maybe he will ask me tomorrow. I will put on my prettiest dress and braid my hair and stand at the door and wait for him . . . Oh look, Grumpy, look, Dopey . . .

HENRY: Oh, shut up. Just shut up. (*Pause. Sulkily*) I'm not proposing to you today anyway. So don't sit around waiting for it. (*Glancing at his watch*) It's too late now. Maybe in the morning.

IMOGEN: (*Drily*) Gosh! Will I sleep?

HENRY: I just feel we ought to wait. People will . . . I mean, it's not going to look very good, is it? I only shot the man a fortnight ago. Now here I am getting engaged to his wife. (*Pause.*) What's another week or two either way? I'm thinking of you, you know. I am. (*Pause.*) Perhaps you'd – would you like me to come and stay here with you? I could move out of Furtherfield House right now. I could do that. Be here with you at nights. Help during the day. With the kids. If that'd be any help.

IMOGEN: I'm not living in sin. If you want your cake you can bloody well eat it as well, mate.

HENRY: (*Grudgingly*) Oh, all right, then. Have it your own way.
Will you marry me, then?

IMOGEN: (*Grumpily*) All right.

HENRY: Is that a yes? Does that mean yes?

IMOGEN: Yes, it means yes. Thank you. Yes.

HENRY: Good. OK? Happy? (*Pause.*) Great Romantic Moments
in History, Number one two seven.

(IMOGEN *relents and comes and kisses him gently.*)

IMOGEN: Do you really want to marry me?

HENRY: Of course I do.

IMOGEN: I'm sorry I proposed. That was terribly rude of me. I
just assumed that was what we'd . . . It was terrible. Terrible
of me. Sorry. (*Pause.*) Do you want to leave it and propose
again tomorrow?

HENRY: No, I certainly don't, thank you. I'm not going through
all that again.

IMOGEN: You're happy?

HENRY: Yes. Over the moon.

IMOGEN: (*Frowning*) Good.

HENRY: My only conditions are that I won't eat lunch, I never do.
And I refuse to shoot squirrels.

IMOGEN: Well . . . The lunch bit's all right. I think with the
squirrels you may find you have to. When they're sitting on
the end of our bed chewing at our toes, you may feel the need
for action.

HENRY: If it gets to that stage, I promise to have a pretty serious
word with them, OK?

IMOGEN: Super.

(MARCUS *enters. He sees them and retreats in embarrassment.*)

MARCUS: Oh, sorry . . .

IMOGEN: Hallo, Uncle. Come in . . .

MARCUS: Sorry, I didn't think. Just barged in the front door,
never thinking . . . Sorry . . .

IMOGEN: Please, honestly. Come in.

HENRY: Please.

MARCUS: Well. Just for a minute. Just wanted to see how you
were.

170

IMOGEN: Oh, we're fine. (*To* HENRY) Aren't we?

HENRY: Yes.

MARCUS: Good.

    (*Pause.*)

IMOGEN: (*Holding Henry's hand*) Do you want to tell Uncle the good news?

HENRY: Yes.

IMOGEN: Or shall I?

HENRY: No. OK. Fine.

    (*Pause.*)

MARCUS: (*Waiting expectantly*) Well. What's the news?

HENRY: (*Muttering, without enthusiasm*) We're getting married.

MARCUS: (*To* IMOGEN) What did he say?

IMOGEN: He said, we're getting married.

MARCUS: Oh. Good. Good. (*He looks enquiringly at* IMOGEN.) Isn't it?

IMOGEN: Yes, I thought it was pretty good. I'm pleased.

MARCUS: Good. (*To* HENRY) What about you?

IMOGEN: Henry's over the moon.

MARCUS: Oh, good. So long as you're both happy. That's the main thing, isn't it?

IMOGEN: I think so. (*Frowning, she gathers up the washing*) Excuse me just a moment.

    (IMOGEN *leaves.*)

MARCUS: You want to marry her, don't you?

HENRY: Yes, I do. Very much. It's just . . . Well, two things really. First, I wish it wasn't quite such a foregone conclusion. I mean, I always think it's good to have at least the illusion of freedom of choice.

MARCUS: Yes, I appreciate that. But I do feel if you don't marry her, people will tend to take rather a dim view. I mean, it's one thing getting rid of her husband for her, but you really can't stand the girl up afterwards, can you? Not when you've wiped out her breadwinner in the first place.

HENRY: Literally a shotgun wedding, isn't it?

MARCUS: Yes, that – pretty well sums it up. What's your other problem?

HENRY: It's more complicated. It involves – other people.

Promises I made . . .

MARCUS: You haven't got a wife already, have you?

HENRY: No. We've split up. Divorced.

MARCUS: Mistress?

HENRY: Not – in the strict sense.

MARCUS: Well, take my tip. Get rid of her – strict or not.

HENRY: I'll try.

MARCUS: (*Indicating* IMOGEN) I don't want her heart broken again, you see.

HENRY: (*With feeling*) No. Nor do I. I promise.

MARCUS: (*Satisfied*) Good. Now, about this other thing.

HENRY: What's that?

MARCUS: As you may know, Anthony was on the board of my company. So now we've got a vacancy. What about it?

HENRY: Well . . .

MARCUS: It won't entail too much. Occasional meetings. It's just that a lot of Imogen's money is tied up in the firm, money that will technically be yours as well, so maybe you'd like to keep an eye on things. We're not that huge so it's not a vast undertaking, as I say. Shouldn't interfere with your other interests in Strewth Street at all. But between you and me, I think our board could do with a spot of new blood. And, of course, your being an accountant isn't at all a bad thing either.

HENRY: I'm not . . . I'm technically not really an accountant –

MARCUS: I thought you were. I understood you were the Knightlys' accountant?

HENRY: No, not really . . .

MARCUS: Well, what are you?

HENRY: (*Picking his way*) I was acting for – as the representative for the Knightlys' accountant.

MARCUS: Really? Trust the Knightlys to have grand accountants like that. They've got a damn sight more money than they know what to do with. Well, anyway, you've got a business head. That's what I'm getting at.

HENRY: Oh, yes.

MARCUS: And that's what my board needs. Desperately. So let's see you at our next meeting, OK?

HENRY: Right.

MARCUS: I can't for the life of me remember when that is but I'll give you a ring and let you know . . .

(IMOGEN *enters, putting on her coat.*)

IMOGEN: I have to collect Lucy from school . . .

MARCUS: Ah, well, I must be off . . .

IMOGEN: Do stay if you want. I'll only be a second. I'll make us some tea . . .

MARCUS: No, no. I'm off. Other furrows. Other burrows. (*Smiling at them both*) I'm delighted. Absolutely delighted. (*He kisses* IMOGEN *on the cheek. As he goes, to* HENRY) I'll call you.

HENRY: Fine.

(MARCUS *goes out.*)

IMOGEN: Do you want to come with me? To collect Lucy? It's only up the road.

HENRY: Yes, of course.

IMOGEN: Since you're going to be her father soon.

HENRY: Yes.

IMOGEN: I do wish you'd look a bit happier about all this. I'm beginning to feel guilty. Please don't marry me if you don't want to. Please, Henry.

HENRY: I love you more than anything in the world. I want to marry you. I want to look after your children. And if you want to some time, we could even have our own children. I love you.

IMOGEN: Then what's the problem, Henry?

HENRY: I'm . . . nervous.

IMOGEN: Of me?

HENRY: Of course not.

IMOGEN: What, then?

HENRY: I don't know precisely. I'm just nervous. Come on, then. (*They go out.* HENRY *still frowning,* IMOGEN *looking at him very concerned. As they do so, the lights cross-fade to* –)

Furtherfield House. The hall. WINNIE *is in her dressing-gown and night attire, doing her rounds with an electric torch. She checks the front door and is heading for the stairs when* HENRY *wanders in, carrying a book.*

WINNIE: Oh. Evening, sir. I thought you were in bed.

HENRY: No, Winnie. I couldn't sleep. Things on my mind, you know.

WINNIE: (*Not very interested*) Oh yes, sir? I was just locking up for the night. You didn't want to go out, did you? Only the front door isn't locked if you want to go out.

HENRY: Really. Do you find you needn't lock it around here?

WINNIE: Well, I normally would, sir. But not on the anniversary. I never lock it on their anniversary.

HENRY: Oh? Whose anniversary's this?

WINNIE: Theirs, sir. Miss Karen and Master Oliver's parents. It's the anniversary of the night they both died, you see, sir. I always make a point of leaving the front door on the latch. Each year I do it. Off my own bat, like. Just in case their spirits are wandering abroad, poor things. Feel like visiting the old place.

HENRY: Ah.

WINNIE: Silly superstitious old woman, you're saying . . .

HENRY: No, no. I'm not saying that.

WINNIE: Will you be going out again tonight, sir?

HENRY: No, I'll just – go for a walk in here for a bit. Perhaps read my book. Master Oliver in bed, is he?

WINNIE: Yes, sir. I took him up his milk and biscuits.

HENRY: Oh?

WINNIE: Always has his milk and biscuits when he's at home. Well, goodnight. I hope you sleep.

(*She switches on her torch and starts to move off.*)

HENRY: Do you find the torch necessary?

WINNIE: It is where I'm going, sir.

HENRY: Where's that?

WINNIE: The servants' wing, sir. Not many light-bulbs still alive down there, not these days.

HENRY: Doesn't that make you nervous?

WINNIE: Nothing for a God-fearing person to be afraid of in this house, sir, I can promise you.

(WINNIE *goes off.* HENRY *stands and looks around for a moment. Outside, the wind moans. He feels nervous. He pulls himself together and sits down, preparing to read. Somewhere, upstairs, a clatter.* HENRY *jumps. He stands. Listens. Reassures himself and settles again. Another sound. This time outside the front door. He moves towards it cautiously. Unseen,* KAREN *appears at the top of the stairs. She is dressed in a long black gown, something rather exotic. She seems rather pale. Tonight she is playing Edgar Allan Poe's weird Mistress of the Manor.*)

KAREN: (*In sepulchral tones*) HenryBell!

HENRY: (*Jumping*) Oh, good grief!

KAREN: Good evening, HenryBell.

HENRY: Karen, please. Don't do that to me again. Ever.

KAREN: (*Approaching him*) You haven't phoned me lately, HenryBell, and you won't answer my calls. I wanted to know how you were. How are you?

HENRY: I'm – very well, thank you. How are you?

KAREN: Me? I'm having a simply wonderful time. You've no idea. I never dreamt big business could be so much fun. You never told me.

(*She reaches* HENRY *and kisses him.*)

(*Softly*) Hello, HenryBell. I've missed you.

HENRY: Thank you.

KAREN: I've missed you terribly. I hope you're not tired tonight because I've missed you terribly.

HENRY: Ah. Well, yes, that's . . . You're looking very . . . very . . .

KAREN: Thank you. I thought we should celebrate.

HENRY: Celebrate?

KAREN: Our revenge. Both our achievements. I'll have some champagne sent upstairs. (*Yelling*) Winnie!

HENRY: No, please, Karen, wait . . .

KAREN: (*Yelling again*) Winnie!

HENRY: (*Loudly*) Karen! Please. Don't wake Winnie, please. We don't want champagne. There's nothing to celebrate, there really isn't.

KAREN: Nothing?

HENRY: No. Even if you feel there is, I can assure you there really isn't. Not from my side. Not as far as you're concerned.

KAREN: HenryBell, you're just being modest . . .

HENRY: No, really –

KAREN: What about Anthony? That was brilliant. I mean, I came down here for the day, just on the offchance to see how you were doing, and there was this funeral in full swing. 'Whose funeral might this be, my good man?' I enquired. 'That be Mr Staxton-Billing's funeral, ma'am. Gunned down in his prime by that furren gentleman from Lunnen.' I consider that rather a brilliant achievement, even if you don't.

HENRY: You're not sorry?

KAREN: Why?

HENRY: That Anthony's dead?

KAREN: No.

HENRY: I thought you loved him?

KAREN: I never said that.

HENRY: You were upset when he left you, though?

KAREN: Not really.

HENRY: Upset enough to want to try and kill yourself . . .

KAREN: I wasn't upset because he left me, I was upset at her for taking him back. But I can see your plan. It's very clever. Better than killing her, far better. Leave the Friesian to pine till her milk turns sour. Now, that is what I call really poetic. HenryBell, you are a true artist. And that is a compliment, believe me. Because it comes from a true artist herself. Do you think there's a chance she'll die of grief? She might, I suppose.

HENRY: Karen, she didn't even like her husband. Imogen didn't take Anthony away from you. Anthony took himself away from you. Imogen had nothing to do with it. She is not to blame in any way for him leaving you. He left you for another woman . . . altogether.

KAREN: Who?

176

HENRY: Councillor Mrs Daphne Teale.

KAREN: Who? Norma's mother?

HENRY: Right.

KAREN: Nonsense. No one would leave me for Mrs Teale. Mrs
Teale? That old tart? No one would leave me for that fat old
tart.

HENRY: I'm afraid Anthony did.

KAREN: Bollocks. It was that wife of his. You're defending her.
Why? Why are you trying to defend her, HenryBell?

HENRY: Because . . .

KAREN: Why? I want to know. Why?

HENRY: Because . . . because, if you must know, we're engaged
to be married. Imogen Staxton-Billing and I are going to be
married. I'm sorry I have to tell you quite as bluntly as that,
but there it is. You'd have found out sooner or later. I'm
sorry. I'm sorry if I've upset you.

(KAREN *stares at him. When she speaks, it is not the reaction that*
HENRY *expects at all. Instead, she sounds faintly puzzled.*)

KAREN: (*Frowning*) I don't get it.

HENRY: You don't?

KAREN: Why you're marrying her. I don't see the point.

HENRY: Well, why does anyone ever marry anyone?

KAREN: To make her miserable?

HENRY: No. Course not. To make her happy.

KAREN: (*Incredulously*) Happy?

HENRY: Yes.

KAREN: Why?

HENRY: Because I love her.

KAREN: You love Imogen?

HENRY: Yes. I've just said. What's the matter with you?

KAREN: (*Smiling in disbelief*) You can't love Imogen. *Imogen?*
How dare you stand there and say things like that? You're
joking. *Imogen*. No, that is out. Sorry. That is out.

HENRY: What do you mean 'out'?

KAREN: That is entirely contrary to what we agreed. I'm afraid
you're not able to do that, HenryBell, that is breaking the
rules. I'm sorry, I can't allow you to break the rules. Out.
Fault. Out.

HENRY: Karen, I'm not talking about rules. I'm talking about real life – this is real life –

KAREN: (*Blazing*) And I'm talking about rules which are a bloody sight more important –

HENRY: Karen, Karen. This is reality. Real, do you understand? It is not a game. Life is not a game, Karen.

KAREN: (*Quietly*) Who told you that?

HENRY: It happens to be the case. There's a much bigger board, for one thing. People keep stealing your counters and changing the rules. Life's a lot more complicated and a good deal harder to play. Take it from me.

KAREN: Wrong, HenryBell. Wrong. It's easy. Easy-peasy. You play by the rules and it's easy . . .

HENRY: But who makes up these rules in the first place?

KAREN: You do. You make up your own rules. That's the joy of it. But you see, HenryBell, once you've made them up, you must keep them. You really must. Otherwise life *is* difficult. If you're finding things difficult, it's only because you're breaking your own rules –

HENRY: But what we're talking about were never my rules, those were your rules . . .

KAREN: They are *our* rules. We agreed them. We made a pact. We started a game together, both of us. It was called revenge. And I insist that you play it to the end. I demand that you do. Now you go over there now and you tell her that the engagement is off, all right? Destroy her. I don't care what you do but you have to destroy her somehow. Now go. Go now.

HENRY: (*Impatiently*) Oh, come on, Karen. Don't be so ridiculous.

(KAREN *starts to try and shove him towards the front door.*)

KAREN: (*Pushing*) Out. Go on. Out now. Out.

HENRY: (*Resisting her*) Now, stop that . . . Karen!

KAREN: (*Pushing him quite savagely*) Do you hear me? I want you out, do you hear? Out, out . . .

HENRY: (*Pushing her away from him*) Look, just stop that, will you?

(*The shove he gives her is harder than he meant. She is also*

178

caught off-balance. She staggers back and sits on the ground. Nothing really hurt except her dignity, she sits there startled, like the school bully who's been unexpectedly punched in return.) I'm sorry, Karen. I didn't mean . . .

(KAREN stares at him. When she speaks, her tone is quiet and very dangerous.)

KAREN: *(Getting up and dusting herself down)* How dare you do that to me, you piddling little – clerk. I make a very bad enemy, HenryBell. Beware. You don't want to play against me, I promise. Never, never try and play against me.

HENRY: I'm not playing at all. I'm finished.

KAREN: Oh no, you're not.

(HENRY does not reply.)

All right. We'll see. *(Screaming at him suddenly)* We'll see!

(OLIVER enters in his pyjamas and dressing-gown.)

OLIVER: What the hell's going on down here? Oh, hi, Ka.

(KAREN does not respond. OLIVER assesses the situation.)

What seems to be the problem?

(KAREN runs to him and buries her head in his chest. From the sounds that emanate from her we can judge that she is crying very angrily, very privately.)

(Who has seen all this before) OK. OK. That's it. No problem. Come on. I'm here.

(HENRY watches, startled. OLIVER holds up a reassuring hand.)

(To HENRY) It's OK. Nothing serious. This happens. *(To KAREN)* There we are. There. There. Come on, then. It's only Olly.

(OLIVER sits on a chair and KAREN sits on his lap. He rocks her gently like a small child.)

Do you want to go to bed, then? Shall I put you to bed?

KAREN: *(Muffled)* No . . .

OLIVER: No? What do you want to do then? Want to play a game?

KAREN: *(Muffled)* No.

OLIVER: *(To HENRY)* Sorry, she'll be all right in a tick.

HENRY: Do you want me to . . . ?

OLIVER: No, she's fine, honestly. *(To KAREN)* What's the problem, then? Tell me the problem?

KAREN: *(Muffled)* He's cheating.

179

OLIVER: What?

KAREN: (*Muffled*) He's cheating. I hate him . . .

OLIVER: No, you don't hate him. You don't really hate him. Old Henry? He's a nice man. You don't hate old Henry.

KAREN: (*Muffled, vehement*) I hate him.

OLIVER: Come on. Stop crying and we'll find you something nice, all right? All right?

KAREN: (*Nodding*) Mmmm.

OLIVER: Tell you what – would you like to have a ride on my bike? What about that? Would you like to do that?

KAREN: (*Nodding*) Mmmm.

OLIVER: Yes, of course you would. (*He gets up.*) Come on, then. I'll get it started, then you can race all over the house. You'd enjoy that, wouldn't you?

KAREN: (*Nodding*) Mmmm.

OLIVER: Come on, then. Come with Olly. (*To* HENRY, *quietly*) Back in a tick.

(OLIVER *takes* KAREN *out, his arm round her shoulders.* HENRY *shakes his head incredulously. In a second, a roar as the motor bike starts up in the billiard room nearby.*)

KAREN: (*Off, a cry of pleasure*) Hey!

OLIVER: (*Off*) There you go. Off you go. Mind the billiard table . . .

(KAREN *gives distant cries of glee as she motors off, all upsets apparently forgotten.* OLIVER *returns. The motor-bike sound continues under the next for a time, receding and approaching as* KAREN *does a few laps of the circuit. Then, unnoticed by the men, it stops.*)

She'll be all right now. Always does the trick. Just take her mind off it with something. Used to do that whenever she fell over as a kid.

HENRY: She's not a kid now, though, is she?

OLIVER: Well, at heart she is. I suppose we both are, really. You mustn't blame her. It's not her fault she behaves like that.

HENRY: Who's fault is it?

OLIVER: Oh, circumstances, you know. All sorts of things. Growing up here, in this house. Big Wendy house really, isn't it? God, we used to have some good games. She's

brilliant, you know. At inventing games. Always told her she ought to be working for John What's-his-name's. You know, those games people. Dressing up. Lot of that. She made us pretend to be different people for days on end. She was terrific. I was no earthly good. I mean, you can do what you like, stick me in a frock, put as many funny hats on me as you like – I'm always exactly the same. Useless. But Karen. Sometimes you couldn't recognize her. Should have been an actress, I suppose. No, not an actress. Nobody else would ever have got a word in, would they? You see, I think the only trouble with Karen is she gets bored rather quickly. She got bored with playing here, eventually. Had to look for new amusements. Other women's husbands. That sort of thing. That's the difference between us. Me, I'm perfectly happy staying here. I'll stay here for ever. No problem. Smaller brain, probably, I don't know.
(*Pause. They are aware of the silence.*)

HENRY: Quiet, isn't it?

OLIVER: She's stopped. Probably stalled. Or run out of petrol.
(*Slight pause*)

HENRY: (*Looking at* OLIVER) Petrol?

OLIVER: (*A nasty thought*) Petrol. Oh, my God. Quickly.
(*They hurry to the door. Before they can reach it,* WINNIE *enters, coughing.*)

WINNIE: Master Oliver! Master Oliver! There's smoke everywhere . . .

OLIVER: Winnie, are you all right.

WINNIE: Thank God you're up . . .

HENRY: (*Who has been looking off towards the billiard room*) We can't go that way, the whole corridor's alight . . .

OLIVER: What about that way?
(*He indicates the way that* WINNIE's *just come.*)

WINNIE: I wouldn't go that way. I only just got through in time. The whole building's ablaze . . .

OLIVER: (*Shouting*) Karen! Karen!

HENRY: (*Shouting*) Karen!

WINNIE: Is Miss Karen here, then?

OLIVER: Of course she's here. Who else do you think would have

181

– Oh, never mind. Come on. We'd better get out of the front door. We might be able to get to reach her through the back . . .

HENRY: Shouldn't we phone the fire brigade?

OLIVER: Well, you can stay and phone if you like. I'm going to stand outside on the hill and wave. It's a damn sight safer.

(OLIVER *goes out with* WINNIE. HENRY *hesitates for a second, considering whether to phone. The room starts to glow red. He decides against it and follows the others out. The flames increase and the roar becomes very loud indeed. Then the sound of fire engines arriving. Maybe some smoke. As this occurs, the location shifts to –*)

SCENE 6
12.30 a.m.

The front drive of Furtherfield House. HENRY, WINNIE *and* OLIVER *stand watching, their faces lit by the fire which rages fiercely some thirty feet away.* OLIVER, *especially, looks totally dazed. Above the roar of the flames, the sound of fire engines working the pumps. A* FIREMAN *rushes past them with a hose.*

FIREMAN: (*Over the din*) Mind your backs, now! Keep well clear!

HENRY: It's hopeless. The whole place is alight. Look at it.

WINNIE: (*Agitatedly*) Miss Karen, is she still in there?

HENRY: I – don't know . . .

WINNIE: She may be trapped in there. What are we going to do?

HENRY: It's all right, Winnie, it's very unlikely she's still in there . . .

WINNIE: How do we know that for sure?

HENRY: We don't know for sure, Winnie, I'm afraid. But there's nothing we can do to help even if she is.

WINNIE: Oh!

HENRY: If it's any comfort, she does seem to have a very strong instinct for self-preservation. Just pin your hopes on that. That's all we can do.

OLIVER: (*Suddenly*) Oh my God, she's still in there . . .

HENRY: No, Oliver, we've just been saying –

OLIVER: (*Very agitated*) She's still in there. I can't leave her in there –
(*He moves forward.*)

HENRY: (*Restraining him*) Listen, Oliver, we just don't know if Karen's in there or not . . .

OLIVER: Not Karen, she'll be OK. It's my bike. My bike's still in there. I can't leave my bike.
(OLIVER *breaks free from* HENRY *and rushes off in the direction of the flames.*)

HENRY: (*Vainly trying to stop him*) Oliver . . . !

WINNIE: Master Oliver, you can't go back in there . . .
(*A commotion and* OLIVER *reappears being physically restrained by the* FIREMAN.)

FIREMAN: Now, come on. Back, back, back, I'm sorry. You can't go back in there. There's no way anyone can go back in there . . .

OLIVER: (*At the same time*) It's my bike, you see. My bike's still in there. It's very valuable. Great sentimental value. I have to get back in there. I must rescue my bike.

FIREMAN: (*Shouting* OLIVER *down*) Look now, listen. Listen. (*To* HENRY *and* WINNIE) Look, could you hold him back for me please, I've got a fire to fight there.
(HENRY *and* WINNIE *do so.* OLIVER *slowly relaxes.*)
Listen, even my own lads can't get near that. Not even with special clothing and breathing apparatus. You get within twenty feet of that you'd go up like a bloody Roman Candle. If there's someone in there, we'll do our best for them. What did you say his name was? Mike, was it?

HENRY: No. Bike. I think he was anxious to rescue his bike.

FIREMAN: His bike? You mean he tried to get back in there for a bloody bike? I don't believe it. What about your roller-skates? You want us to have a try for them as well? I don't know. (*Calling to one of his men*) Take that one round that way. Where Harry is. Link up with Harry. Try and keep it off them outbuildings there. (*To them*) We're not going to save a lot of this, I'm afraid.

HENRY: No?

183

FIREMAN: Too late, you see. Time we got the call. Lucky someone in the village saw the blaze. Or we wouldn't be here still.

HENRY: Yes, yes.

FIREMAN: Mind you, we nearly weren't anyway. Half-way up the hill. This maniac coming the other way in an open sports car. I ask you. Open sports car, middle of the night. Nearly had us in the ditch . . .

HENRY: Did you happen to see if it was a man or a woman?

FIREMAN: Don't know. Couldn't tell. Had a crash helmet on. We'd better get you people somewhere safe . . . Got anywhere we can take you? Otherwise we'll knock up the hotel . . .

HENRY: Well, I . . .

(IMOGEN *appears, anxiously. She has her coat on over her night things.*)

IMOGEN: Henry? Oh, Henry . . .

HENRY: Imogen?

IMOGEN: (*Rushing to him*) Darling, you're safe?

HENRY: (*Holding her*) We're OK. We're all all right. Don't worry. We're all safe.

IMOGEN: (*Slightly delirious with relief*) Thank God! I woke up and I saw the whole sky was alight. I knew what it was at once. And I knew you were here and I was so frightened.

HENRY: (*Reassuringly*) It's all right. We're perfectly safe. Nothing to worry about.

IMOGEN: I was so frightened. How did it start? Do you know?

HENRY: (*With a glance at* OLIVER) We're – not a hundred per cent sure . . . (*Looking at her feet*) Darling, you've got no shoes on, what are you doing?

IMOGEN: (*Vaguely*) Oh, no. Nor I have.

HENRY: You're shivering . . .

WINNIE: I should come nearer the fire, miss . . .

HENRY: Darling, is there a chance you could put us three up? Just for tonight . . .

IMOGEN: Yes. Of course. Yes. We'll have to improvise a bit. There may not be quite enough beds.

HENRY: Well, maybe we could squeeze up a bit . . . .

(*He smiles.*)

IMOGEN: (*Smiling*) Yes. That would be nice.

HENRY: Good. (*Calling to the* FIREMAN) Excuse me! I say.

FIREMAN: Hallo!

HENRY: We're OK. We're fixed up. We'll be down at the farm there. When you need us . . .

FIREMAN: Right. Tomorrow morning. Someone'll need to talk to you tomorrow morning.

HENRY: Right. Thank you for everything. All you've done. (*To* IMOGEN) One doesn't need to leave something for firemen, does one?

IMOGEN: No, I don't think so.

FIREMAN: (*Moving off*) Bring that round. Bring that right round now, Ray. On to the base. The base of it . . . That's it!
(*The* FIREMAN *goes off.*)

IMOGEN: Poor Oliver! That's his home, isn't it, gone for ever.

HENRY: (*Concerned*) Yes. (*Calling gently*) Oliver.

OLIVER: (*Who has been staring at the fire throughout*) Hallo?

HENRY: Imogen wondered if you wanted to – come back to the farmhouse . . .

IMOGEN: For the rest of the night, anyway. Have a cup of tea or something . . .

OLIVER: Terrific. That'd be terrific. Do you happen to carry any hot milk . . .

IMOGEN: Yes. We can run to that.

OLIVER: Terrific.

WINNIE: (*Gently*) I'll bring it up to you, Master Oliver.

OLIVER: Terrific.
(*He still continues to stare, fascinated, at the flames.*)

HENRY: (*To* IMOGEN, *indicating* OLIVER) You wait in the car.

IMOGEN: OK. It's just down the drive a little way. They wouldn't allow me any closer. Don't be long.
(IMOGEN *and* WINNIE *go off towards the car.*)

HENRY: Oliver? Olly?

OLIVER: Yah?

HENRY: You all right?

OLIVER: Oh, yah. It's just a bit . . . A bit, you know . . .

HENRY: Yes.

OLIVER: Hell of a blaze. Oh, well. It's only a building, isn't it?

HENRY: That's a very healthy way of looking at it . . . Are you coming?

OLIVER: Yah, sure. (*Looking back at the building as he goes, half to himself*) I'll have to find somewhere else to go, I suppose . . . (OLIVER *and* HENRY *go off to the car. As they do so, the lights cross-fade to –*)

SCENE 7
11.00 a.m.

The sitting room of Imogen's farmhouse. In a second, MARCUS *enters, followed by* HENRY, *who seems very abstracted throughout.*

HENRY: After you.

MARCUS: Thank you. (*Continuing their conversation*) Yes, as I say, I spoke to Percy Cutting yesterday and he said he'd be very honoured to be a witness for you.

HENRY: Oh, good. Thank you. I'd hoped to persuade Oliver Knightly to do it but I can't seem to trace him. No one's seen him for at least a fortnight.

MARCUS: Probably spending all his money somewhere.

HENRY: Do you think so?

MARCUS: Well, that house was pretty well covered, I believe. Miraculously, they paid up. That was all his, of course.

HENRY: Not hers?

MARCUS: No, no. They both had money in trust – the parents were pretty sensible in that respect – but the house was Oliver's. I haven't seen either of them, actually, come to think of it. Have you seen her at all? Karen?

HENRY: (*Troubled*) No. No, I haven't.

MARCUS: Well, good riddance . . .

HENRY: She's – around, though . . .

MARCUS: Around?

HENRY: Yes.

MARCUS: Here?

HENRY: Not far away. I don't know, it's just a feeling.

MARCUS: I should forget her, if I were you. This time in a fortnight you'll be married to Imogen. A new life.

HENRY: (*Unenthusiastically*) Yes.

MARCUS: Did you have a look at those figures?

HENRY: (*Blankly*) What?

MARCUS: The ones I gave you? My company books?

HENRY: Oh, yes. Sorry. Yes, I did.

MARCUS: What's your verdict?

HENRY: Well, it's – er – I mean, as I say, I'm not an accountant – but I would say, from a very cursory first glance – without in any way committing myself to a definite judgement . . .

MARCUS: The firm's in a spot of trouble, is that it?

HENRY: I'd say a fairly big spot.

MARCUS: Yes?

HENRY: Desperately big.

MARCUS: Yes. (*He worries.*) I was hoping that the – whajercallit – general upsurge in trade that's been apparently happening of late – might have carried us with it . . . But we seem, as a firm, to have been left a bit high and dry . . . Very disappointingly.

HENRY: The thing is, you see – it would appear to me that your basic problem – please, this is just one man's opinion –

MARCUS: No, carry on. Carry on . . .

HENRY: Your basic problem is that you're producing something – much more expensively than anyone else is producing it . . .

MARCUS: Ah well, there are sound reasons for that, of course . . .

HENRY: And on top of that, you're not really producing enough of them . . .

MARCUS: (*Recognizing the truth in this*) Yes, yes . . . That's an excellent point.

HENRY: And, if that wasn't enough, nobody seems to want them anyway.

MARCUS: Yes. I think you've put your finger on it. This is just the sort of talk I wanted to hear . . .

HENRY: So far as I can see, the only reason you haven't yet been declared bankrupt is that the Inland Revenue and the Customs and Excise are in nearly as much chaos at present as you are.

MARCUS: (*Thumping the furniture*) I said it, you see, I said this –
almost these exact same words – at our last board meeting.
We need substantial capital investment. We need to
modernize the plant, drastically reduce the cost per unit and
on top of that –

HENRY: – make sure you're producing something that people
want . . .

MARCUS: Oh, don't worry about that. As my grandfather said to
me, 'Don't worry. People will always need pipes.' So long as
there's a civilization they're going to need some way of
pumping it in and then some way of pumping it all out again
afterwards. No, it's capital, that's what we lack. We're
crippled without it.

HENRY: How much do you need?

MARCUS: About a million and a half.

HENRY: Well, we can't help you. You've had most of Imogen's
money.

MARCUS: She'll get that back, don't worry . . .

HENRY: Oh, I'm sure . . .

MARCUS: With interest. Don't you worry about that. Maybe not
immediately but – never fear. No, I've got – feelers out. In
the City.

HENRY: Really?

MARCUS: In the next day or two – I'm fairly confident we'll get a
nibble from someone.
(IMOGEN *comes in.*)

IMOGEN: OK. We're there. Coffee's coming. Sorry for the delay.

MARCUS: Oh, grand.

HENRY: (*Nodding towards the kitchen*) All right?

IMOGEN: (*Inexpressively*) Yes.

HENRY: Good.
(*They all sit down and wait. No one speaks.*)

MARCUS: (*After a pause*) Er . . .

IMOGEN: Sorry?

MARCUS: Where is it? The coffee?

IMOGEN: Winnie's bringing it.

MARCUS: Winnie? The woman who used to work for the
Knightlys?

IMOGEN: That's right. She came to us the night of the fire. And we seem to have – inherited her rather.

HENRY: She's jolly useful.

IMOGEN: (*With less conviction*) Oh, she is.

HENRY: Doesn't cost us much. Board and lodging.

MARCUS: Good arrangement then.

IMOGEN: Yes.

(*A pause.*)

HENRY: What's she doing?

IMOGEN: I don't know. I made the coffee. I just left her to bring it in.

(WINNIE *appears in the doorway, empty-handed.*)

WINNIE: Excuse me, madam?

IMOGEN: Yes?

WINNIE: (*Confidentially*) Could I have a word . . . ?

IMOGEN: (*Rising and going to her*) Yes, Winnie, what is it?

WINNIE: It's just that I'm finding the tray just a little too heavy to carry, you see, madam . . .

IMOGEN: Yes, all right . . .

WINNIE: It's just my left wrist, you see, madam. My right one's as strong as an ox . . .

IMOGEN: (*Shooing her out*) Yes, come on, then. Come on.

(IMOGEN *and* WINNIE *go out.*)

MARCUS: Have you decided where you're going for your honeymoon?

HENRY: Yes. Here, I think.

MARCUS: Here?

HENRY: Yes. We thought, you know, with the children. And the animals. More trouble than it was worth. We thought, why sit and be miserable in a hotel when we could be . . . be here? Instead.

MARCUS: Pleasant enough, here.

HENRY: It is.

MARCUS: (*Staring at him*) You're looking rather pale, Henry. If you don't mind my saying so.

HENRY: Am I? Oh. I'm not sleeping perhaps as well as I should . . .

MARCUS: Oh dear. Why's that? Guilty conscience?

(*He laughs.*)

HENRY: (*Smiling feebly*) Possibly.

(IMOGEN *returns, carrying the coffee tray.* WINNIE *shadows her.*)

IMOGEN: Here we are.

(*She starts to unload the tray on to the table.*)

WINNIE: (*In an undertone*) I'd put the coffee pot just there, madam . . . And then the milk just next to it there . . .

IMOGEN: (*Irritably*) Yes, all right, Winnie. Thank you . . .

WINNIE: The cups can go along here then, madam . . .

IMOGEN: (*In a sharp undertone*) I said thank you very much, Winnie. I can manage, thank you.

WINNIE: (*A little hurt*) Thank you, madam.

(WINNIE *goes out.* IMOGEN *pours the coffee.*)

IMOGEN: White, Uncle?

MARCUS: Fairly dark, thank you. (*To* HENRY) How are you coping with the farmer's life? Keeping your head above the muck?

HENRY: Yes, I think I'm . . . I'm coping, aren't I?

IMOGEN: Henry's especially good with chickens.

MARCUS: Chickens? Really?

HENRY: Yes, we seem to have an affinity. I can chat to them for hours.

IMOGEN: Don't get too friendly. We may have to get rid of a few soon.

HENRY: Oh, Lord. Couldn't we possibly wait till they die naturally?

IMOGEN: (*Admonishingly*) Henry . . .

HENRY: Sorry.

IMOGEN: He's completely hopeless. He can't bear to kill anything.

(HENRY *sags. A pause.*)

(*Smiling awkwardly*) Much. (*Looking at the coffee tray, irritably*) Oh, there's no spoons. She hasn't brought any spoons.

MARCUS: Oh, we don't need spoons . . .

IMOGEN: Of course we need spoons . . .

HENRY: I'll get them. Don't worry. I'll get them.

(HENRY *goes out to the kitchen.*)

IMOGEN: (*Muttering*) If I was only allowed to do this myself, we'd have spoons in the first place.
(*The doorbell rings.*)
Now who is that? The front door. Excuse me a moment.
(IMOGEN *goes out of the other door.* HENRY *returns almost at once with some teaspoons.*)

HENRY: (*To* WINNIE, *who is apparently following him*) It's all right, Winnie. I can carry them. Thank you. (*Looking round the room, concerned*) Where's Imogen?

MARCUS: She's –
(*A clatter of somebody tripping over a tin in the hall.*)

IMOGEN: (*From the hall, angrily*) Oh, for heaven's sake . . .
(HENRY *puts down the spoons and runs to the door.*)

HENRY: (*Alarmed*) Imogen?
(IMOGEN *enters before he can leave the room. She carries a square parcel about the size of a biscuit tin.*)
You all right, darling?

IMOGEN: Yes, I just fell over that damned can. I meant to take it out to the barn.

HENRY: Can?

IMOGEN: Yes. Petrol can.

HENRY: Petrol can?

IMOGEN: Yes.

HENRY: In the hall?

IMOGEN: Yes.

HENRY: What's a petrol can doing in the hall?

IMOGEN: Well, it wasn't in the hall until I put it there. It was on the front step.

HENRY: The front step?

IMOGEN: Yes. This morning. When I opened the front door. It was just sitting there. Someone must have left it.

HENRY: Who?

IMOGEN: I don't know.

HENRY: Someone must have done.

IMOGEN: Yes, I said, someone obviously did.

HENRY: Who?

IMOGEN: I said. I haven't the faintest idea.

HENRY: Who'd leave a petrol can on the front step?

MARCUS: (*Helpfully*) A passing motorist?

HENRY: Was it full?

IMOGEN: No, empty.

HENRY: Empty? (*In fresh panic*) Then where's the petrol gone?

IMOGEN: Henry! What the matter with you?

HENRY: What have they done with the petrol?

MARCUS: They possibly put it in their car, old chap.

HENRY: (*Laughing, slightly hysterically*) A likely story.

> (IMOGEN *and* MARCUS *exchange glances.*)

IMOGEN: (*Soothingly*) Well, let's have our coffee, shall we?

MARCUS: (*Adopting her tone*) Good idea.

IMOGEN: Did you get the spoons, darling? Oh good, you did. Thank you, darling.

HENRY: (*Calming slightly*) They're the right ones, are they?

IMOGEN: They're lovely, darling. Perfect spoons. (*Handing a cup*) Uncle?

MARCUS: Thank you.

IMOGEN: Help yourself to sugar. Darling?

HENRY: (*Taking his cup*) Thank you.

IMOGEN: Well. (*She sips her own coffee.*) That's better.

MARCUS: Very nice. What's in your parcel?

IMOGEN: I don't know. I'd better see. It's addressed to me, anyway.

HENRY: (*Alert*) Parcel?

IMOGEN: Yes. Probably an early wedding present.

MARCUS: Oh, that's nice.

HENRY: (*Tense again*) Where did that parcel come from?

IMOGEN: I just brought it in here, just now.

HENRY: Just now?

IMOGEN: You saw me bring it in here. Just now.

HENRY: Where did it come from?

IMOGEN: Out there. The postman brought it – darling, what is the matter with you?

HENRY: How do you know he was a postman?

IMOGEN: Because I opened the door to him . . .

HENRY: (*Shouting*) What proof did you have he was a postman? Did you ask him for proof?

IMOGEN: (*Shouting back at him*) No, I'm afraid I didn't ask him for his birth certificate. He was wearing a postman's uniform, a postman's hat, a postman's badge, driving a postman's van and delivering parcels as he has been doing for the past ten years. That seemed good enough to me, all right? (*Calmer*) Now, really . . .

(*She shakes the parcel. It rattles.*)

What on earth can it be?

(*She starts to untie the string.*)

HENRY: (*In a low, urgent tone*) Imogen, just put it down there. Very gently.

IMOGEN: (*Startled*) What?

HENRY: Do as I say, please. Put it down. (*Sharply*) Now, please.

IMOGEN: (*Doing so, alarmed*) What's the matter?

MARCUS: What's wrong, old chap?

(HENRY *moves to the parcel, cautiously.*)

HENRY: I'm . . . just . . . going to . . . take this . . . outside . . .

(*He takes up the parcel.*) All right?

IMOGEN: What on earth are you doing? Where are you taking my parcel?

HENRY: (*Moving to the door, very carefully*) Trust me darling. Don't try to follow me, anyone. And please keep away from the windows . . .

IMOGEN: (*Indignantly*) But Henry, it's for me. It's addressed to me.

HENRY: Please!

(HENRY *goes out slowly to the front door. Slight pause.*)

MARCUS: Imogen, do you think – just before you finally tie the knot – you might – he might be persuaded to have a medical? I mean, it's just . . . If you were . . . Children. Hereditary and so on . . . Just a thought.

IMOGEN: (*Rather dazed*) I don't know what's come over him.

MARCUS: Poor old darling. You've not had an awful lot of luck with your men so far, have you? One libertine and one lunatic. Not a good score.

IMOGEN: He's . . . Henry's changed. He's got some terrible problem he doesn't seem to want to talk about . . . And he's so jumpy . . . He's hardly sleeping . . .

193

MARCUS: No, he said he wasn't.

IMOGEN: When he does, he has these terrible dreams. During the day, he spends most of his time patrolling the yard with that gun of Anthony's. I don't know why, he can't fire it anyway. And at night we have to have all these buckets of water round the bed . . .

MARCUS: Buckets of water?

IMOGEN: Yes?

MARCUS: Does he get very thirsty?

IMOGEN: No, in case of fire.

MARCUS: Oh, fire. I see. He worries about fire.

IMOGEN: Yes. I thought it was – just a reaction to the fire up at the house but it's been going on for weeks. (*She rises and goes to a window.*) I don't know why, but I have this feeling that Karen Knightly might have something to do with all this . . .

MARCUS: Karen Knightly, but how –

IMOGEN: (*Looking out of the window.*) Dear God, what on earth is he doing now?

MARCUS: Imogen, he asked us to stay away from the windows. Don't you think you ought to humour him?

IMOGEN: (*Watching*) I think he's gong to shoot my parcel.

MARCUS: What?

(*He rises to join her.*)

IMOGEN: Yes, look. He's put it on the wall there, see? He's going to shoot at it.

MARCUS: Good Lord, so he is . . . Duck! He's going to shoot!

(MARCUS *and* IMOGEN *crouch below the window. From outside, a shotgun is fired, followed immediately by a clang. They both peer cautiously back over the window ledge.*)

Good God, he hit it. Better not stand here. He'll see us.

(*They sit. As they are doing so,* WINNIE *comes in.*)

WINNIE: I heard a shot, madam. Was that a shot?

IMOGEN: It's all right, Winnie, it was just Mr Henry again.

WINNIE: (*Darkly*) Oh, yes? I see.

(WINNIE *goes out again.*)

MARCUS: What makes you think Karen Knightly's behind this?

IMOGEN: I don't know. It's just a – feeling. (*Suddenly, very anxious*) Uncle, I've got the most dreadful fear I'm going to lose him, somehow. I think I'll die if I lose him.

MARCUS: (*Uncertain*) It'll be all right. I'm sure it'll be all right.

(HENRY *comes in. He carries a crumpled gift card in one hand and a 13-amp plug attached to a short length of tattered flex in the other.*)

HENRY: (*Casually*) Hallo.

IMOGEN: Hallo, darling.

MARCUS: Hallo, there.

(*Pause.*)

What was in the parcel, then? Anything nice, was it?

HENRY: Yes, it's . . . It was an electric toaster. (*Handing the card to* IMOGEN) From Betty and George.

IMOGEN: Oh, lovely. How kind of them.

HENRY: Yes. I – (*Holding up the flex*) I saved the plug.

(*He smiles at them rather feebly. They smile back, encouragingly. As they do so, the lights cross-fade to –*)

SCENE 8
11.00 a.m.

Lembridge Tennit. The waiting area just outside the boardroom.
EUGENE CHASE, *a young executive, is waiting with his briefcase.*
PERCY *enters. He too carries a briefcase.*

EUGENE: Ah! Good morning. Are you one of the gentlemen representing J. W. Lipscott's?

PERCY: Indeed I am. How do you do, Percy Cutting's the name. (*They shake hands.*)

EUGENE: Eugene Chase. How do you do? Welcome to Lembridge Tennit, Mr Cutting.

PERCY: Thank you, Mr Chase.

EUGENE: Are your colleagues with you, Mr Cutting, or –

PERCY: Yes, yes, they're just behind me, Mr Chase. I took an earlier lift . . .

(*Slight pause.*)

EUGENE: Good trip up, was it?

PERCY: In the lift?

EUGENE: Well, I meant on the train really, but . . .

PERCY: Oh, on the train? Yes, splendid. Bang on time.

EUGENE: Oh well, that's nice. Makes a change, doesn't it?
> (*He laughs.* PERCY *laughs.*)
> Nice and warm today, anyway.

PERCY: Yes, indeed.

EUGENE: Was it warm down there?

PERCY: Oh, it was very warm down there.

EUGENE: Mind you, it's warm up here.

PERCY: Yes, yes. It certainly is warm up here.

EUGENE: Makes a change, anyway.
> (*He laughs.* PERCY *laughs with him.*)
> (*Seeing someone along the corridor*) Ah, these look like your colleagues now, Mr Cutting.
> (MARCUS *and* HENRY *enter. Both carry briefcases.*)
> Welcome to Lembridge Tennit, gentlemen. (*Extending a hand*) Eugene Chase. How do you do?

MARCUS: How do you do? (*Taking his hand*) Marcus Lipscott.

EUGENE: (*Taking his hand*) Eugene Chase. Oh, you're the Mr Lipscott in person. How do you do?

MARCUS: Colonel Lipscott.

EUGENE: Colonel Lipscott, I beg your pardon. Must get that right, mustn't we? I'm Eugene Chase. Part of the Lembridge Tennit negotiating team. I'm sure we'll be seeing a lot of each other over the course of the next few weeks.

MARCUS: You've met my colleague, have you? Mr Cutting?

EUGENE: Indeed I have met Mr Cutting.

MARCUS: My general manager. And this is Mr Bell. One of our directors.

EUGENE: (*Staring at him*) Ah, you're Mr Bell. Yes. How do you do? Eugene Chase.

HENRY: How do you do?

EUGENE: Just to fill you in, gentlemen. Just as soon as the rest of our negotiating team arrive, we'll be going into the boardroom there in order to commence our discussions. (*Glancing at his watch*) I think, in essence, you may just be a shade early.

MARCUS: Yes, we are. I think. Just a fraction. Thank British Rail for that.

EUGENE: Makes a change, anyway.

(*He laughs. They all laugh.*)

I think – I don't want to anticipate, obviously, what's going to be said in there – but I think we'll be discussing the general outline of how control is to be satisfactorily transferred.

MARCUS: You talked in your last letter about personnel changes. What are you anticipating there, exactly?

EUGENE: Well, as I say, let's not pre-empt the meeting itself, shall we?

MARCUS: Are you talking about management? Or the workforce? Or what? I mean, some of those chaps have been with us practically from birth. I don't want to see them on the scrapheap, you see.

EUGENE: I'm sure none of us want to see anyone on the scrapheap, do we, if it can possibly be avoided? There may inevitably be an element of purely unavoidable wastage as a result of rationalization, but then – I regret to say that can happen to anyone at any point in time, can't it?

HENRY: (*Grimly*) Oh, indeed it can.

EUGENE: Indeed.

HENRY: Especially at Lembridge Tennit, I seem to remember.

EUGENE: Ah. Yes, I read you'd . . . Of, course, you were once one of ours, weren't you?

HENRY: Yes, I was.

EUGENE: Yes.

HENRY: Now I'm one of theirs.

EUGENE: Yes, yes . . . (*Seeing rescue*) Ah. Here they come. Here are my colleagues now.

(KAREN *arrives. She is the very essence of a top executive. She is followed by* JEREMY, *who carries her briefcase.*)

KAREN: Good morning, Eugene. Good morning, gentlemen.

HENRY: (*Softly*) Good God!

EUGENE: I don't know if you already know any of these gentlemen, Miss Knightly . . . ?

KAREN: (*Nodding at them all but not shaking hands*) Yes, I think I know everyone. Hallo, Percy.

PERCY: Percy Cutting, yes. Hallo, Karen.

(*He shakes hands.*)

KAREN: Colonel Lipscott.

MARCUS: Hallo, Karen. This is a surprise.

KAREN: Mr Bell . . .

HENRY: Miss Knightly . . .

KAREN: May I introduce my assistant, Jeremy Pride.

JEREMY: Hallo.

KAREN: Well, this is all very exciting, isn't it?

MARCUS: Oh, yes.

KAREN: A new era, gentlemen, don't you agree? Well, shall we go on in?

EUGENE: Yes, indeed . . .

(EUGENE *holds the door open.* KAREN *sweeps in. She is followed by* PERCY, HENRY *and* JEREMY *with* MARCUS *bringing up the rear.*)

KAREN: (*As she goes*) Did you have a pleasant trip up?

PERCY: Oh yes, thank you. Arrived bang on time.

KAREN: Oh, good. That does make a change, doesn't it?

(*She laughs.* PERCY *and* JEREMY *also laugh.* MARCUS *is about to follow them in when* EUGENE *stops him.*)

EUGENE: Just a warning. I didn't like to say anything in front of your colleagues, but be warned, I think she's going to insist on a great deal of strengthening at board level.

MARCUS: Oh, yes?

EUGENE: I think she feels that people like, say, your Mr Bell, for instance, could usefully be replaced by someone with a shade more technological know-how . . .

MARCUS: Henry's a very good man, you know . . .

EUGENE: Ah yes, no doubt. Would that goodness were enough in itself, Colonel. But sadly not . . .

KAREN: (*Off*) Are you coming in to join us, Eugene, or would you prefer us all to meet in the passageway?

(*A lot of appreciative male laughter.*)

EUGENE: Coming, Miss Knightly. (*To* MARCUS) Whatever you do, don't underestimate her, will you? Or she'll have you for breakfast.

MARCUS: (*Grimly*) Yes, I can well imagine she might.

(*As* MARCUS *and* EUGENE *enter the boardroom, the lights change to –*)

Dusk.

The fire-damaged remains of Furtherfield House. HENRY *stands in what was once the hall. He stares about him for a moment. Suddenly* OLIVER *appears from somewhere within the house.*

OLIVER: (*Unsurprised to see him*) Oh, hi.

HENRY: Oliver! Good Lord. Haven't seen you for a bit.

OLIVER: No. I was just – taking a last look at the old place.

HENRY: Yes.

OLIVER: Hell of a mess. Not a lot left really. I tried going upstairs but it's far too dangerous. I wouldn't advise it.

HENRY: I won't try.

OLIVER: Terrible mess. What are you doing these days, then? Busy?

HENRY: I'm – Well, I was working for Marcus – for Colonel Lipscott's firm but – I've just been removed from the board, so . . .

OLIVER: Oh? Oh, bad luck.

HENRY: So. Sort of unemployed really.

OLIVER: Aren't you getting married? Didn't I hear that?

HENRY: Er . . . I'm not sure about that, either. Probably. I don't know.

OLIVER: Oh. Mine of misinformation, aren't I? Comes of – I don't know what it comes of, really.

HENRY: What are you doing then?

OLIVER: Well . . . Not a lot, like you. I've been settling the insurance on this place. Persuading them to smile and pay up.

HENRY: They have, I hope?

OLIVER: Oh, yes. Eventually. After a good deal of argy-bargy. And then I've been selling the place.

HENRY: This place?

OLIVER: Well, what's left of it. The land, you know.

HENRY: All of it?

OLIVER: Yes. I didn't want to stick around here any more. Too many memories. Thought I'd go and settle somewhere else entirely. No idea where. And I was offered a pretty fair sum for this lot actually.

HENRY: Who's bought it?

OLIVER: Oh . . . God, I never remember their name . . . Somebody. Something.

HENRY: Lembridge Tennit, by any chance?

OLIVER: Lembridge Tennit. Absolutely. Got it in one.

HENRY: What are they going to do with it? Do you know?

OLIVER: Oh. A factory, I think. A plastics factory.

HENRY: Here?

OLIVER: Yes. Be absolutely ghastly, I should think.

HENRY: Yes, it will. Not very nice to live next door to, either.

OLIVER: I believe they're putting a slip road through the wood just along there. And then . . .

HENRY: Down past the farm?

OLIVER: Yah. They need to go that way because, of course, all down there they want to build the new industrial estate.

HENRY: Industrial estate?

OLIVER: Yah.

HENRY: Where the meadow is now?

OLIVER: That seems to be the scheme. I've told them, I don't think they stand a hope in hell of getting permission for the heliport but they're going to try.

HENRY: Oh, I dare say they'll get it. I dare say they will.

OLIVER: Anyway. All I can say is, I'm glad I'm moving.

HENRY: Yes. I bet.

OLIVER: Well, I'll see you around, I expect.

HENRY: Yes, I've no doubt, Oliver.

OLIVER: Think I'll stroll gently down the hill. I don't like it here at night. Gives me the creeps. Too many ghosts, you know. Just – full of ghosts. Bye.

HENRY: Bye.

(OLIVER *strolls off into the night.* HENRY *stands and shakes his head. A man finally admitting defeat. Suddenly, there is the sound of a motor bike nearby. In the darkness, it is quite eerie. It startles* HENRY. *He looks about him to see if he can locate it. It seems to be circling round him but he can't see it. He runs one way. Then another. But the bike sound is all around him, getting*

200

*louder and closer. He is on the verge of panic. Suddenly, as
unexpectedly as it had started, the noise stops.* HENRY *stands
listening. Silence, then the sound of footsteps slowly approaching.
Heavy feet crunching over the debris.* HENRY *stands alarmed. A
figure appears. A tall* MOTOR-CYCLIST *all in black. Sinister and
menacing in his gleaming helmet with impenetrable tinted glass.
The figure stops as it sees* HENRY, *then starts to approach him.*
HENRY *draws back but doesn't dare turn and run. He braces
himself as the* MOTOR-CYCLIST *reaches him and stops. He
reaches in his pocket and* HENRY *watches terrified, expecting the
worst. The* MOTOR-CYCLIST *produces an envelope and hands it
to* HENRY, *without a word.* HENRY *takes it.*)
(*Hoarsely*) Is this for me?
(*The* MOTOR-CYCLIST *does not respond.* HENRY *opens the
envelope and reads the note. Despite his nervousness, he gives a
brief laugh and shakes his head.*)

MOTOR-CYCLIST: (*In a perfectly ordinary sort of voice*) Any reply at
all?

HENRY: No. No reply. Thank you.
(*The* MOTOR-CYCLIST *turns and goes off the way he came.*)
(*Laughing slightly hysterically*) No reply.
(*He starts to move off as the lights cross-fade to –*)

SCENE 10
7.00 p.m.

*Imogen's kitchen. She enters with some toys which she is evidently
tidying away. She treads in something and looks at her feet in disgust.*

IMOGEN: Uggghh! It's Marmite. I know it, it's Marmite. God, I
hate it.
(*She dumps down the toys, finds a floorcloth and scrubs at the floor.*)
I hate it. How I hate it.
(*She is scrubbing away when* HENRY *enters. He stops when he sees*
IMOGEN. *She eventually straightens up and sees him.*)
(*Angrily*) Henry, where have you been? Where the hell have
you been?

201

HENRY: What?

IMOGEN: I've been frantic. I thought you were in an accident or something.

HENRY: How do you mean?

IMOGEN: You don't say anything, you just vanish all day. I thought you'd been hurt –

HENRY: Hurt?

IMOGEN: Knocked down or something. I don't know what I thought. God, why do you do this to me, Henry?

HENRY: (*Shrugging*) I'm sorry . . .

IMOGEN: I've been worried sick. Don't you care?

HENRY: I'm here now, anyway.

IMOGEN: Well, thank you. Thanks very much. (*Composing herself slightly*) Do you want something to eat then?

HENRY: No.

IMOGEN: You can't have eaten since this morning, can you?

HENRY: I don't know, I can't remember. Probably not.

IMOGEN: You didn't have much then, either. (*Slight pause.*) Where have you been?

HENRY: Oh, just walking around.

IMOGEN: All day? Where?

HENRY: I don't know. Up at the old house.

IMOGEN: Furtherfield?

HENRY: Yes.

IMOGEN: Why were you up there?

HENRY: Just looking.

IMOGEN: I see. (*Slight pause.*) Are you going to take your coat off or are you going to sit in it all evening?

(*Pause.* HENRY *slowly takes off his coat.*)

What are we going to do, Henry? Please talk to me. What are we going to do? You won't tell me what's worrying you . . . I feel so helpless. I don't know what to do for the best. (*Pause.*) Tell me. Do you want to leave me? Is that it? Do you want to go? (*Slight pause. More urgently*) Henry. Tell me! Please, talk to me. I don't care what you want to do, but you must talk to me about it.

HENRY: (*Slowly*) You see, everything that's happened between us is based on – lies, really.

IMOGEN: Us? Our relationship, you mean?

HENRY: Yes.

IMOGEN: Based on lies?

HENRY: Yes.

IMOGEN: (*Coldly*) Oh, thank you. Terrific.

HENRY: No, I didn't mean . . .

IMOGEN: Bloody terrific. Thank you.

HENRY: Imogen . . .

IMOGEN: Great. Thank you. You . . . pillock!

HENRY: (*Going to touch her*) Imogen . . .

IMOGEN: (*Moving away, savagely*) Go away! Get away from me!
(*They stand apart.*)
(*Tearful*) What did you mean, lies? How can you say lies?
How can you say that to me? I never lied to you. Ever.

HENRY: I didn't mean you were lying, Imogen. It was me. I was
the one who was lying . . .

IMOGEN: How? What were you lying about?

HENRY: Oh, almost everything.

IMOGEN: You mean you didn't love me?

HENRY: No, of course I loved you. I still do love you. It's just –
the reason I came here – why I got to know you – how I came
to be engaged to you – all of it's based on a deceit.

IMOGEN: It's that bloody girl, isn't it? Karen Knightly? I don't
know what she's done to you, what she's holding over you,
but . . . What is it, Henry? What is there between you two?
There's something, isn't there? You're not lovers, I know
that much.

HENRY: (*Alarmed*) No.

IMOGEN: But it's something almost as strong as that. Stronger.
Because it's pulling us apart, isn't it? She's doing that. Not
you.

HENRY: It's . . . We had an arrangement. An agreement between
us. And I can't break it. I've asked her to release me from it
and she won't. The problem is that if I stick to the letter of
our agreement, hers and mine, then it's in direct conflict
with what I feel for you.

IMOGEN: What are you talking about? What sort of an
agreement?

HENRY: It's a pact. It's – revenge.

IMOGEN: Revenge?

HENRY: Oh, it all sounds so ridiculous now – but, six months ago – seven months – I don't know – it was the lowest point in my life and I decided the only thing left for me, frankly, was to jump off a bridge.

IMOGEN: Jump off a bridge? Which bridge?

HENRY: What does it matter which bridge –

IMOGEN: I want to know. Which bridge?

HENRY: Albert Bridge. Anyway, there I was. And there was Karen Knightly also busy apparently jumping off.

HENRY: (*Disbelievingly*) Karen Knightly?

HENRY: Well, I – Maybe she wasn't, I don't know. Anyway –

IMOGEN: Wait a moment. Was this the same night she dragged Anthony up to town in order to stop her?

HENRY: That's right, it was.

IMOGEN: Then she certainly had no intention of jumping. If you're really seriously considering it, you don't issue invitations, I can promise you that.

HENRY: Well. Whatever. The fact was we were both very low, she and I. And we both felt that our respective worlds had treated us very badly. So we decided to – hit back at them. Get our revenge. Only the twist was – and it did seem a brilliant idea at the time – we'd swap revenges.

IMOGEN: Swap?

HENRY: I'd take her revenge and she'd take mine.

IMOGEN: I see. And who was your revenge to be against?

HENRY: Oh, just people in my office, that's all. People I felt had done me down. Pathetic really.

IMOGEN: And has she taken your revenge?

HENRY: My God, she has. She's decimated the building. Lembridge Tennit is operating on a skeleton staff.

IMOGEN: You mean she killed people?

HENRY: Only one or two.

IMOGEN: One or two?

HENRY: Well, she didn't kill them, I don't think. No, she just – caused them to die.

IMOGEN: I can't quite see the difference, but never mind. So that

204

was your revenge. What was hers? Who were you supposed to kill?

HENRY: No one. I wasn't supposed to kill anyone . . .

IMOGEN: I'm sorry. I'll rephrase that. Who were you supposed to cause to die then? (*A slight pause.*) Anthony? Was it Anthony?

HENRY: I swear to you that was an accident. You have to believe that.

(*Another pause. The truth sinks in.*)

IMOGEN: (*Staring at him*) It has to be me, then, doesn't it?

HENRY: No. . . .

IMOGEN: (*Feeling weak*) Oh, my God . . .

HENRY: Imogen.

IMOGEN: (*Sitting*) I feel sick. I actually feel sick.

HENRY: Imogen, listen. Listen to me.

IMOGEN: (*Her hands to her head*) You'd better go. You'd better leave now, Henry, please.

HENRY: Imogen, you have to believe that . . .

IMOGEN: (*Screaming*) Henry, please go away. Please. I am very frightened. I am terrified. Now, please go! Now! (*Pause.*) Now!

(HENRY *stares at her.*)

HENRY: (*At length*) Yes. OK. I'll – may I just – I'll just pack a couple of things – May I?

IMOGEN: (*Huddled*) Be quick. Be quick. Be quick.

HENRY: Yes.

(HENRY *leaves the room.* IMOGEN *gives a shudder. She is shivering from the shock of all this.*)

IMOGEN: Oh. (*She clasps her arms round herself.*) Oh. Oh, dear. (*She gets to her feet, uncertain what to do for the best.*) Oh! Oh, dear. Oh.

(*Her teeth chatter slightly. Rather more for something to do than for any other reason, she picks up Henry's coat and prepares to put it tidily over a chair. She sees the corner of the note* HENRY *received earlier, sticking out of one of the pockets. She puts the coat down so that the note is uppermost. She attempts to look at it without touching it. Then she flicks it casually once or twice, hoping to open it enough so she can read it. Finally, she takes it*

*by the corner and twitches it clear of the pocket and on to the floor.
She ambles past trying to read it as it lies there, but it remains
obstinately folded. She gives up, retrieves it and allows it to fall
open in her hand.)*
(*Reading*) 'HenryBell. The game proceeds until I choose to
stop it. Admit defeat and I may show you mercy. Meet me
where it all began at midnight. K.'
(IMOGEN *looks thoughtful as the lights change to –)*

SCENE 11
Midnight.

Albert Bridge SW3. *As before at the start of the play.* HENRY *wanders
on to the middle of the bridge and contemplates the murky depths.*

KAREN: (*Off*) Henry! HenryBell!
HENRY: Karen?
(KAREN *appears at the other end of the bridge. She is dressed in
evening dress.*)
KAREN: Good evening, HenryBell, I hoped you'd come. I really
hoped you would.
HENRY: (*Wearily*) What do you want, Karen? Just tell me.
KAREN: I told you that in my note, HenryBell. Did you like my
messenger I sent? I chose him specially.
HENRY: Terrific. Terrific bloke. We had a load of laughs
together.
KAREN: Now don't be sulky, HenryBell. I came to show you
mercy. I told you. I bring you a choice.
HENRY: Oh, yes? What might that be? Pistols or poison?
KAREN: Choice number one. We continue to play the game as
we're doing at present . . .
HENRY: No. No more.
KAREN: (*Smiling*) No. I didn't think you'd choose that one. In
which case, HenryBell, you have to stand by the agreement,
don't you?
HENRY: Listen, Karen . . .
KAREN: Wait! In which case you have choice number two, don't

206

you? If Imogen loves you – as you say she does and I'm sure it's true – then it's obvious what you do next, isn't it?

HENRY: Nothing's obvious to me any more, Karen, I'm sorry.

KAREN: You jump, HenryBell, you jump.

HENRY: (*Incredulously*) What?

KAREN: Jump and break her heart. Isn't that brilliant?

HENRY: You're joking.

(*A pause. She waits.*)

Is that the choice? Is that all? Thanks very much.

KAREN: (*Slowly*) Not – quite all.

HENRY: Well?

(IMOGEN's *voice is heard in the distance.*)

IMOGEN: (*Calling, off*) Henry!

HENRY: (*Surprised*) Imogen?

KAREN: What the hell's she doing here? Why did you bring her?

HENRY: I didn't bring her, she must have . . .

IMOGEN: (*Closer*) Henry!

KAREN: Oh, well. It doesn't matter. All the more fun, really.

(IMOGEN *appears at the other end of the bridge from* KAREN.)

IMOGEN: Henry, what are you doing?

HENRY: Imogen, I'm . . .

KAREN: Ignore her, HenryBell.

HENRY: (*To* IMOGEN) Just a second, wait there.

IMOGEN: Henry!

HENRY: (*To* IMOGEN) Wait there! I won't be long.

KAREN: And so to your third and final choice, HenryBell. All the best things come in threes, isn't that the case?

HENRY: What is it, then? Come on.

KAREN: You change sides and join me.

HENRY: What?

KAREN: We play on the same side. For ever. As a team.

HENRY: A team.

KAREN: You and me. (*She holds out her hand.*) I'm inviting you to join me, Henry. For ever. Isn't that the best? It's a great, great honour.

(HENRY *stares at her.*)

What do you say? Wouldn't we be fabulous? Just think of it . . .

HENRY: You and me?

KAREN: Me and you.

HENRY: That's my third choice, is it?

KAREN: Yes.

(*She smiles at him.*)

IMOGEN: (*Anxiously*) Henry, please. I'm sorry . . .

HENRY: In that case, I unhesitatingly choose to jump off the
bridge . . .

(*He starts to climb up on to the parapet.*)

KAREN: What?

IMOGEN: Henry!

HENRY: I'm sorry, it's the only choice that's even remotely
attractive . . .

KAREN: (*Outraged*) What are you talking about?

HENRY: All in all, I think jumping sounds by far the best.

KAREN: (*Incredulously*) You'd rather be dead than with me . . . ?

HENRY: I didn't want to put it as crudely as that, but absolutely,
yes . . . Cheerio, then!

(*He appears to be about to jump.*)

IMOGEN: (*Screaming*) Henry!

KAREN: (*Yelling*) Henry . . . !

HENRY: (*Stopping*) What?

KAREN: HenryBell, you can't.

HENRY: Why not? What's to stop me? It's what you wanted, isn't
it?

KAREN: No. No, I didn't.

HENRY: Why not?

KAREN: Because . . . (*In a small voice*) Because . . . I love you,
HenryBell.

HENRY: You what?

KAREN: (*A little girl*) I love you.

IMOGEN: Don't believe her.

HENRY: I don't. Not at all.

KAREN: Of course you do. You know I do. It's true. It's true,
HenryBell. It is, I swear it.

HENRY: You don't love me. You just want to take me away from
Imogen, any way you can. You don't love me, you just want
to hurt her . . . That's not love . . .

KAREN: I love you.

HENRY: I'm sorry, Karen, no, you don't.

KAREN: (*Angrily*) I don't care about hurting her. Do you think I care about her? I love you for you.

HENRY: Wait a minute. Are you saying you don't care whether we hurt Imogen?

KAREN: I love you.

HENRY: And you don't care if that love hurts her or not?

KAREN: No. Why should I care?

HENRY: You don't even care if you hurt Imogen any more or not?

KAREN: I've said no. No.

HENRY: And so you no longer care if I hurt her or not? You won't even mind if I don't hurt her?

KAREN: She's irrelevant . . . Forget her. I don't want to see or hear about her ever again. I just want you, HenryBell.

HENRY: And that's all you want?

KAREN: (*Shouting*) Yes, yes, yes!

HENRY: (*With a cry*) Terrific! Well, that's settled then.

KAREN: Is it?

HENRY: Game's over, isn't it?

KAREN: (*Blankly*) How do you mean?

HENRY: You no longer want me to hurt her. Then I'm free to love her . . .

(*He starts to climb down.*)

IMOGEN: (*In breathless admiration*) Oh, Henry, you're brilliant.

KAREN: (*Realizing*) Oh, now wait. Oh, no . . . Oh, no . . .

HENRY: Oh yes, Karen. Oh yes . . .

HENRY: You can't do this. I forbid you to do this.

HENRY: Now, now, we play by the rules, Karen, remember? You taught me that. There's nothing you can do. It's all strictly legal, I've stuck to the letter.

KAREN: What are you doing?

HENRY: I love you, Imogen. Forgive me.

IMOGEN: Oh, Henry . . . I love you too much to care.

KAREN: (*Outraged*) What are you doing? You can't let her do this . . . You can't do this.

HENRY: (*Falling into Imogen's arms*) Oh, Imogen . . .

IMOGEN: (*Blissfully*) Oh, Henry . . .

(*They kiss.*)

KAREN: This is disgusting! This is revolting! Get back on that bridge at once, do you hear me? I'd sooner you jumped.

IMOGEN: Are you coming home?

HENRY: Take me home, now . . .

(HENRY *and* IMOGEN *walk slowly away from* KAREN.)

KAREN: (*Screaming after them, as they go*) If you do this . . . if you do this to me . . . I swear you'll never sleep again without dreaming of me . . . you'll have me on your conscience for ever . . . for the rest of your lives . . . (*She climbs up on the bridge, the better to shout after them.*) Oh, yes. Go on then. Go home to your cosy little country cottage with your pigs and your cows and your hideous children. You'll never be free of me. You'll remember me with guilt in your hearts for ever. For ever . . . Ever . . . HenryBell!

(IMOGEN *and* HENRY *have evidently vanished from her view.* KAREN *stands perched on the bridge, undecided what game to start next. She seems momentarily at a loss.*)

(*In her little voice*) HenryBell.

(*She pouts. Then, slowly, a smile crosses her face. She laughs to herself with childish delight as she thinks up a new game.*)

(*Delightedly*) Of course. Of course!

(*She looks at the water, then in the direction in which* IMOGEN *and* HENRY *have gone. She braces herself to jump.*)

(*Softly*) Revenge. (*A little louder*) Revenge! (*As she jumps off the bridge, with a great triumphant cry*) Reve–e–e–n–g–e! (*She vanishes out of the light. As she hits the water, a distant splash and, almost simultaneously, blackout.*)